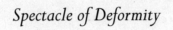

Spectacle of Deformity

The publisher gratefully acknowledges the generous support of the Humanities Endowment Fund of the University of California Press Foundation.

Spectacle of Deformity

FREAK SHOWS AND MODERN BRITISH CULTURE

Nadja Durbach

UNIVERSITY OF CALIFORNIA PRESS

BERKELEY   LOS ANGELES   LONDON

University of California Press, one of the most
distinguished university presses in the United States,
enriches lives around the world by advancing scholarship
in the humanities, social sciences, and natural sciences. Its
activities are supported by the UC Press Foundation and
by philanthropic contributions from individuals and
institutions. For more information, visit
www.ucpress.edu.

University of California Press
Berkeley and Los Angeles, California

University of California Press, Ltd.
London, England

Library of Congress Cataloging-in-Publication Data

Durbach, Nadja, 1971–.
    Spectacle of deformity : freak shows and modern
British culture / Nadja Durbach.
        p.   cm.
    Includes bibliographical references and index.
    ISBN 978-0-520-25768-9 (cloth : alk. paper)

    1. Abnormalities, Human—Great Britain—History—
19th century.   2. Freak shows—Great Britain—
History—19th century.   3. Human body—Social
aspects—Great Britain—History—19th century.
I. Title.

QM691.D87   2010
616'.0430941—dc22   2009009244

Manufactured in the United States of America

19 18 17 16 15 14 13 12 11 10
10 9 8 7 6 5 4 3 2 1

This book is printed on Cascades Enviro 100, a 100%
post consumer waste, recycled, de-inked fiber. FSC
recycled certified and processed chlorine free. It is acid
free, Ecologo certified, and manufactured by BioGas
energy.

For Ben—amazing, wondrous,
extraordinary . . .

CONTENTS

ILLUSTRATIONS

ACKNOWLEDGMENTS

If Blanche DuBois always depended on the kindness of strangers, I have depended entirely on the kindness of archivists. Without their help this book would not have been possible. Although I have tried to use as many different types of historical documents as possible, this book has largely been written from thousands of scraps of paper—handbills, posters, tickets—that have been lovingly preserved by archivists who recognize the value of this type of ephemera. I am extremely grateful to Jonathan Evans of the London Hospital Museum and Archives, Julie Anne Lambert of the John Johnson Collection at the Bodleian Library at Oxford University, Helen Peden of the British Library's Evanion Collection, Jeremy Smith of the Guildhall Library, and Vanessa Toulmin of the National Fairgrounds Archive at the University of Sheffield. Each of these individuals went above and beyond the call of duty to make source material available to me and to answer countless questions. I would also like the thank the staff of the British Library, the Wellcome Library, the London Theatre Museum, the Newspaper Library at Colindale, the National Archives, the Natural History Museum, the Royal College of Surgeons, the City of Westminster Archives, the Royal Anthropological Institute, the London Metropolitan Archives, the Ashmolean Museum, and the Circus World Museum in Baraboo, Wisconsin. I am also grateful to Fred D. Pfening, who kindly gave me copies of circus contracts from his personal collection, and to Shane Peacock, who sent me copies of many photographs of Krao.

Many friends and colleagues have read parts of this book, some of them more than once, and offered insightful comments at different stages. I would particularly like to thank Matt Basso, John Belchem, Beth Clement, Paul Deslandes, Joy Dixon, Jim Epstein, Christopher Hamlin, Anne Keary, Seth Koven, Gretchen Krueger, Philippa Levine, Leslie Reagan, Angela Smith, Janet Theiss, Marlene Tromp, James Vernon, and Maryann Villarreal. Judy Walkowitz deserves special mention; not only did she read chapters for me, but she has continued to be a source of great moral support over the many years she has mentored me. During my semester as a fellow of the University of Utah's Tanner Humanities Center I was lucky enough to have a captive set of dedicated and thoughtful readers. Many thanks to Vince Cheng, Marian Eide, David Hawkins, Joe Metz, Jennifer Ritterhouse, and Carolina Webber.

This project has also benefited from conversations with John Gillis, Tom Laqueur, Pamela Scully, Martha Stoddard Holmes, Vanessa Warne, Ina Zweiniger-Bargielowska, and audience members at a variety of conferences and presentations. I would also like to thank Mara Keire and Chris McKenna, who repeatedly housed me in Oxford. Melanie Clews both put me up and put up with me, and she deserves special thanks for making room in her flat for my freaks on multiple visits to London.

The funding for this project came from two grants from the University of Utah's University Research Committee. The time for research and writing also came in the form of a Faculty Fellowship from the University of Utah, a Tanner Humanities Center Fellowship, and a visiting appointment at the Center for British Studies at the University of California, Berkeley.

I am very grateful to Niels Hooper, who has been enthusiastic about this project from our very first correspondence; he has offered wonderful guidance along the way. I would also like to thank Caroline Knapp, Sharron Wood, and the staff of the University of California Press. Peter Bailey, Ellen Ross, and an anonymous reviewer for the University of California Press provided very helpful advice and suggestions for revisions. The book is much better, I am certain, for their input, though its shortcomings are of course all my own.

My families—Durbachs and Cohens—have provided welcome and much-needed support and encouragement throughout this process. My parents have been unrestrainedly enthusiastic about my work and endlessly tolerant of my unusual interests. My brother Andrey has been helpful in more ways than he can possibly imagine. He continually reminded me that, although I was engaged in a serious academic enterprise, it was important to take the time to acknowledge that freaks are also fun. Most of all I thank my husband, Ben, who has been living with my freaks much longer than anyone should have to. He has not only read many drafts of this book in its various incarnations, but he has listened to countless outlandish theories over the many years that I have had the pleasure of his very good company. When our own little experiment in "maternal impression" arrived on the scene, he spent many hours performing a variety show of his own so that I could have time to finish this book. For that, and many other things, I am eternally grateful.

Exhibiting Freaks

IN 1847, UNDER THE HEADING "The Deformito-Mania," the popular periodical *Punch* bemoaned the public's "prevailing taste for deformity, which seems to grow by what it feeds upon." "Poor MADAME TUSSAUD, with her Chamber of Horrors," it continued, "is quite thrown into the shade by the number of real enormities and deformities that are now to be seen, as the showmen say 'Alive, alive!'"[1] *Punch,* ever the shrewd social commentator, was noting the widespread British fascination with, and demand for, "monsters," "human oddities," "*lusus naturae,*" "prodigies," "novelties," and "freaks." Although most of these words had been used interchangeably for centuries to refer to those who displayed their unusual bodies to the curious for entertainment purposes, the term "freak"—short for "freak of nature"—only began to be used consistently in this context around 1847,[2] the very same year that *Punch* lamented the public's "morbid appetite" for the "frightful" and the "horrible." In the period between 1847 and 1914—the heyday of the modern freak show—it quickly became the most common way to refer to the hundreds of individuals across the United Kingdom who exhibited a congenital bodily anomaly for profit. This book argues that these shows should not be dismissed as merely marginal, exploitative, or voyeuristic forms of entertainment. In fact, displays of freakery were critical sites for popular and professional debates about the meanings attached to bodily difference. It is no coincidence that freak shows reached their zenith at the height of Britain's modern and imperial self-fashioning.

The display of the monstrous body was not new in the nineteenth century, nor was it confined to the United Kingdom. In medieval Europe monstrous births were often interpreted as divine signs, omens that warned of impending danger. But as many scholars have noted, by the sixteenth century they were beginning to lose their portentous status, becoming objects of curiosity and wonder as well as tropes rich in metaphorical and political resonance. Representations of monstrous bodies, rather than the physical bodies themselves, circulated freely within and beyond Europe in the print culture that witnessed an explosion in the early modern period.[3] The particular meanings attached to these monstrosities were easily shaped precisely because the consumers of these texts rarely had an opportunity to see the body in question itself. While some monsters could be viewed in the flesh by the lucky few who lived in the vicinity,[4] most early modern Europeans had access only to carefully crafted visual and textual representations of monstrosity that were tailored to serve a particular political, moral, or religious purpose.

If metaphorical and mythical monsters ran rampant through early modern texts, live freak shows were also common from the Iberian Peninsula to Russia in the early modern era. Although, as Kathryn Hoffmann has argued, some of these exhibitions featured fakes,[5] genuine human anomalies of all shapes and sizes could increasingly be seen at fairs, marketplaces, coffeehouses, and taverns across Europe in the seventeenth century. By the eighteenth century these horned men, hairy women, giants, dwarfs, and double-bodied wonders had become staples of both popular and elite culture, appearing not only in entertainment venues but also in scientific spaces.[6] Distinguishing between sites of leisure and those of learning can, however, be misleading, for many displays of monstrous bodies successfully married the scientific to the spectacular. Peter the Great's Kunstkamera, for example, which housed his personal collection of anatomical preparations, natural history specimens, and other curious objects, also included living freaks of nature who could be seen not only by the scientists using the museum as a research facility but also by curious members of the Russian public.[7]

The diversity of human anomalies on display increased over the course of the nineteenth century, in part because of developments in transportation. With the emergence of railways and steamships in the 1830s and 1840s, Europeans became much more mobile, and long-distance travel became a regular phenomenon in service of both tourism and the mainte-nance of empire. Freak shows flourished in this environment because they were no longer dependent upon local anomalous births. Instead they could draw upon a larger pool of performers who came not only from other European countries but also from the Americas, Asia, and Africa—locations that sometimes yielded genetic mutations that resulted in anomalous bodies that were unfamiliar, and therefore intriguing, to those of European descent. By the mid-nineteenth century the freak show had become a truly international institution. Human oddities from around the world, and increasingly from the colonized areas with which Europeans had the most regular contact, crisscrossed the Atlantic, appearing in both North American and western European cities and towns. Some continued on to Russia or even Constantinople, tracing and retracing what had become an established freak show route.

While acknowledging that the Victorian and Edwardian freak show was part of a much longer and global history of the exhibition of human bodily anomalies, this book focuses on Britain from the mid-nineteenth to the early twentieth century. This is in part because it was here and during this moment of "taxonomic frenzy"[8] that the European freak show arguably reached its apotheosis. But it is also because the meanings invested in monstrous bodies are culturally contingent. Rather than interpreting freaks as archetypal and thus transhistorical phenomena that provide access to a widely shared "secret self,"[9] this book suggests that the signifi-cance attached to anomalous bodies, and thus the lessons they embodied, were never stable. As Jami Moss contends, living monsters, like their tex-tual representations, were infinitely "malleable, capable of being rewritten according to the needs of a particular cultural moment."[10] It is therefore crucial to understand the specific context that produced certain types of bodies as aberrant and the ways in which their display operated as both an index of, and a strategy to cope with, larger cultural anxieties.

Scholars have often argued that the discourse of monstrosity functions as a gauge of broader social unease and provides a ritualistic mechanism for dealing with this discomfort.[11] Judith Halberstam maintains that "the monster functions as monster . . . when it is able to condense as many fear-producing traits as possible into one body."[12] The freak was mon-strous precisely because of the instability of its body: the freak could be both male and female, white and black, adult and child, and/or human and animal at the same time. Indeed, this ability to inhabit two categories at once, and thus to challenge the distinction between them, was the hallmark of the nineteenth and early twentieth-century freak show performer, common to each of the acts discussed in this book. And it was precisely this corporeal and cultural volatility—this refusal to uphold the natural order, that in turn sanctioned the social order—that made the freak so socially and politically disruptive and thus so frightening.

To defuse the tensions inherent in the challenge presented by this category confusion, both the exhibitors and the consumers of spectacular bodies often turned to humor. As Roger Lund has demonstrated, the English had a long tradition of laughing at those with physical deformities. This type of humor, he argues, was in the eighteenth century part of an "ideology of form" that dismissed the deformed as "foreign, transgressive, ugly and inherently worthy of contempt." The purpose of ridicule, he suggests, is to "clarify difference in order that it can be excluded."[13] Similarly, Matt Houlbrook has argued with respect to the cross-dresser that the individual who contravenes norms is often simultaneously "a source of massive cultural anxiety and a figure of humour and intrigue."[14] The freak, while monstrous, was thus also a comic character precisely because his or her physical difference was transgressive and therefore inherently ridiculous. Humor and horror coexisted in freak show performances, for both of these genres served as a means to express and to manage the cultural anxieties that human anomalies literally embodied. *The Spectacle of Deformity* thus explores the modern British freak show as a contested space in which showmen, spectators, scientists, and freak performers themselves used the "comic horror of monsters"[15] to negotiate around what it meant to be "normal," and thus what it meant to be British, at a critical juncture in the making of modern Britain.

THE FREAK SHOW AND COMMERCIALIZED LEISURE

In 1859, commenting on the closing of the infamous Bartholomew Fair, the journalist Henry Morley declared that the British nation had "recovered" from its "taste for Monsters," which had become "a disease."[16] This proclamation was, however, premature. Far from witnessing the decline of the freak show, the second half of the nineteenth century saw its steady growth. Fifteen years later Thomas Frost, the Chartist writer and chronicler of fairs and circuses, insisted that "public interest in . . . monstrosities remains unabated."[17] Indeed, although the French strictly controlled the exhibition of what they termed *phenomènes*,[18] in the United Kingdom anyone could see armless men, hairy women, giants, dwarfs, conjoined twins, half-animal half-human wonders, and other amazing bodies any day of the year, as there were no laws that specifically regulated the display of human oddities. By the middle of the nineteenth century the freak show had thus become firmly embedded within, and inseparable from, the burgeoning industry of cheap Victorian entertainment.

Richard Altick's *The Shows of London* identifies the display of human oddities as one of countless types of entertainment that the inhabitants of Europe's largest metropolis could consume in the heyday of the expansion of the commercial leisure market. Britain had become a consumer society in the eighteenth century, but it was in the middle of the nineteenth century that the rapid growth of the middle class and the institutionalization of the Saturday half-holiday (which gave the working class more time for leisure) led to the widespread demand for inexpensive popular entertainments. This spurred the rise of music halls, theaters, circuses, seaside resorts, aquariums, zoos, pleasure gardens, and popular museums, which sprang up across the urban landscape over the course of Victoria's reign.[19] While home to their unique forms of entertainment, these venues were also showcases for freak performers. Indeed, it was these new permanent institutions, argues Julia Douthwaite, that allowed the exhibition of anomalous bodies to reach its apogee in the nineteenth century.[20]

But human oddities could also be seen in temporary "show shops," unused storefronts easily converted into exhibition rooms and just as easily abandoned when the landlord found a more respectable tenant.[21] The London barrister and former actor, dramatist, and journalist Montagu Williams described a popular Whitechapel venue that had been variously used by a greengrocer, an undertaker, and a pawnbroker before being taken over by a showman. In the late 1880s it was one of four or five show shops in the neighborhood. The lineup, Williams maintained, included a "black dwarf" who shared the bill with a "fat lady," an armadillo, some snakes, and a waxwork exhibition of the victims of Jack the Ripper, all of whom had been murdered within blocks of the shop.[22] In the nineteenth and early twentieth centuries freaks could thus be found not only in established entertainment venues, but also behind almost any door. The commodification of their unusual bodies was part and parcel of a pervasive, though not necessarily new, desire for the spectacular and the curious.[23]

While show shops, aquariums, music halls, and other new entertainment spots were largely metropolitan phenomena, freak shows were highly mobile spectacles that visited not only cities but also towns and sometimes villages across the United Kingdom. The annual calendar of fairs and

Figure 1. Sideshow at Hull Fair, 1914. Mary Evans Picture Library, Barry Norman Collection.

wakes established a predictable route for traveling shows. Dating back to the medieval period, fairs had begun as trade marts and hiring venues, but by the nineteenth century they had largely become sites of popular amusement. Wakes—originally religious festivals to honor a parish saint—had also lost their spiritual significance and been transformed into local carnivals.[24] The itinerant freak shows that appeared at these events (dozens of which took place across the United Kingdom) were thus able to draw in a much broader public than many other nineteenth- and early twentieth-century commercial entertainments, which often catered only to the urban spectator.

Exhibitions of human oddities were more widely accessible than other entertainments, not only because they were peripatetic, but also because they were inexpensive to attend, at times costing as little as a penny. Many acts even offered discounts for servants and the working classes in order to attract the widest audience possible. Indeed, freak shows appealed to individuals across the economic spectrum. In the 1850s, John Fish—owner of a cotton mill in Bury and an enthusiastic follower of P. T. Barnum—closed his factory when Tom Thumb came to town, presenting each of his employees with a ticket to the exhibition.[25] This did not mean, however, that the industrialist and the mill hand (let alone the pauper and the prince) rubbed shoulders at these shows. By offering the working class cut-rate admission only at certain hours of the day or in certain sections of the venue, and by staging private performances in the drawing rooms of the rich and famous, exhibitors ensured their elite clientele a degree of social segregation while at the same time providing inexpensive amusement for the masses.[26]

As well as catering to a socially and economically diverse audience, freak shows, unlike many other leisure activities, also appealed to both men and women. Showmen actively courted a female clientele, for in the late nineteenth century women were emerging as important consumers of urban pleasures. By providing private viewing rooms "for ladies only," freak show entrepreneurs created safe spaces within potentially dangerous urban centers for middle-class women to relax and enjoy the spectacle without fear of male "pests."[27] Promotional materials for Barnum's 1889 London circus—which featured a substantial freak show—stressed that "unattended ladies and children can visit it with perfect propriety and safety."[28] By offering half-price tickets for children, freak show managers also suggested to women that this was a respectable family entertainment. They implicitly contrasted their shows with the "nearly naked dancing girls" and "poses plastiques"—in which women became "living statues" by assuming the poses of classical sculpture clad in bodystockings that simulated nudity—that were also enjoying a renaissance in the late nineteenth century.[29] Indeed, showmen like P. T. Barnum often advertised their acts as "clean, wholesome, amusing and highly instructive" and explicitly marketed them not only to parents, but also to teachers.[30] When the bearded lady Madame Fortune exhibited herself in 1852 her handbill maintained that "Ladies and Gentlemen who have the direction of Boarding Schools and Academies are particularly invited to visit her and her Child, with their Pupils and Children, in order to satisfy their curiosity on the subject of this most Wonderful Phenomenon."[31] Similarly, a giant and a fat lady on exhibit in a beer shop in Lambeth advertised in 1875 that their show was "CLEAN AND RESPECTABLE" and that "SCHOOLS AND PUBLIC PARTIES" would be "LIBERALLY TREATED WITH."[32]

This attempt to construct freak shows as respectable entertainment suggests that showmen understood that their exhibitions might draw in not only those seeking cheap thrills, but also elite consumers. In fact, the propriety of particular freak acts was heavily dependent on how they were packaged and the nature of the spaces they occupied. When "the Aztecs," the subjects of chapter 4, were exhibited to Queen Victoria—who was not only the head of state but a model of domesticity—the act immediately acquired the stamp of respectability. This royal sanction and that of the

"Emperor Napoleon and Imperial family of Russia, also Prussia, Austria, Holland and Denmark, [and the] King of the Belgians" was then used in their publicity materials to promote the act as suitable for even the most sophisticated audiences.[33] Scarcely a decade later, however, when "they had lost their celebrity and had fallen very low indeed," the Aztecs were being exhibited in a shop at the New Cut market on London's South Bank, a decidedly working-class venue where hucksters sold cheap food and utilitarian items and the entertainment cost little more than a penny.[34] Although the act itself had changed very little, its new physical location rendered the performance no longer suitable for bourgeois audiences. As chapter 4 will detail, when the act was repackaged yet again in the late 1860s and properly placed within the more fashionable spaces of the city, it once again attracted a "better clientele."

There was thus nothing inherent in the anatomical anomalies themselves that made an act more or less respectable, or indeed more likely to appeal to one audience than another. Rather, it was the ways in which acts were marketed as entertaining and educational and their ability to be manipulated and reshaped that made freak show performances popular across the social spectrum. Freak shows were thus one of only a few kinds of Victorian and Edwardian entertainment that explicitly catered to, and succeeded in attracting, an extremely broad audience that cut across lines of class, gender, age, and region. Male and female, young and old, rich and poor, and rural and urban alike stepped right up to see the tall and short, fat and thin, hairy and scaly bodies, "alive, alive!"

Showmen satisfied this seemingly boundless demand for freaks of nature with a steady supply of dwarfs, midgets, giants, conjoined twins, bearded women, skeleton dudes, fat ladies, albinos, and "savages." As I will discuss in greater detail below and again in chapter 5, "primitive" or "savage" Others were central players in nineteenth-century freak shows, their racial and cultural differences cast as a bodily anomaly analogous to physical deformation. But regardless of whether freaks had excess body hair, atypical skin, misshapen limbs, or merely skin color and other physical traits uncommon among their "Caucasian" audiences, human novelties often enhanced their performances by adopting the persona of a liminal being that occupied the borderland between human and animal. The Bear Lady, the Lion-faced Man, the Leopard Boy, the Frog Man, the Tiger Lady, and the Lobster Claw Lady all had popular acts in the last decades of the nineteenth century.[35] As Robert Bogdan, Elizabeth Stephens, Rosemarie Garland Thomson, and other scholars of the American freak show have argued, this persona was central to the act: when exhibiting themselves for profit these performers became freaks, assuming characters for the purposes of entertainment. It was the "techniques of exhibition in which corporeal difference is literally staged"—techniques that included costumes, choreography, and supporting materials such as souvenir photographs and pamphlets—that in the end constructed the anomalous body as freakish.[36] For, as Thomson has argued, the freak was "fabricated from the raw material of bodily variations" for entirely social purposes; the "freak of nature," she insists, was always in fact a "freak of culture."[37] The "freak" was, therefore, both an occupation—like "actor," "dancer," or "acrobat"—and a role that was produced in collaboration with the audience whose spectatorship itself shaped the construction of the performer's body as aberrant.[38] This was well understood, at least by a portion of the show-going public. In an 1898 article entitled "'EVEN AS YOU AND I' At Home with the Barnum Freaks," Arthur Goddard stressed the performative nature of the freak role. "In public they are 'freaks,'" he wrote, "but when they are off their platforms and their pedestals it is pleasant to find that, with the one particular reservation in each case, they are just men and women, normal and healthy, 'even as you and I.'"[39]

While freaks were performing a role, they were also interacting with audience members as individuals. Exhibitions were often called "levees," suggesting that freaks were receiving guests rather than merely showing their bodies to strangers. In fact, few freaks mutely and passively displayed their abnormalities on a stage removed from the spectators. Instead they conversed with the audience, often in more than one European language, moved among them, and invited the visitors to touch them, shake their hands, and even to kiss them. They usually performed songs, dances, or tricks to amuse the public, and at times they encouraged audience participation in their acts. A handbill for Julia Pastrana, "the Bear Woman," who sang songs in English and Spanish and danced the Highland Fling, advertised that "after each performance, [she] comes among the audience to converse and answer questions."[40] Madame Fortune's promotional material similarly maintained that "everybody will also be allowed to touch her Beard, so as to be convinced that it is perfectly natural."[41] As Rachel Adams has demonstrated in the context of the United States, the freak show experience was in fact far more interactive than critics have typically allowed.[42]

In fact, although primarily the objects of the gaze, freaks sometimes returned it. Chang and Eng, the original "Siamese twins," treated their spectators as spectacle: their biographers have noted that the twins carefully

Figure 2. Barnum and Bailey program, 1889. Guildhall Library, City of London.

observed and listened to their audience and commented to each other after the show about their own impressions of the crowd that flocked to see them.[43] Similarly, when "the Aztecs" first appeared in London they were immediately taken to the Royal College of Surgeons' Hunterian

Museum to gaze at the anatomical anomalies on display. The *Lancet* reported that they were "much struck" by the skeletons of Charles Byrne and Caroline Crachami, a giant and a dwarf who had been stars of the Regency freak show, and they "peered with great curiosity" at the mummies in their cases.[44] That they were allowed—in fact, invited—to look at other freaks rather than merely serving as the objects of curiosity suggests that "staring at the Other" sometimes went both ways.[45]

Not only were professional freaks invited to look at others, but, like other performers, they largely maintained control over their own exhibition and could negotiate the terms and conditions of their display. When Joseph Brice, "the French Giant," was exhibited in a private "Indian Temple" in Cremorne Gardens in 1862, he became indignant when his manager tried to introduce "the Woolly Woman of Hayti" into his show space, and he refused to perform until she was removed.[46] Indeed, according to classified ads placed in *The Era* and *World's Fair* in the late nineteenth and early twentieth centuries, freak performers—at least those who were adults, mentally competent, and came from developed Western societies—were clearly free agents who could ask for either a flat salary or a share of the profits. Some freaks used booking agents such as Count Orloff, "the Human Ostrich," whose act involved devouring strange objects. Orloff ran an international agency for freaks and "working acts" like himself,[47] but classified advertisements in the showmen's trade journals were the primary means by which freak performers found engagements. Ads frequently stated that the costs of traveling on tour—whether by train or in "comfortable wagons"—would be paid by the manager, that freaks were responsible for their own posters (or "flash," as they were called in the trade), and that they were required to send their publicity photos to prospective employers. This suggests that experienced freaks generally had enough capital to invest in the production of good-quality photographs and attractive posters and that they took responsibility for securing their own appearances on their own terms.[48]

That venue managers and touring shows sought to entice performers by paying their traveling expenses and offering them the choice between a salary and a share of the profits also suggests that this was a competitive market where freaks (who, unlike other laborers, were not a dime a dozen) could earn a decent income.[49] According to the showman Tom Norman, often the freak "could buy and sell the showman, by whom they have been engaged, because they are, or were, engaged on a salary, and apart from that, they generally had the privelidge [sic] of selling either pamphlets of their lives, or else photographs of themselves."[50] Indeed, souvenir photographs provided freak performers with "a virtually unending source of capital."[51] In addition, they could also pass the hat at the end of the show and pocket this income without paying any to the venue manager, the "taking of private collections being a weakness," according to the writer A. St. John Adcock, "inherent in all freaks and living sideshows from time immemorial."[52] Working as a freak thus appears to have been a fairly lucrative business, the work much easier and better paid than other types of relatively unskilled labor.

Even those who came from non-Western countries seem to have been able to make choices about their performances. As Roslyn Poignant has argued, aboriginal peoples whose lifeways had been destroyed by colonialism sometimes consented to join traveling shows, though this was often the best of very limited options. Her chronicle of the "Australian Cannibal Boomerang Throwers" reveals that although this group of indigenous Australians was essentially "abducted" and always underpaid for their labor, they were not mere victims of an avaricious showman. Instead Poignant maintains that the Aborigines were invested in their identities as performers, suggesting that they were not entirely without agency.[53] Similarly, a group of Zulus exhibited at Earl's Court in 1899 apparently chose to perform traditional dances in England rather than work in the dangerous mines of South Africa. According to *The Era,* the men seemed to relish their performance and refused to take direction from their manager, extending their songs and dances as long as they saw fit and thus exerting a degree of control over the manner of their exhibition.[54]

Managers were in fact often required by the government to provide proof that their performers had willingly agreed to contract themselves for entertainment purposes. When a group of Zulus appeared at the Royal Windsor Castle Menagerie in Shrewsbury the press noted that their exhibitor had to provide a deposit of almost £1,000 for their return and produce documentation that showed that the men had been taken before a "diplomatic agent" to swear that they were voluntarily agreeing to be exhibited.[55] Clifton Crais and Pamela Scully have demonstrated through a study of Sara Baartman—a Khoikhoi woman exhibited in London between 1810 and 1811 as "the Hottentot Venus"—that it is difficult to know whether these agreements really reflected informed consent.[56] However, the British government was clearly sensitive to the issue of exploitation, particularly in the wake of the abolishment of the slave trade in 1807 and of slavery itself in 1833. The state intervened in cases in which it believed that showmen were mistreating their "primitive" performers, recognizing that it was easy for exhibitors to take advantage of those who were far from home, spoke little English, and had no access to family or other safety nets. In 1890 the Home Office and the Foreign Office jointly helped to repatriate a group of Ona Indians back to Chile after they had arrived from a tour of Belgium destitute and had taken shelter in the Dover workhouse.[57] Similarly, in 1934 the Metropolitan Police stepped in to aid a dwarf woman from South Africa return to Pietermaritzburg. Exhibited as Princess Ubangi, the woman had been forced to perform while seriously ill due to a growth in her pelvis.[58]

Although Victorian and Edwardian freak shows were subjected to only minimal government regulation, it would nevertheless be historically inaccurate to position them as nothing more than an unscrupulous institution with greedy managers that held the most vulnerable members of society hostage. As Matthew Sweet has argued, to reduce the relationship between spectator and freak to patronizing voyeur on the one hand and "pathetic victim of exploitation" on the other oversimplifies the complexities and ambiguities of the freak show.[59] But in resisting this simplistic reading of the freak show as always already exploitative one runs the risk of substituting an equally naïve interpretation that champions the freak (or, indeed, the showman) as the real hero of this story and the public as his or her dupe. While it is important not to romanticize the show world—especially given the paucity of reliable sources produced by freaks themselves—it is nevertheless critical to allow for the agency of freak show performers. This is not merely in order to "rescue them from the enormous condescension of posterity,"[60] but rather to situate the freak show properly within the larger history of Victorian and Edwardian entertainment, and in relationship to British labor, social, and economic history.

Most freaks, whether British or foreign, though subject to the vagaries of the economy, were, like other types of performers, active agents in the marketplace for commercialized leisure.[61] Victorian critics of the freak show often assumed that freaks earned little money for their performances, "live[d] in a deplorable manner," and were regarded by their drunken managers as "valuable cattle."[62] But this is merely one reading of a much more complex relationship. The showman Tom Norman asserted that "95% of the freaks, novelties, etc. are very content."[63] Although the testimonials of showmen who profited from the exhibition of strange bodies are not sufficient evidence that freaks were not exploited, neither should this position be categorically dismissed. Some acts, such as "Krao, the Missing Link" and "the Aztecs" (discussed in chapters 3 and 4), did not elect to become freaks, and in fact appear to have been sold by their parents for the purposes of exhibition. But many people born with congenital anomalies clearly chose to perform as freaks—and stressed this in their promotional materials[64]—rather than seek out other forms of financial support or submit to institutionalization. If scholars such as David Gerber have quite rightly problematized the meaning of choice and consent in the case of the severely deformed, they have also often ignored the realities of the Victorian economy and of the social welfare system, both of which impacted not only those born with limiting disfigurements but also the working poor in general.[65] Tom Norman's son, George Barnum Norman, claimed that many "novelties" were "unwanted and cast out by their own families." They were, he insisted, "grateful for the opportunity to achieve some degree of independence—their only alternative being starvation or the workhouse."[66] While it would be misleading to celebrate the freak show as the only real sanctuary for the physically deformed, this is an important alternative reading of its role in Victorian and Edwardian society, and something I will explore in greater detail in chapter 1.

This book, however, also seeks to move beyond the binarism of victim and agent, arguing that this mode of analysis tends to close down any real discussion of the freak show's cultural work. As Scully and Crais have noted with respect to the large body of scholarship on "the Hottentot Venus," focusing on whether she possessed agency or did not forecloses our ability to ask more complicated questions about this type of historical subject and ultimately inhibits our ability to "develop analytical models that allow us to better explore the complexities of power, individual motivations, and social ascriptions, which we concede perhaps more clearly in the present than we can render in the past."[67] To understand the Victorian and Edwardian freak show as a cultural institution that in fact served a social purpose requires moving beyond debates about exploitation and instead foregrounding the meanings attached to particular anomalous bodies that were being produced, reproduced, and endlessly reworked by a variety of historical actors. *The Spectacle of Deformity* is intended to be a step in this direction.

THE FREAK SHOW AND THE BODY

Many historians and literary critics have found it difficult to move beyond these debates over victimization precisely because they have positioned freaks as "disabled people" and therefore maintain that their display must be construed as exploitative.[68] The most vocal critique of the freak show comes from scholars identified with the developing field of disability studies. Disability studies, which emerged in the 1970s from within the disability rights movement, seeks to explore "how different cultures, historical eras, and individuals have defined, understood, and experienced corporeal norms and corporeal deviances."[69] This work has been critical in shifting from the "medical model" of disability, which seeks to correct the disabled body in order to make it conform to social norms, to the "minority model" or "social model," which locates the "major disadvantage of disability in prejudicial social attitudes and exclusionary institutions rather than in bodies that have traditionally been cast as aberrant markers of inherent inferiority and personal misfortune."[70]

Catherine Kudlick has prompted historians to engage with the field of disability studies. She argues that disability is a "key defining social category" that, like race, class, and gender, is a valuable analytical tool for interrogating Otherness. It is crucial, she maintains, to understanding how societies have organized themselves hierarchically, and how the modern state in particular has emerged in relationship to the idea of the "capable citizen." Indeed, for Kudlick disability is not merely another "Other," but instead "reveals and constructs notions of citizenship, human difference, social values, sexuality, and the complex relationship between the biological and social worlds."[71] Kudlick's call is critical for, as David Mitchell and Sharon Snyder have argued, historians have too often deployed race, class, sexuality, and gender as categories of analysis without attending to the ways in which these categories are imbricated in discourses of ability and disability. Conversely, they argue, scholars who have foregrounded bodily aberrance often understand it merely as a signifier of race, class, gender, and sexual deviance rather than as its own distinct axis of difference that, although intricately related to these other categories, nevertheless leads to particular kinds of social and political exclusions.[72]

The intervention of historians is also critical because although disability studies scholars have demonstrated that disability is a "socially constructed identity that changes over time,"[73] they have been less attentive to historicizing the constructed nature of the physical body itself. Disability studies scholars frequently distinguish between "impairment" and "disability," as feminist scholars used to differentiate "sex" from "gender." If "impairment" is the "lack of a limb or part thereof or a defect of a limb, organ, or mechanism of the body," then "disability," activists and academics have argued, is a "form of disadvantage which is imposed on top of one's impairment."[74] But if historians of the body have in recent years argued that sex as much as gender is a historical production,[75] "impairment" often stands in disability studies discourse as a biological reality. The social model of disability, argue Mairian Corker and Tom Shakespeare, "sees disability as *socially created,* or constructed on top of impairment," implying that impairment is not in fact a social product.[76] While highly critical of the "medical model," disability studies have nevertheless, as Shelley Tremain argues, assumed that impairment is an "objective, transhistorical and transcultural entity which biomedicine accurately represents," thus inadvertently reifying medical interpretations of bodily difference. The term "impairment," Tremain maintains, is not value-neutral; as much as "disability," it is the product of historically contingent relations of power.[77]

But if impairment is a problematic term, so too is disability, for it evokes an understanding of bodily difference that began to take shape only in the early part of the twentieth century and thus expresses a specific, historical relationship between the self, the state, and the social. To speak of a group of people whose bodies have been deemed aberrant as "the disabled" is not merely to identify them as the "*objects* of institutionalized discourses" produced through historical, social, and political "narratives of malignancy, excessive dependency, and . . . parasitism."[78] Rather, it is also to identify this understanding of bodily difference as the product of a particular historical moment, something that disability studies scholarship has often overlooked. In an otherwise theoretically rich study of the American freak show, Rosemarie Garland Thomson has argued that the "wondrous monsters of antiquity, who became the fascinating freaks of the nineteenth century, transformed into the disabled people of the later twentieth century," suggesting that although the terms may have changed, the cultural meanings attached to physical difference have remained constant.[79] Rather than argue that freaks were transformed into the disabled, this book maintains that "freakery" and "disability" were radically different ways of dealing with difference that should not be collapsed.

"The disabled"—as distinct from "the deformed," "the infirm," "the impotent," or "the crippled," terms with their own discrete meanings—emerged as a category in Britain only around the turn of the century, in the years after the outbreak of the Boer War. It referred specifically to wounded soldiers and sailors, particularly the limbless, who, having sacrificed their bodily integrity for the safety of the nation, could now make demands upon the state.[80] The term "disabled" was not widely used, though, until the First World War, when it was sometimes used interchangeably with "handicapped," a term taken directly from the world of sports (according to the *Oxford English Dictionary*, "handicapped" was applied to the "physically or mentally defective" and especially to children beginning around 1915). As Seth Koven has eloquently argued, the relationship between wounded soldiers and handicapped boys was in fact encouraged by the state during and after the First World War as a way for both parties to recoup their masculinity.[81] The category of "the disabled" took shape, then, at a particular historical moment when the British government was forced to reevaluate the rights and responsibilities of citizenship, and when British society was compelled to rethink the social meanings attached to bodily disfigurement. The disabled thus only became a socially relevant category in the second decade of the twentieth century, when thousands of wounded soldiers returned from the front and needed to be "rehabilitated" and reincorporated into British society.[82]

The problem with using disability to interrogate the Victorian and Edwardian freak show, then, is that scholars have often collapsed the analytical category and the specific meanings and connotations of this word. To understand the freak show we must deploy the analytical category of disability, for freaks were eagerly consumed by a broad public precisely because of the cultural significance attached to their bodily difference. As this book will argue, displays of "human oddities" functioned as important spaces for negotiations over the class, gender, racial, ethnic, and sexual meanings of "normal" and "abnormal" bodies, terms that, as Georges Canguilhem has argued, are as much social as scientific.[83] Freaks were thus key to the production of the categories of "the self" and "the other."

But the tendency of scholars to apply late twentieth-century conceptions of disability to the bodies of nineteenth-century freaks obscures the fact that the ways in which difference is categorized is never self-evident but rather always culturally contingent. If we historicize "the disabled" and understand the concept as a twentieth-century category that took shape in the context of wartime bodily sacrifice and state compensation for injuries, then nineteenth-century freak performers were not "disabled." Historians working under the rubric of queer studies have demonstrated that "homosexual" is not an identity or social category that can usefully be mapped back onto sexual practices and subjectivities before the late nineteenth century. Likewise, "disabled" is not a particularly useful term for freak show performers as it masks more than it reveals and subsequently closes down historical analysis of the meanings invested in the display of human anomalies. To speak of freak show performers as "disabled" thus works against the purpose of the field of disability studies, which seeks to reveal the ways in which perceptions of bodily difference are culturally conditioned.

Some disability studies scholars, particularly those working in the American context, have been extremely sensitive to issues of language.[84] Historians of modern Britain, however, have tended to be less invested in historicizing the concepts and terms associated with bodily aberrance. In Britain, according to the *Oxford English Dictionary*, the word "disability" originally denoted an incapacity to hold political office, referring to a legal disqualification from the duties and privileges accorded only to certain kinds of citizens. No later than the seventeenth century the word "disabled" also came to mean incapacitated because of physical injury, but it was not widely used in this sense. The more common term for this condition was "cripple," a term that had been employed since at least the tenth century to refer to those lacking full use of their limbs.

The social category of "the cripple" was well established in British culture by the Victorian period, in part through characters such as Dickens's Tiny Tim. Indeed, crippled beggars were highly visible members of the urban populace throughout the nineteenth century. Like freaks they, too, displayed their non-normative bodies to strangers. But unlike freaks— who cast themselves as professional entertainers and rarely attempted to solicit pity from their audiences[85]—crippled beggars hoped to evoke empathy and thus receive alms precisely because they were unable to labor. This appeal to a generous public for financial support, or indeed to the state itself for some form of relief, placed "cripples" in an entirely separate category from freak show performers, as the distinction between "able-bodied" and not was rooted not in the deformity of the body per se but rather in understandings of its capacity for labor.

If the term "disability" was not frequently used in the nineteenth century to refer to physically compromised bodies, "able-bodied" was a widely understood concept and category because of the term's associations with the New Poor Law. Clause twenty-seven of the 1834 Poor Law Amendment Act distinguished between the "able-bodied" poor (those who could work) and those who "from old Age or Infirmity of Body" were "wholly unable to work." Although the latter were permitted to receive "outdoor" poor relief—food, money, or medicine while remaining in their own homes— the former could seek aid from the government only if prepared to give up their independent existence and enter a workhouse. The opposite of "able-bodied" in the nineteenth century, then, was neither "disabled" nor "deformed" but "infirm."

According to Sidney and Beatrice Webb—the Fabian socialists who became experts on poor law policy—"infirm" was defined as "permanently incapacitated, whether from old age, physical defect, or chronic debility, from obtaining any paid employment."[86] The term was used alongside "impotent," which suggested bodily weakness, particularly in relation to the limbs. Indeed, the term used in the poor laws that is closest to the twentieth-century category of "the disabled" is "defectives." This initially referred only to the blind, deaf, and dumb, but after 1847 included also the lame and the deformed. Deborah Stone has argued, therefore, that "English Poor Law policy dealt with disability as a variety of very separate conditions."[87] More to the point, the crucial distinction made in Victorian society was between those who could work, and were thus by definition able-bodied, and those who could not and were thus, whatever their specific capacities or incapacities, classified as infirm.

As I will argue in more detail in chapter 1, the mere fact that they were working, being paid to exhibit their bodies, meant that freak performers were classified as able-bodied. By working, freaks demonstrated their respectable status as self-sufficient laborers and resisted the idea that they were dependents suffering from what the poor law termed "infirmity of the body." In fact, freaks were heavily invested in their status as "able-bodied," which, as I have suggested, had particularly important political and social ramifications in the age of the workhouse. The armless and legless invariably incorporated into their acts demonstrations of their skills and capacities. Charles Tripp, "the Armless Wonder," had, according to his publicity materials, "educated himself to use his feet with a deftness that few men of even mechanical bent attain with their hands." He could light a cigarette with his feet and demonstrated his "superior penman[ship]" on a writing desk that was "entirely the construction of his nimble and well-trained toes."[88] Similarly, Herr Unthan, also advertised as "the Armless Wonder," could shake hands, offer a glass of wine, roll a cigarette, play cards, play the violin and cornet, and "shoot the spot out of the ace of hearts," all with his feet.[89] The "Lobster Claw Lady," exhibited during Easter week in 1898, apparently had full use of her severely deformed hands: "when this most wonderful lady is knitting, sewing, crocheting, and doing all kinds of pretty embroidery work," her handbill proclaimed, "she does so with the same freedom and accuracy as any other lady might with their hands and fingers."[90]

But freaks did not perform only menial activities that reduced them to the "lowest common denominator" of humanity, as some scholars have suggested.[91] At Barnum's Greatest Show on Earth in London in 1889 the legless performed as aerial gymnasts, displaying their skill at feats that most people with all their limbs intact would not dare to attempt, while the armless were advertised as "artistic workmen" who could do crafts that required considerable expertise.[92] When Chang and Eng, the original "Siamese twins," exhibited themselves, they amazed the audience with their acrobatic tricks, leaping from their feet to their hands in unison.[93] Those exhibited because of their strange appearance or size but whose deformities did not interfere with their capacity to lead otherwise ordinary lives also demonstrated their particular talents in front of eager audiences. "The Great Chak-A-Nooray," whose only extraordinary characteristic seemed to be a huge head of frizzy hair, advertised that he would demonstrate his skill at archery and Japanese top spinning at each performance.[94] The diminutive Tom Thumb not only posed as different characters but also recited Napoleon's "celebrated Speech to his army," sang a variety of patriotic songs, played the hornpipe, and performed the "Jockey Dance."[95] Thus freaks of all varieties tended to construct themselves as skilled performers whose bodies allowed them to lead normal, if not extraordinary, lives, a fact that was clearly central to their public personae.

In a publicity stunt orchestrated by the Barnum and Bailey Circus for its London show in 1899, the sideshow performers issued a manifesto that made this point explicit. Some of the performers, the statement declared, "are really the development of a higher type, and are superior persons, inasmuch as some of us are gifted with extraordinary attributes not apparent in ordinary beings." Freaks were not lacking in any way, according to the manifesto. Rather, the fact that they were "possessed of more or less limbs, more or less hair, more or less bodies, more or less physical or mental attributes than other people," might in fact "be taken as additional charms of person or aids to movement, as the case may be."[96] Indeed, freak performers often drew a clear distinction between themselves and those whom they considered physically disadvantaged. When a one-eyed man attended Chang and Eng's show in New York the twins insisted that he pay only half price, as "he had not had the same advantage as the others."[97] A souvenir pamphlet sold at their 1830 London show claimed that "being visited by a cripple, who had lost both arms and feet, they told him how sincerely they pitied him, and that as they had four hands and he none, it was their duty to assist him and immediately made him a present of a crown, and some cigars."[98] Freaks thus did not necessarily think of themselves as physically compromised and actually often saw others as much less able. Many freaks, in fact, had bodily anomalies that in no way interfered with their cognitive or physical abilities. They often possessed excess hair, unusual pigmentation, extra appendages, or other physical traits that even today would not be categorized as a disability, for the freak show was a space to exhibit bodily differences of all varieties.

Those who displayed themselves as freaks in the nineteenth and early twentieth centuries were, therefore, often "deformed" but neither "infirm" nor "disabled." It is only by unpacking the much more precise and complicated meanings attached to bodily difference in the heyday of the modern freak show that we can hope to understand the cultural significance of these exhibitions. The purpose of this book is not to "reflect critically on the utility of the freak show for understanding the contemporary predicament of disabled people," as some members of the disability studies community have approached this topic.[99] Rather, it is to account for the modern British freak show's widespread appeal by understanding it as a product of its time and place. It is precisely because human oddities were always open to a variety of interpretations that the freak show is such an important site for interrogating the specific ways in which nineteenth- and early twentieth-century Britons differentiated between "normal" and "abnormal" bodies and the significance that they attached to these distinctions.

THE MEDICALIZATION OF MONSTROSITY

As Lennard J. Davis has argued, the word "normal," denoting conforming to the common type, didn't emerge in the English language until around 1840; its derivatives "norm," "normality," and "normalcy" followed shortly afterward. It is thus possible, argues Davis, "to date the coming into consciousness in English of an idea of 'the norm' over the period 1840–1860."[100] The widespread fascination with bodily anomalies that, as *Punch* shrewdly noted, seemed to have intensified around the 1840s was therefore a response to not only the expansion of the leisure market but also changes in scientific understandings of the body. The concept of "the norm" emerged in Britain in relationship to the science of statistics, which, as Davis points out, was central to eugenics. The science—or, perhaps more accurately, the pseudoscience—of the betterment of a race through selective breeding practices, eugenics explicitly sought to encourage the reproduction of the fittest members of society and thus to eliminate freaks. The construction of the category of "the normal," and consequently "the abnormal" or "the freak," was thus intimately related to an increased concern about the health and fitness of the white British body.[101] Freak shows were thus part of a much larger scientific discourse of the corporeal norm that arose around the middle of the nineteenth century.

Scholars have generally tended to agree that by the eighteenth century, at the very latest, gazing at "monsters"—the medical term used at the time for those born with significant anomalies—had become not only a popular pleasure but also a scientific pursuit incorporated into the study of anatomy and natural history.[102] With the emergence of teratology and teratogeny (the sciences of birth defects) in the nineteenth century, the study of monsters evolved into a medical specialty in its own right. Since the 1830s Isidore Geoffroy Saint-Hilaire—who with his father Etienne developed the field of teratology—had argued that congenital anomalies were not random but rather fell into clear categories that could, in fact, be scientifically classified. Anomalous bodies were thus not symptomatic of a chaotic universe, but rather they offered an opportunity "to understand the natural order more fully and to define it with greater precision."[103] Saint-Hilaire's 1832 book on the subject, *Histoire générale et particulière des anomalies de l'organization chez l'homme et les animaux,* theorized that even monstrous bodies conformed to natural laws and, if correctly examined, would reveal their principles of organization. An 1833 review of the book in the *Lancet,* the prestigious British medical journal, while lamenting the woeful inadequacy of English embryology, championed this new science of teratology, arguing that increased "scrutiny and observation" had allowed the study of congenital anomalies to become more scientific and thus freed from superstition.[104] The work of Saint-Hilaire marked the consolidation, historians have repeatedly argued, of the medicalization of the freakish body that characterizes the modern period, the moment when all forms of bodily difference were scientifically catalogued and subsumed within knowable categories.[105]

But the medicalization of the anomalous body was far from complete by the nineteenth century, as the persistence of freak shows suggests. The idea that after 1820 the "cultural differences between kinds of curiosity became more easily classifiable as either professional or prurient"[106] is in fact itself a product of the nineteenth century. This narrative was constructed during the late Victorian period by medical practitioners themselves as part of their assertion of their own relatively new professional identity. In fact, throughout the nineteenth century expert knowledge about the natural world continued to be produced in a dynamic relationship to popular ideas and discourses.[107] The nineteenth century was a watershed not because of the success of the pathological categorization of bodily anomalies, but rather because it marks a key moment of contestation between popular and professional ideas. Scientific practices and theories in this period were rarely the property of the privileged few but grew out of negotiations between newly emerging professionals and the general public who were equally, but differently, invested in understanding nature. While attempting to construct themselves as experts with specialized knowledge, Victorian scientists nevertheless incorporated vernacular categories into their classificatory systems and used technologies and techniques of display familiar to a public who had by the first decades of the 1800s become accustomed to being called upon to witness, and to participate in, the production of scientific knowledge.[108]

Indeed, the scientific study of bodily anomalies, even when conducted within the confines of medical schools and professional societies, continued to rely heavily on their display as wonders, a commercial and cultural practice that, as we have seen, dates back at least as far as the sixteenth century. Medical researchers used the freak show as a source of raw material. Saint-Hilaire himself had been eager to bring the conjoined twins Chang and Eng to Paris but had been refused by the government, which instituted a ban on this particular act that remained in place almost five years.[109] In Britain, no legislation or government interference prevented the exhibition of human curiosities until the labor and alien laws of the interwar period. Thus, like the curious public, medical professionals were free to visit any number of freak shows, at which they could see and sometimes even examine the anomalous bodies on display. In his textbook on skin diseases, H. Radcliffe Crocker, the most distinguished British dermatologist of his day, described not only "the Elephant Man," but also other acts he had personally seen exhibited in Barnum's circus and at the Westminster Aquarium.[110] As chapters 1 and 2 illustrate, the surgeons Frederick Treves and John Bland Sutton both made a habit of scouting these exhibitions for pathological cases. An 1898 article in the *Guyoscope*, a medical *Punch*, satirized this scientific obsession with sideshow acts by describing the efforts of "a senior physician on the staff of the leading London Hospital" who attended Barnum's show in order to "inspect the freaks in the scientific interest."[111] The naturalist Frank Buckland, although admittedly more curious and adventurous than most Victorian scientists, proudly declared, "I always go into caravan exhibitions at fairs, &c."[112] Indeed, he became friends with conjoined twins Millie-Christine and Chang and Eng, as well as the giants Joseph Brice and Anna Swan.[113]

George M. Gould and Walter L. Pyle's *Anomalies and Curiosities of Medicine,* published in the United States in 1896 and released in a London edition the following year, maintained that "hardly any medical journal is without its rare or 'unique' case."[114] Even the *Lancet*—which by the late nineteenth century had firmly established itself as a serious medical journal—regularly published case reports on freak exhibitions, accompanying the description of the fantastic body on display with a medical diagnosis.[115] In a series of lectures at the City Orthopaedic Hospital, which were later published in 1862, the surgeon E. J. Chance detailed the case of "the Porcupine Man," a popular freak show performer whose skin was "bristly."[116] Similarly, in his manual on antenatal pathology, the well-known British obstetrician J. W. Ballantyne repeatedly drew on examples from the show world. In his discussion of congenital hypertrichosis (the superabundance of hair) he mentions the Sacred Hairy Family of Burma, Krao the Missing Link, Julia Pastrana, and Adrian and Fedor Jeftichew, "the Kostroma people," all popular sideshow attractions.[117]

By the end of the nineteenth century, medical textbooks and encyclopedias regularly used images of freaks to illustrate various congenital conditions.[118] Gould and Pyle included in their text souvenir photographs of well-known freak acts, often erasing their frames and thus effacing the commercial origins of the illustrations. The Elephant Man, Lalloo, the Aztecs, and Krao, the Missing Link all appear in *Anomalies and Curiosities of Medicine,* which at first glance might seem to be a compendium of sideshow acts rather than a medical textbook. The circulation in obstetrical journals of graphic images of monstrous births—little different from the "pickled punks" on display at sideshows—was in fact central to the emergence of obstetrical specialization in the early twentieth century. Publishing case reports distinguished the obstetrician from the general practitioner who was not engaged in scientific research.[119] The freak exhibition thus provided scientists and medical professionals access to what they perceived as medical specimens. This enabled them to assert their authority over the deformed body, despite the fact that scientific medicine could often do very little to treat either the symptoms associated with or the underlying causes of these types of anomalies. Far from being "a throwback to some barbaric past," the Victorian freak show was, therefore, "an adjunct to the culture of scientific rationalism."[120]

But however much scientific medicine, which was only beginning to become professionalized in the second half of the nineteenth century, sought to control how the public interpreted deformities, they were only

Figure 3. Poster for Adrian and Fedor Jeftichew, the Kostroma People, South London Palace, 1874. Wellcome Library, London.

marginally successful in doing so. In 1898 the *Lancet* claimed to have received letters from the public asking for a medical explanation for the freaks on display at the Barnum and Bailey Circus.[121] However, the obstetrician J. W. Ballantyne admitted that the public was not in fact always interested in medical interpretations of human anomalies but rather "look[ed] upon monstrosities to-day very much in the same way as did the general public and the [medical] profession as well in the Middle Ages."[122]

This was in part precisely because the medical community had not been particularly successful in either diagnosing or curing what they claimed were pathological disorders. But it was also because showmen were able to perpetuate a fantastic reading of the freakish body and thus succeeded in discouraging audiences from seeing their exhibits as diseased. The extraordinary bodies they displayed were wondrous, promoters maintained, precisely because they defied scientific classification. Their exhibits were not examples of known medical conditions, showmen argued, but instead were "unique," "singular," and "rare." Terms like "nondescript" were frequently applied to such acts to emphasize their inability to be accurately categorized.[123] This, of course, was a marketing strategy: to insist that your act was the only one of its kind ensured a larger audience. At the same time, though, it challenged the medical profession's attempt to classify these bodies as medical cases and thus to close down other interpretations of their deformities.[124]

Not only did freak acts and their managers resist a medical diagnosis, but they took great pains to establish that they were not exhibiting a diseased or unhealthy body. Freaks often maintained that they were in good health. Mr. Tipney, the Skeleton Man, announced that he had a robust appetite and good strength and, despite his emaciated form, was in surprising "health."[125] Miss Annie Jones, Barnum's bearded lady, sold a souvenir pamphlet in the United Kingdom that maintained that she "enjoys the best of health."[126] Miss Bounds, the Bear Lady, who walked on all fours, announced in her souvenir autobiography that although she had severely deformed limbs, in all "other parts of my body I am full grown and healthy, and I am not behind other ordinary built ladies." She declared, "I enjoy excellent health and have a good appetite."[127] "The Human Tripod," a three-legged child exhibited in 1846, was described as "being otherwise a very fine, well-made, healthy, and lively boy" aside from "having THREE LEGS, AND TWENTY TOES . . . a BIPENIS, AS WELL AS A TRISCELES."[128] When Lalloo, the subject of chapter 2, was exhibited in the 1880s with a parasitic twin protruding from his abdomen, his pamphlet insisted that "his health is excellent."[129]

This emphasis placed upon the health of freak show acts suggested that although it may have been indecent to gawk at the sick, the deformed body excited a healthy curiosity that there was no need to deny. Erin O'Connor has argued that Victorian critics of the freak show maintained that it led to "aesthetic aphasia," erasing the need to distinguish between the beautiful and the ugly. The countless exhibits of monstrosities, accessible to all through the advent of a new mass commodity culture, produced, she insists, a "public sensibility so dull, that it could not even register disease as disease."[130] However, just as freak performers did not consider themselves disabled, so too did they resist being categorized as diseased. As this litany of proclamations of health makes clear, freaks did not consider themselves sick or in need of medical treatment.

This did not mean, however, that they completely shunned the medical profession. Rather, they often used the language of medicine and appealed to its emerging authority for their own ends. Doctors and surgeons, whether real or fake, were called on to verify the authenticity of the body on display and to testify to its health. Their expertise, however, was otherwise irrelevant, as there was nothing, the publicity materials implied, that required medical intervention. Freak show entrepreneurs regularly used the testimonials of doctors, which as often as not were completely fabricated, to support their claims about the uniqueness and authenticity of their acts.[131] When Tom Thumb was exhibited in 1846 his handbill proclaimed that "Her Majesty's Physicians, have pronounced him the most symmetrical Dwarf in the world!"[132] The poster for a "Full-Grown Female CHILD WITH TWO HEADS" exhibited in London's Drury Lane in 1853 testified that she had been pronounced by "the most eminent physicians and surgeons in London" to be "the most wonderful production nature ever produced."[133] Both "the Double Man," who not only had two hearts but whose right side was muscular and masculine while his left was undeveloped and dainty, and "Master Esau Battae," whose upper body was apparently covered in flexible rainbow-striped hair, and countless other freaks advertised that they had been examined by medical professionals and certified as authentic.[134]

Although some freak entrepreneurs were deliberately vague in their publicity materials, mentioning "Medical Gentlemen" and "eminent Surgeons" without naming any names, a significant number drew on (or invented their own) experts with the appropriate credentials, such as Member of the Royal College of Surgeons (MRCS), Fellow of the Royal College of Physicians (FRCP), or Fellow of the Royal College of Surgeons (FRCS). This suggests that they and their audiences were sensitive to the professional distinctions that separated the reliable, licensed practitioner from the mere quack. Many advertisements claimed that their freaks had been examined by the "medical faculty" at London's most prestigious hospitals, such as St. Thomas', St. Bartholomew's, and Guy's.[135] In 1850 a handbill for the "Fairy Queen" asserted that she was not only "acknowledged to be the smallest living child in the world" but that she had "been exhibited at the University College, London, before 500 medical gentlemen."[136] Similarly, James Paine, "the Giant Boy," was pronounced "perfectly healthy" by the "most eminent of the Faculty." A testimonial from a Fellow of the Royal College of Surgeons maintained that he was "free from dropsy, and all other disease."[137] Freak shows thus used the language and growing authority of professional medicine to promote their acts and attract spectators. For this reason, having the certification of the medical faculty became an asset in the show world: a classified advertisement for "High-Class Prodigies" in *The Era* in 1899 declared that it "will always pay a fair price for all who have testimonials from Schools of Medicine."[138]

These shows, however, were more careful than medical professionals to differentiate between deformity, which they implied could be displayed, and disease, which they appeared to agree could not. While doctors sought to diagnose bodily anomalies and thus explain them scientifically, exhibitors had a clear stake in resisting any attempt to pathologize the freak, which would render their display unseemly and undermine their status as wondrous, unique, and thus marketable. But by advertising freaks as healthy rather than diseased, and as remarkable rather than disgusting, these types of exhibitions also allowed for human diversity and celebrated bodily variation. They thus served as spaces of resistance to what Leslie Fiedler calls "the tyranny of the normal."[139] For, unlike medical science, the spectacle of the freak exhibit "tries to expand the possibilities of interpretation" of the deformed body rather than containing its definition and meaning "through classification and mastery."[140] Far from being merely exploitative, these types of shows, therefore, allowed for and in fact promoted discussion about the potential meanings attached to bodily anomalies. This did not mean that they suggested an innate equality between all bodies, for freak shows clearly distinguished between the normal and the aberrant and often upheld the hierarchies so central to modern British culture. Nevertheless, they invited multiple interpretations, not limited to the medical, of the significance of physical difference and thus opened up public debate about the ramifications of where the boundary between the self and the other could be, and should be, drawn.

Distinguishing between the self and the other was critical in the Age of Imperialism, as the maintenance of Britain's far-flung empire was dependent upon establishing and, crucially, naturalizing the difference between ruler and ruled, a project that by the middle of the nineteenth century was intimately bound up in the discourses of bodily norms. It is no coincidence that the heyday of the commercial freak show was also the moment when Britain consolidated its imperial might. Crucial to empire building was the establishment of Britain's ability to defend its expanding territory by advertising to itself and to the world that it had fit, healthy, capable citizens at its disposal. Accounting for the physical differences among races and for bodily deformities that occurred even among the more "favored" races was central to British attempts to manage anxieties around bodily fitness at a crucial moment in its history. The freak show was part and parcel of this process, as it explicitly underscored the distinction between civilized and savage, modern and ancient, evolved and primitive, white and black, and, by implication, governing and governed. It is for this reason that so many of these shows featured not only those born with congenital anomalies, but also non-Western peoples.

Exotic peoples from far-flung places had been exhibited in the United Kingdom since the early sixteenth century. As early as 1501 a group of Inuit were on display in Bristol; in 1603 indigenous Virginians could be seen canoeing on the Thames.[141] When Trinculo stumbles upon Caliban, a classic "wild man" character, in Shakespeare's 1610 play *The Tempest,* his first thought is to take him home in order to display him as a novelty. In England, he declares to Stephano, "any strange beast makes a man: when they will not give a doit [a trifling sum] to relieve a lame beggar, they will lay out ten to see a dead Indian." In the eighteenth century, with the expansion of overseas travel, exploration, and colonization, exotic others began to be exhibited more frequently as living curiosities. In 1787 "three MOST WONDERFUL WILD BORN HUMAN BEINGS," supposedly from South America, each with a "monstrous CRAW under the Throat," could be seen in London for two shillings.[142] The availability of foreign performers only increased during the nineteenth century as contact between Britain and the wider world became more commonplace, in part as a result of colonial relationships.

Scholars have often argued that the freak show and the ethnographic show represent two different "traditions of human display," and thus have tended to treat them separately.[143] But exhibitions of exotic peoples were not, in fact, a wholly distinctive category of performance.[144] In his 1902 account of "sideshow London," A. St. John Adcock described a typical show that featured both "a bearded lady" and "three reputed Africans [who] lick red-hot pokers that sizzle on their tongues, and quaff boiling lead out of rusty ladles with manifestations of keen enjoyment."[145] This aggregation of *lusus naturae* and ethnographic "specimens" in one show space is crucial to understanding the nature of the Victorian and Edwardian freak show and the ways in which it operated as a site for the construction of racial and imperial ideologies. By displaying people of color alongside bearded ladies, armless men, and conjoined twins, sideshow performances explicitly configured racial otherness as freakish bodily difference and thus normalized the white British body.

The exhibition of "the Leopard Boy" in 1881, for example, helped to establish for a broad British public the normative nature of the "Caucasian," and thus the intrinsic aberrance of all Others. A twelve-year-old boy whose base skin color was that of "the ordinary African negro bronzed black," "the Leopard Boy" had "a multitude of white spots, in size varying from that of a threepenny piece to the palm of one's hand," all over his body and hair. Advertised as likely a "hybrid between two races of people of totally different colours," this act unequivocally represented the product of racial mixing as freakish, and thus warned spectators of the physical repercussions of cross-breeding and the necessity for preserving the purity of the white body.[146] These anxieties about miscegenation were played out on stage at a moment in which Britain's relationship to Africa was intensifying as the population of white settlers in southern Africa expanded in the wake of the discovery of gold and diamonds. Displays of bodily difference were thus part of the discourse of imperial superiority that rested on seemingly scientific studies of race.

The emergence of anthropology as a scientific discipline—one that attempted to account for the disparities among the so-called "varieties of mankind"—was thus intimately connected to sideshow spectacle.[147] Impresarios in fact often cast themselves as anthropologists: A. E. Pickard—"the Barnum of the North," who ran the largest freak museum in Glasgow—claimed that his exhibitions were not merely entertaining but contributed to the production of knowledge about mankind. The man who wishes to succeed in the freak business, claimed an article about Pickard in *World's Fair*, "is the one who studies every point of Anthropological and Ethnological Science, without this he cannot call himself a real showman, but will only find a back seat as an exhibitor."[148] Showmen often employed ethnologists to find them specimens for display.

G. A. Farini, who was charged with stocking the Westminster Aquarium with human and animal novelties, regularly contracted with explorers, some of whom were coming to define themselves as anthropologists. He frequently obtained the services of Carl Bock, a Norwegian naturalist whom Farini described as an "ethnological research[er]."[149] Bock's sensational book *The Head Hunters of Borneo* was reviewed by Alfred Russel Wallace—cofounder of the theory of evolution—who considered it a valuable text; indeed, it continues to be used by anthropologists today.[150] In these early days of anthropology there was, therefore, no clear distinction between the mere freak hunter and the true ethnographer.

While showmen relied on anthropologists to track down exotic peoples and to provide testimonials that corroborated the authenticity of their acts, anthropologists at the same time used the showmen's exhibitions to gain access to ethnological "specimens." John Conolly, president of the Ethnological Society, was adamant that his colleagues should examine and report on these types of exhibits. "If such an examination and report would be useful and instructive as respects exhibitions of a genuine and honest character, it might still more serve to inform the public . . . and to guard them from imbibing erroneous information, whether arising from ignorance, or offered to them by impudence and fraud."[151] The Ethnological Society, and later the Anthropological Society (which broke away from the former group in 1863), frequently examined foreign performers, both at their shows and at their societies' headquarters, debated their origins and authenticity, and wrote extensively about how these acts contributed to knowledge about racial difference. Like the nascent medical profession, the emerging field of anthropology was thus heavily invested in the freak show and attempted not to close them down, but rather to exploit these exhibitions for their own purposes.

Freak shows thus served as important venues for the production of both popular and professional racial discourses, as they explicitly rendered non-white peoples as aberrant. Indeed, as the case of "the Leopard Boy" reveals, this message was reinforced not merely by the fact that non-Western peoples shared the stage with *lusus naturae,* but also because many acts were simultaneously congenitally anomalous and racially other. This conflation of "freak" and "type" had been commonplace since at least the early years of the nineteenth century, when Sara Baartman appeared in London, Manchester, and Limerick as "the Hottentot Venus." Baartman was a Khoikhoi woman who attracted curious crowds eager to see a "Hottentot" exhibited with the appropriate trappings of Africanness. But she also had what appeared to European audiences to be unusually large buttocks, which were read by some as a freakish mutation and by others as merely typical of Khoikhoi women. To accentuate her buttocks she appeared in a tight-fitting costume that closely matched her skin color, thus creating the illusion of nakedness. According to contemporary reports her dress was "intended to give the appearance of being undressed."[152] As Bernth Lindfors has argued, Baartman thus "offered the British public at least three kinds of sideshow stimulation: she was part freak, part savage, part cooch dancer."[153] As I have suggested, however, these categories were not easily distinguishable from each other, or from the larger colonial narrative that ultimately framed the show. Zine Magubane has persuasively argued that Baartman's exhibition must be understood within the context of larger imperial debates over slavery and the expansion of empire in the Cape Colony.[154] But Baartman's physical peculiarities, appearance of nakedness, and implied hypersexuality in and of themselves also served to justify Baartman's colonial subjugation. The character of "the Hottentot Venus," as well as many of the case studies in this book, ultimately collapsed the categories of the ethnographic type and the freak of nature and discouraged audiences from distinguishing between a body that was anomalous in relation to the human species and one that merely diverged from the white British "norm." These shows reveal, therefore, that racial difference was produced in dynamic relationship to other forms of corporeal "deviance" and cannot be divorced from the discourses of deformity more generally.

Whether displaying "Siamese twins," "missing links," or savage "cannibal kings," freak shows raised, and often attempted to answer, critical questions about the social and political meanings attached to human bodily variation. This book investigates the cultural construction of these corporeal hierarchies from within the historical context of the nineteenth and early twentieth centuries. It argues that between roughly 1847, when the term "freak of nature" began to be widely used, and 1914, when the First World War radically reconfigured how society would manage bodily deformity, the British were heavily invested in clarifying the boundaries between normal and abnormal bodies and that the freak show was central to this process. *The Spectacle of Deformity* posits that Victorian and Edwardian freak shows were popular not merely because they were voyeuristic venues that offered a rare glimpse of the grotesque. Rather, by exploring the imprint of class, gender, sex, race, and ethnic difference on the body, freak shows helped to articulate the cultural meanings invested in otherness—and thus clarified what it meant to be British—at a moment in which Britain was constructing itself as a modern and imperial, and thus model, nation.

ONE

Monstrosity, Masculinity, and Medicine

Reexamining "the Elephant Man"

IN FEBRUARY OF 1923 TOM NORMAN, one of the best known showmen of his day, wrote to the showmen's trade journal *World's Fair*. He was responding to an article about the surgeon Frederick Treves's recently published memoir, *The Elephant Man and Other Reminiscences*, which the weekly claimed "tells a true story [of a freak] that surely has never been equalled in any tragedy or romance ever written as fiction."[1] Norman, who had served as one of four business managers for Joseph Merrick, "the Elephant Man," during the brief period that he had exhibited himself in England, sought "to point out some mistakes" in Treves's account, which he suggested *World's Fair* had uncritically reproduced. Norman objected to Treves's condemnation of the institution of the freak show and his assumption that Merrick had been mistreated by his exhibitors, claiming that "the big majority of showmen are in the habit of treating their novelties as human beings, and in a large number of cases as one of their own, and not like beasts." Indeed, Norman declared, as far as "his comfort was concerned while with us, no parent could have studied their own child more than any of all the four of us studied Joseph Meyrick's [sic]."[2]

Tom Norman's account of "the Elephant Man"—which appears not only in his letter to *World's Fair* but also in the showman's own memoirs—contrasts sharply with that of Treves. Treves positioned Merrick as an abandoned, friendless, and exploited misfit who had been exhibited as "an object of loathing." "He was shunned like a leper," declared Treves, "housed like a wild beast, and got his only view of the world from a peephole in a show-man's cart."[3] He had "lived a life that was little better than a dismal slavery," Treves maintained, until the surgeon himself had rescued Merrick and given him "a home of his own for life" at the London Hospital.[4] Norman, however, challenged Treves's sensational contention that he had, as Norman sarcastically recounted, "rescued this freak from the clutches of showmen, and was able to bring undreamed of happiness into the life of a hideously deformed creature who would otherwise have perished without ever knowing what happiness meant."[5] Instead, Norman asserted that Merrick had contacted the showmen on his own initiative, that there had always been a "spirit of friendship"[6] between them, and that he had, in fact, made a tidy profit off his own exhibition. Norman argued that in the end the hospital was much more degrading than the freak show and insisted that Merrick's agency was compromised not at the moment he was compelled to exhibit his deformity for profit, but rather once he became a permanent resident of the London Hospital and relinquished all control over the manner in which is body could be viewed. Norman constructed Merrick not as a helpless victim but as a fellow working man whose choice to perform as a freak enabled him to maintain his independence and in the process, crucially, to assert his own version of working-class masculinity.[7]

By juxtaposing these competing narratives of Victorian Britain's most famous freak, this chapter offers a reappraisal of the place of the freak show within the social, cultural, and economic history of labor, charity, and the state. This reading of "the Elephant Man" argues that despite its inherent prejudices, Norman's interpretation of Merrick's life is a critical historical document as it insists that we interrogate the assumption that the freak show is always already exploitative, offering instead a more nuanced understanding of its economic and social role in the lives of deformed members of the working poor. In addition, this analysis of "the Elephant Man" interrogates late nineteenth-century medicine's relationship to deformity—which Treves uncritically championed as purely scientific, objective, and explicitly redemptive—suggesting that scientific medicine's engagement with human anomalies was dependent upon and deeply enmeshed in more popular and commercial discourses and practices surrounding the display of spectacular bodies.

Joseph Merrick, better known as "the Elephant Man," has in recent decades come to represent the paradigmatic Victorian freak. The mythic tale of his exploitation by ruthless showmen and his rescue by Frederick Treves, a compassionate young doctor, has survived in popular culture largely through anthropologist Ashley Montagu's *The Elephant Man: A Study in Human Dignity* and David Lynch's 1980 film. Lynch's representation of Merrick as a refined soul trapped in a monstrous body, freed from a life of degradation by Treves, who gave him permanent shelter at the London Hospital, is much more mawkish and moralizing than one would expect from the leading postmodern surrealist filmmaker. Indeed, historian Raphael Samuel has suggested that if an "upper-class evangelical of the 1880s had possessed a cine-camera, this is the film he might have made."[8]

The film is unashamedly sentimental precisely because, like Montagu's book, it is based heavily on Treves's own memoir, *The Elephant Man and Other Reminiscences,* in which he positions himself as Merrick's savior from exploitative "vampire showmen."[9] Treves's melodramatic story begins with his initial encounter with Merrick in the winter of 1884 at a cheap freak show directly across from the London Hospital, where Treves was employed as a surgeon and lecturer in anatomy. Treves recalled that his first impression of Merrick was of a "little man below the average height":

> The most striking feature about him was the enormous and misshapened *[sic]* head. From the brow there projected a huge bony mass like a loaf, while from the back of the head hung a bag of spongy, fungous-looking skin. . . . From the upper jaw there projected another mass of bone. It protruded from the mouth like a pink stump, turning the upper lip inside out and making the mouth a mere slobbering aperture. . . . The back was horrible, because from it hung, as far down as the middle of the thigh, huge, sack-like masses of flesh covered by the same loathsome cauliflower skin. The right arm was of enormous size and shapeless. . . . The lower limbs . . . were unwieldy, dropsical looking and grossly misshapened *[sic]*.

Treves immediately requested that this "strange exhibit" cross the road to the hospital, as he was "anxious to examine him in detail and to prepare an account of his abnormalities." "I made a careful examination of my visitor the result of which I embodied in a paper," Treves maintained, and after taking a series of clinical photographs, he returned Merrick in a cab to the "place of exhibition," assuming that he had "seen the last of him."[10]

Treves reported that the show was soon "forbidden by the police" and that Merrick was taken to the Continent, where he was robbed by an unscrupulous showman who eventually abandoned him in Belgium. The narrative resumes with Merrick's return to London in the summer of 1886. By then he was destitute, Treves declared, having in his pocket only a few shillings and "a ray of hope," "my [business] card," which Treves claimed "was destined to play a critical part in Merrick's life." Arriving at Liverpool Street Station in the heart of London's East End, Merrick was mobbed by a crowd eager to see what was beneath his voluminous hat and cloak. When the police arrived on the scene Merrick apparently produced the card and the surgeon was summoned. Treves then recalled that he admitted him to an isolation ward in the attic of the hospital and, after conferring with Francis Carr Gomm, chairman of the hospital's House Committee, decided that "Merrick must not again be turned out into the world."[11] Although his condition was incurable, Merrick remained a permanent resident of the London Hospital, where, according to Treves, he was "happy every hour of the day" until his death in 1890.[12]

Treves's sentimental narrative has become the official version of the history of "the Elephant Man." Indeed, Peter Graham and Fritz Oehlschlaeger have maintained that Treves was the best "articulator" of Merrick's life story. Despite "considerable differences of education, class, health, and fortune," they argue, Treves and Merrick were both "denizen[s] of the same culture" and thus their "biases were largely the same."[13] To claim that Treves and Merrick came from the same "culture," however, is misleading. Merrick was a working-class man from northern England who had labored at unskilled jobs since the age of eleven, first in a cigar factory and later as a peddler. Forced out of his home by his stepmother, who found him grotesque, he had taken shelter with a kind uncle who was employed as a hairdresser. But, refusing to be a burden on his uncle, Merrick had also lived in cheap lodging houses before eventually checking himself into the Leicester workhouse where he remained for almost five years.[14] Treves, in contrast, grew up in the comfort of a middle-class family in Dorset and later in South London, eventually settling with his wife and children in a house on the prestigious Wimpole Street. An expert on appendicitis, he became surgeon to King Edward VII, who knighted him in 1902.[15] To assert that Treves and Merrick shared similar life experiences, values, and attitudes, then, is disingenuous. Although Treves may have been the best articulator of Merrick's bones, which he eventually had boiled down and put on display in the London Medical

College's Pathological Museum, he was not necessarily the best interpreter of Merrick's life story.

Treves's memoirs are in fact only one account of a complex series of events and interactions. Tom Norman, Merrick's London manager, also wrote a memoir in which he challenged Treves's interpretation of the freak show as exploitative and indecent. Norman was the son of a butcher and, like Merrick, had supported himself from an early age. He left home at fourteen, working as a butcher's assistant in London before entering the show world. When he first met Merrick, in 1884, Norman was only twenty-four years old, but he was already well on his way to becoming one of the most respected showmen of his day. Known as "the Silver King," he was operating thirteen show shops in London, staging performances at the Royal Agricultural Hall in Islington, and traveling the fair circuit with other acts.[16] Norman's account of Merrick, which provides valuable insight into the nature of the Victorian show world, contrasts sharply with Treves's. Norman locates exhibitions of anomalous bodies within the broader economic history of nineteenth-century Britain, stressing the importance of these shows as a source of livelihood for deformed members of the working poor who struggled to support themselves while remaining independent of state welfare.

Norman thus positions Merrick not as a helpless invalid but as a fellow working man who successfully and shrewdly capitalized on an expanding consumer culture by selling the only thing he had left to commodify: his extraordinary body. Merrick's choice to perform as a freak, Norman maintained, was central to his sense of self, as it enabled him to maintain his status as an able-bodied laboring man. Norman argues that in fact the hospital was much more exploitative than the freak show. As a freak, Merrick governed his own bodily display, profited from his exhibition, and thus reestablished himself as an independent man who exercised masculine control over his own person. Norman argued that Merrick, as a hospital "inmate" for whom there was no hope of a cure, became a dependent charity case whose continuing support was contingent upon relinquishing all control over his body and its uses.

Written at the end of successful careers, Treves's and Norman's memoirs were intended to establish their authors as leaders in their respective fields. Their stories about "the Elephant Man" were in both cases central to their articulations of their own professional identities and thus tell us much more about themselves than about Merrick.[17] Both of these sources must therefore be treated as narrative reconstructions of past events and relationships that reflect personal and professional prejudices and cater to the demands and expectations of their very different audiences, which in both cases consisted primarily of their authors' professional colleagues. Treves's melodramatic account foregrounds his empathetic nature and promotes the hospital as a redemptive institution while at the same time downplaying the Victorian medical profession's competitive—and thus, at times, exploitative—element. Similarly, in his attempt to defend "the penny showman" against recriminations that he merely profited from the ills of others, Norman recasts himself as "the people's friend" and disinterested guardian of his freak show exhibits. Both men thus underscore their emotional, rather than professional and thus economic, relationships to Merrick, attempting to deflect attention away from his clear use-value as a "monster."

But if the showman's autobiography is as biased as the surgeon's, Norman's lesser-known account of Joseph Merrick nevertheless offers a compelling, and historically significant, counternarrative to Treves's didactic rescue story. As a fellow working-class man, Norman understood and articulated the important social and economic role that the freak show played in Victorian and Edwardian working-class culture. As Treves's rival for the right to exhibit "the Elephant Man," he also provides an astute analysis of the place of anomalous bodies within the culture of medical science.

SCIENCE AND THE SIDESHOW

When Frederick Treves described his initial encounter with "the Elephant Man" in the winter of 1884, he returned repeatedly not to an objective scientific discourse but to the emotional language of horror and disgust. He was, Treves claimed, a "degraded," "perverted," "repulsive" "thing," "the most disgusting specimen of humanity that I have ever seen." Although this "creature" was "already repellent enough," Treves claimed, "there arose from the fungous skin-growth with which he was almost covered a very sickening stench which was hard to tolerate."[18] Andrew Smith has argued that Treves deployed a "Gothic discourse" to describe "the Elephant Man" because medical language could not sufficiently account for the "horrors" of his deformity.[19]

· The medical and the Gothic were not, however, separate discourses. Even in the 1880s the word "monster," long associated with both religious omens and popular entertainment (as its root in the Latin for "to show" and "to warn" suggests), remained the clinical term for those born with severe physical deformities. In fact, the use of the term in British medical journals increased over the course of the nineteenth century, reaching its peak in the period between 1870 and 1890.[20] The obstetrical columns in the *British Medical Journal* at the end of the nineteenth century were replete with descriptions of "foetal monsters," "double monsters," and other cases of congenital "monstrosity." Religious, moral, and commercial ways of figuring bodily difference thus survived within, and were perpetuated by, modern medicine, despite its claim to be a scientific, and thus morally neutral, enterprise. Treves's portrayal of Merrick reveals not so much the limits of medical language, but rather the ways in which the scientific and commercial discourses and practices around deformity were in the late nineteenth century symbiotic and even parasitic.

It was not merely that medicine borrowed the language of monstrosity from the freak show; it also borrowed its monsters. The practice of exhibiting human oddities for profit had been part of English entertainment dating back to the Elizabethan period, and medical men had been exhibiting, collecting, and cataloguing freakish bodies since at least the eighteenth century.[21] The surgeon and anatomist John Hunter had gone to great lengths to acquire the skeletons of two early nineteenth-century human oddities, Caroline Crachami, "the Sicilian Fairy," and Charles Byrne, "the Irish Giant," for his extensive private collection of medical curiosities, which he bequeathed to the Royal College of Surgeons. Indeed, even the eminent surgeon John Bland Sutton maintained that this collection was "little better than a freak-museum."[22]

In the late nineteenth century medical men continued to use the freak show to advance their own knowledge of teratology, the science of birth defects. They sought out extreme bodies in order to better understand pathology, using people displayed for entertainment purposes for entirely other ends. Bland Sutton recalled that, particularly in the early years of his career, he "often visited the Mile End Road, especially on Saturday nights, to see dwarfs, giants, fat-women, and monstrosities at the freak-shows. There was a freak-museum at a public-house—The Bell and Mackerel, near the London Hospital; this museum attracted customers." Bland Sutton had himself encountered "the Elephant Man" on one of these freak-finding forays.[23] Norman reported that several medical students had come to see "the Elephant Man" before Treves made his appearance. In fact it was Reginald Tuckett, Treves's house surgeon, who alerted him to the exhibition. Norman's location of the show directly across from the London Hospital's main entrance was, therefore, strategic: he was explicitly catering to scientific medicine's reliance on the freak show for its raw material.

The sciences of teratology and pathology and the leisure industry's commercialization of extraordinary bodies had for some time, then, been equally invested in the practices of bodily display. If, as Lisa Kochanek has argued, "the case history must recreate the freakish as a medical commodity," Treves's "riveting" and repeated presentations of his medical specimens at meetings of the Pathological Society of London necessarily echoed the sensationalism of the sideshow. The subjects he chose were reportedly "gruesome" and, according to his biographer, what his follow-up articles "lacked in a wider readership they made up for in horror."[24] But while Treves sharply contrasted his own "careful" and scientific examination of "the Elephant Man" within the privacy of the London Hospital with Merrick's public—and, in his opinion, obscene—display across the street, he omitted from his memoirs his own role in the exhibition of "the Elephant Man" as a live specimen before the Pathological Society. As the *British Medical Journal* reported, "Mr. Treves showed a man who presented an extraordinary appearance, owing to a series of deformities, . . . the patient had been called 'the elephant man.'"[25]

This was clearly a highly competitive environment, for in 1888 Bland Sutton exhibited Lalloo, the subject of chapter 2, whom he had seen on show in Tottenham Court Road.[26] In his memoir Bland Sutton effaced the distinction between the sideshow and the scientific space, claiming with pride that his "anatomical demonstrations got the name of Bland-Sutton's entertainments."[27] As Bernard Lightman has argued, this blending of education and entertainment was common in the scientific lectures of the period. Scientific lectures, whether delivered in established museums or more ephemeral exhibition halls, were part of a new marketplace in which the pursuit of knowledge about the natural world became as much a leisure activity as a visit to a pleasure garden. Professional lecturers understood, Lightman claims, that they were competing for the attention of a fickle public and thus borrowed heavily from the culture of display and from oratorical styles associated with the music hall and the fairgrounds.[28] Indeed, performances, argues Iwan Rhys Morus, were "part and parcel of the business of making science and its products real to [nineteenth-century] audiences."[29]

This overlap between professional and more popular modes of display and public speaking was evident among those in the medical field, as Bland Sutton's comments make clear, even when their audience was limited to students and colleagues and did not include the general show-going public. One of Treves's medical students fondly recalled his "racy descriptions of the more abstruse parts of the human body. He often had us in fits of laughter, which is more than most teachers of anatomy today manage to do, I fancy."[30] In displaying "the Elephant Man" in front of his professional colleagues, then, Treves—who was clearly also known for his amusing presentations—was both entertaining his audience and enhancing his reputation for "'discovering' more unusual cases than anyone else."[31] Exhibiting the freakish body was thus as central to Treves's professional identity as it was to Norman's, for it was through these practices of bodily display and the lectures that framed them that medical professionals staked their claim to be experts on monstrosity and attracted paying students to their lectures.

Treves not only exhibited Merrick's strange body, but later he also circulated his image as a photographic souvenir. In 1889, three years after he was admitted as a permanent resident of the hospital, Merrick posed for a studio portrait. The photograph depicts Merrick dressed in his "Sunday Best" posing in a traditional Victorian portraiture stance, the three-quarter profile position that accentuated the monstrous aspects of his body. Had the photographer placed Merrick facing the other direction, his "normal" side would have dominated the image and the opposite effect would have been created. This monstrous image of Merrick was made into a *carte de visite,* a small card-backed photograph. *Cartes de visite* were extremely popular collectibles beginning in the 1860s; indeed, freaks regularly sold *carte de visite* portraits of themselves to earn extra money.[32] The inscription on the back of the *carte* in the hospital's archives proclaims this to be a portrait of "The Elephant Man given to me by The Rev. H. T. Valentine who was Chaplain at the London Hospital at this time." It was owned by Miles H. Phillips, a gynecologist, who long after Merrick's death attended lectures at the London Hospital Medical College.[33] This portrait of "the Elephant Man," which clearly was circulated at least among the hospital population and was perhaps also given to Merrick's patrons, was thus little different from the souvenirs hawked at fairgrounds and sideshows. It suggests that the hospital itself was complicit in commodifying Merrick's monstrosity, using techniques borrowed directly from the show world.

If medicine appropriated the practices of bodily spectacle so central to the freak show, freak show entrepreneurs also regularly exploited the tropes of scientific medicine for their own purposes. While physicians and surgeons were not particularly forthcoming about their interactions with, and reliance upon, sideshow performers, freaks often advertised that they had

Figure 4. *Carte de visite* of Joseph Merrick in his "Sunday Best," ca. 1889. Courtesy of Royal London Hospital Archives.

been examined by medical professionals. Whether real or fake, these testimonials, a common feature of the freak poster and handbill, reveal a growing public trust in the opinions of the medical profession. But they also suggest that the discourses of professional medicine were not in fact exclusive and could also be exploited for other ends entirely.[34] When Norman introduced "the Elephant Man," he declared that Merrick was intended "not to frighten you but to enlighten you," suggesting that this was an educational exhibit that could contribute to the production of knowledge.[35] By effectively turning his show shop into a scientific space, Norman was also participating in what Lightman has called the "spatial economy of science," leaving it to the public to attempt to distinguish his presentation from that of other popular scientific demonstrators.[36]

This blurring of the boundaries between the professional and the popular was also evident in the manner in which the show world borrowed from science's own visual culture. In 1885 an engraving of Merrick's misshapen body was added to the cover of his souvenir pamphlet. The illustration had been made from one of the photographs that Treves had taken to accompany his report in the Pathological Society's journal. Merrick and one of his later managers manipulated the image to exaggerate Merrick's "trunk," a thick piece of skin that grew from his upper lip, and thus to enhance his persona as "the Elephant Man."[37] Ironically, Merrick's promoters challenged Treves's construction of Merrick as a medical case by using a scientific illustration to support their reading of Merrick as a "monster half-man half-elephant."[38]

While the freak show used the medical profession for its own purposes, it also actively contributed to debates about the root causes of congenital abnormalities. In his public presentation Norman attributed the cause of Merrick's deformities to "maternal impression," which theorized that the form of an unborn child could be altered by something the mother experienced while pregnant.[39] Merrick's mother, Norman declared, had been frightened by a circus elephant; her baby had thus been imprinted with the form of an elephant. Taking this theory to its logical conclusion, Norman typically warned the crowds waiting outside the shop that women in a "Delicate State of Health" should not attend the show for fear that this victim of maternal impression could cause another monstrous birth, for women and doctors alike reported that monstrous births could be caused by a "morbid desire" to see a *lusus naturae*.[40]

Throughout the nineteenth century responsibility for the production of a human monstrosity was regularly placed squarely on the shoulders of women. Women's active and powerful imaginations, it had been argued for centuries, made their babies susceptible to alteration inside the womb. If a woman experienced a fright, longed for a particular food, or witnessed something unusual, her baby could be marked. A black baby born to a white mother could be accounted for by the mother being startled by a "Blackmoor" during gestation; a child born bright red with claws in the place of hands could equally be explained away by the mother's insatiable desire for lobster during pregnancy. This was alarming, Marie-Hélène Huet has argued, because instead of "reproducing the father's image," the monstrous birth "erased paternity and proclaimed the dangerous power of the female imagination," something that neither husbands nor medical practitioners could control.[41]

Under the heading "Maternal Impressions," the 1897 encyclopedia *Anomalies and Curiosities of Medicine* maintained that it was the "customary speech of the dime-museum lecturer to attribute the existence of some 'freak' to an episode in the mother's pregnancy."[42] But this dismissal of maternal impression as a superstitious belief—an explanation for deformity found credible only by the most gullible—belied the fact that in the 1880s, at the time of Merrick's exhibition, the subject continued to be seriously debated in the pages of the *British Medical Journal* and the *Lancet*. It was not uncommon in this period for doctors reporting on cases of monstrosity to mention whether the mother had experienced a fright or a bad dream during pregnancy.[43] In an article devoted to maternal impressions published in the 1889 *Cyclopaedia of the Diseases of Children*, Willam C. Dabney maintained that "impressions made upon a pregnant woman are capable of causing mental and bodily defects in her child." A careful study of ninety cases drawn from European and American medical journals led him to conclude that pregnant women should avoid "all violent and emotional disturbances."[44] By using maternal impression as an explanatory device, Norman thus affirmed the audience's own knowledge about bodily deformity. At the same time he perpetuated a theory that still had currency within medical circles, thus bridging the divide between lay and professional understandings of the origins of the freakish body.

The freak show's ability to influence professional medicine is also evident in the fact that medical professionals repeatedly diagnosed "the Elephant Man" as suffering from elephantiasis, a parasitical disease that did not in fact match Merrick's puzzling disorder. Treves initially admitted Merrick to the hospital in 1886 as a case of elephantiasis, a misdiagnosis that was repeated in a report on Merrick's death published in the *East London Advertiser*, in the article on Treves's memoirs that appeared in *World's Fair* in 1923, in Norman's response to that article, and even in a 1959 memoir written by D. G. Halsted, who as one of Treves's medical students had cared for Merrick at the London Hospital.[45]

While little about Merrick actually suggested an elephant (indeed, declared Halsted, he looked more like a "Tapir Man" than an "Elephant Man"), the name derived from the trunklike piece of skin that protruded from his upper lip. Although it had originally been removed during his residency in the Leicester workhouse, before he began to show himself for money, it had begun to reappear by the mid-1880s. Merrick's promotional material accentuated his so-called elephantine qualities in order to promote this particular reading of his body, for "the Elephant Man" was a role that Merrick and his managers carefully crafted for their audience. In his autobiographical souvenir pamphlet Merrick maintained that his right hand was almost the size and shape of an "Elephant's fore-leg" and that his "thick lumpy skin" was like "that of an Elephant."[46] His poster reinforced this description by depicting a "monster half-man half-elephant rampaging through the jungle."[47] Although the construction of Merrick as a half-human, half-animal wonder was a conceit of sideshow exhibition, it significantly influenced even the medical interpretation of Merrick's deformity. Treves vividly remembered Merrick's canvas poster, which depicted "the figure of a man with the characteristics of an elephant,"[48] and his pamphlet, both of which structured his and others' reading of Merrick as a case of elephantiasis.

Despite the fact that popular and professional interpretations of deformity could not always be clearly divorced from each other, by the end of the nineteenth century the medical profession was asserting its proprietary right to explain the nature and meanings of bodily difference. Scientific medicine, which began to emerge in eighteenth-century hospitals and was cemented with the rise of germ theory and the laboratory in the late Victorian period, sought to diagnose and to cure diseases. The hospital was critical to this process of organizing groups of symptoms into discrete nosological categories because it allowed for the centralization of the sick, and thus provided doctors and medical students access to a wide variety of illnesses and to multiple cases with similar symptoms.[49] Although Merrick could not be cured, Treves and his colleagues did seek to diagnose him as suffering from an identifiable disease that only medical professionals could interpret.

The medical profession, however, was not particularly successful at determining either the nature or the cause of Merrick's disfigurement, nor that of other performers. This allowed the freak show to flourish precisely because it offered a different interpretation of deformity and resisted the medicalization of monstrosity. Unlike scientific medicine, which drew a firm line between the healthy observer and the diseased object of the medical gaze, the freak show actually discouraged audiences from interpreting "the Elephant Man" as pathological. Merrick's promotional pamphlet maintained that he was "exhibiting" a "deformity" and assured the public that he was "as comfortable now as [he] was uncomfortable before," suggesting that he was neither ill nor in pain. Although this was of course a clever strategy that served to assuage any discomfort associated with staring at someone who might indeed be suffering, it was also an attempt to draw a commonality between Merrick and the audience. Norman promoted this by introducing his exhibit as "Mr. Joseph Merrick, the Elephant Man." While "there was always the gasp of horror and shock, and sometimes the hurried exit of one or more of the audience" when he unveiled "the Elephant Man," Norman instructed the crowd "not to despise or condemn this man on account of his unusual appearance." "Remember," he asserted, "we do not make ourselves, and were you to cut or prick Joseph," alluding to Shylock's famous speech, "he would bleed, and that bleed or blood would be red, the same as yours or mine." Rosemarie Garland Thomson has argued that "freaks and prodigies were solely bodies, without the humanity social structures confer upon more ordinary people."[50] But by using Merrick's proper name, rather than his show title, in order "to impart [him a] little dignity," and by gesturing to his blood, a synecdoche of his humanity and identity, rather than focusing on his outward appearance, Norman claimed that he encouraged the crowd to see Merrick as "the most remarkable human being ever to draw the breath of life" rather than as a monstrosity, in either sense of the word.[51]

The claim that Treves actually rescued Merrick from the "dismal slavery"[52] of the freak show thus requires further scrutiny. From this perspective it is medicine itself that appears to constrain, fix, and dominate bodies that transgressed the boundaries of "the normal." Indeed, the hospital, as we shall see, did not necessarily liberate "the Elephant Man," but rather might in fact have compromised his identity as an able-bodied, self-governing working-class man.

LABOR, CLASS, AND THE MASCULINE BODY

Before his hospitalization in 1886 Merrick had had a successful career as a freak. After almost five years in the Leicester workhouse he had taken the initiative to contact the local variety theater to seek employment as a novelty act. He had then struck a deal with a consortium of showmen, including Norman, who agreed to exhibit him as "the Elephant Man" in several cities across Britain. Norman, although he had seen "many curious people before, some really repulsive," initially believed that Merrick was too grotesque to be entertaining. He nevertheless later admitted, gesturing to his own considerable talent for marketing anything from "a flea to an elephant" to an "Elephant Man,"[53] that their partnership was reasonably profitable. "The takings at the door were quite good," he recalled, "and we were both satisfied in that respect."[54] The takings were so good that Merrick was able to save "considerably more" than £50—a sizable nest egg for a working-class man—during the first five months that he exhibited himself. Norman suggested that Merrick in fact earned more from his own exhibition than Norman himself did. While they shared the take evenly, Norman alone paid for the rent of the show shop, food, and lodging, he claimed.[55]

This ability to earn a steady wage was, according to Norman, crucial to Merrick's sense of self. As Heather McHold has noted, half of Merrick's six-page pamphlet for his show was devoted to his employment history, detailing the ways he had earned a living—as a cigar roller, a peddler, and a hawker—and thus identifying him as an independent laborer.[56] Norman reported that Merrick had declared, "I don't ever want to go back to that place," meaning the workhouse.[57] For working men, independence, "the capacity to make one's own way in the world and to be one's own master," which John Tosh has identified as the core tenet of Victorian manliness,[58] was inextricably bound up in demonstrating one's distance from reliance on the poor law. Throughout the nineteenth century the ability to earn enough to support oneself and one's family was essential to working-class notions of masculinity, which were often expressed through the demand for a family wage, that is, a large enough income to make ends meet without wives also working outside the home. While work proved to be the chief sphere in which middle-class men demonstrated their good character, the claim of working-class men to be literally *working* men was also central to their identities as citizens and as *men*.[59] If middle-class morality-mongers rejected the freak show as a degraded form of prurient entertainment, for working-class performers it could in fact represent the route to respectability, as it allowed them to demonstrate that they were independent laborers, and thus to articulate their moral worth.

Norman's memoirs explicitly locate Merrick within this discourse of working-class masculine self-reliance. According to his son, Norman adopted the motto "Be your own man" and taught his children never to become dependent on any form of state relief or charity, to make an "Honest Bob" without the help of "Hand-outs." His memoirs, which reflect what his son identified as his "spirit of independence," stress that Merrick "was a man of very strong character and beliefs—anxious to earn his own living and be independent of charity." Norman claimed that Merrick refused to work the "Nobbings," in other words, to pass a hat around at the end of a show to collect extra money. He proudly proclaimed, "We are not beggars are we, Thomas?" To Norman this was a "noble gesture," a sign of Merrick's manly character.[60] Affirming Merrick's status as an independent man, Norman always announced to the spectators that "Joseph, not content to live off charity," had himself "seized the opportunity of joining the showmen who secured his release, and was now able to pay his way and be independent of charity."[61]

Norman's narrative stresses that in contrast to the workhouse, which was dehumanizing and demoralizing, the freak show permitted Merrick to become an active economic agent who could assert his own working-class version of masculine independence. While it suited Norman to deflect the more troubling issue of exploitation by underscoring Merrick's agency, his account of "the Elephant Man" explicitly challenges the assumption that the freak show is *necessarily* abusive and immoral and suggests instead that for the working class in particular it may have been a, if not the only, means to autonomy. It was in fact the hospital rather than the freak show, Norman insisted, that compromised Merrick's dignity by preventing him from laboring and by transforming him into a member of the deserving poor.

When Francis Carr Gomm, chairman of the hospital's House Committee, wrote to the *Times* to appeal for funds for Merrick's upkeep, he represented him as an ideal object of charity. Since this was a "case of singular affliction brought about through no fault of himself," Carr Gomm argued, the "charitable people" of London should show their empathetic nature and help this "poor fellow." Merrick deserved financial assistance, the letter suggested, because he was not "able-bodied" (a key poor law term), which meant that he was physically unable to work rather than unwilling. He was "debarred from seeking to earn his livelihood in any ordinary way," as "only one arm [was] available for work," argued Carr Gomm, who assumed that the only labor he could perform would literally be manual. Treves's 1888 account of Merrick's case reiterated this position, declaring that Merrick was "unable to follow any employment and physically prevented from learning any trade" because of the extent of his deformities.[62]

Indeed, when he admitted Merrick to the hospital, Treves listed him as having "no occupation," despite the fact that he knew that Merrick had been employed as a freak performer.[63] Merrick's status as a charity case was thus intimately bound up in the presumed incapacity of his body to undertake the physical labor deemed appropriate to his class.

Merrick was, however, more than capable of continuing to work as a show freak, and thus he could have preserved both his independence and his social status as an able-bodied laborer dependent on neither charity nor state relief. But both Carr Gomm and Treves suggested to the public that his profession was irregular and indecent, maintaining that the police "rightly prevent his being personally exhibited again."[64] For middle-class Victorians, selling one's labor power for manual tasks was appropriate within the industrial capitalist system, but other forms of bodily commodification, such as prostitution—or, in this case, the exhibition of a freakish body—challenged norms of respectable behavior.[65] Treves and Carr Gomm, then, called on the public for charitable donations to prevent what they considered an unacceptable method of exploiting one's body for profit.

It was Norman's belief that Merrick's "only wish was to be free and independent." This could not be achieved, however, as long as Merrick remained an inmate of the hospital, which to Norman seemed little different from the workhouse. Merrick must have felt, Norman insisted, as if "he were a prisoner and living on charity."[66] Carr Gomm claimed that Merrick was always a "free agent" and entitled to leave at any time, even proposing that the hospital would turn over the funds they had collected on his behalf to his uncle if he wished to return to Leicester.[67] But according to the testimony of a hospital porter, Merrick had asked on more than one occasion, "Why can't I go back to Mr. Norman?"[68] Norman's memoirs suggest that Merrick saw the hospital, like the workhouse, as a temporary solution to poverty and that he had intended to resume the life of an able-bodied wage earner rather than remain under the care of the hospital or a family member. That he was prevented from doing so reveals a profoundly middle-class misreading of the freak show as inherently exploitative rather than as central to Merrick's articulation of his distinctly working-class masculinity.

By casting Merrick as a charity patient the hospital transformed him from a wage earner into a member of the deserving but dependent poor, a position that was inherently emasculating and infantilizing. Seth Koven has argued that Merrick can be read as a "Barnardo-boy manqué," a "rough lad" rescued from the streets who, like other "ragged" youths, became the object of benevolent efforts to "succor the bodies and spirits of poor boys."[69] Treves accentuated the paternalism of the charity hospital, where patients were expected to be deferential to the medical staff, by positioning himself not only as Merrick's physician, but also as a father figure who cared to his needs, bestowed gifts, and financially supported him. He repeatedly characterized Merrick as "childlike" or "boyish," stressing his immaturity: in his "outlook upon the world," Treves argued, Merrick "was a child." His "rapture" at being taken to a pantomime was even more intense, Treves claimed, than the "unconstrained delight of a child."[70]

This immaturity and childishness also had racial overtones, as colonial subjects in the age of imperialism were consistently figured as younger siblings to be educated and civilized. As Jami Moss has argued, while Treves, the "white male doctor," emerged in his narrative "as the model of civilized humanity," "the Elephant Man," "in his more 'animal' state," was linked to "so-called savages who lived in the British colonies."[71] Merrick's poster, with its "primitive colours" and palm trees, suggested to Treves that this "perverted object" "roamed" the "wild[s]" of a "jungle."[72] Treves further racialized Merrick by characterizing him as a "primitive creature" and an "elemental being" whose speech was so slurred that "he might as well have spoken in Arabic." Treves claimed to have "learnt his speech," as a missionary might, so that he could talk freely with Merrick and serve as an "interpreter" for the hospital staff.[73] Writing in the tradition of the social investigators and journalists who imagined the East End as an outpost of empire, Treves explicitly Orientalized "the Elephant Man" by likening him to the Indian elephant god Ganesh. He was "a monstrous figure," Treves recalled, "as hideous as an Indian idol."[74]

This passivity, dependence, and racial positioning was also explicitly feminizing. Like the Victorian feminine ideal, the angel in the house, Merrick was kept sequestered in his rooms. When he ventured too far outside them he was quickly shepherded back, lest he scare the other patients.[75] The bulk of his time, therefore, was spent within his private space, where he received visitors, read, or performed handicrafts like building models or weaving baskets. When he left the hospital grounds it was to attend a Christmas pantomime or to travel to the country, where he was sent on summer holidays. Merrick's life at the London Hospital thus conformed to the middle-class domestic ideal and cast Merrick in a decidedly feminine role. As William Holladay and Stephen Watt have argued, Treves's account can be read as a domestic melodrama in which Merrick figures as the heroine.[76] Indeed, Treves often accentuated what he saw as Merrick's feminine nature. Despite his deformities and troubles, Merrick was a "gentle, affectionate and loveable creature, as amiable as a happy woman."[77] When Merrick shyly asked for a dressing bag, a traveling case for toiletries, as a Christmas gift, Treves compared him to a "small girl with a tinsel coronet and a window curtain for a train."[78] Treves recounted that Merrick sobbed in a womanly way, picked flowers in the countryside, and read love stories to pass the time. Treves characterized Merrick as a passive, domestic, sentimental, and feminine "creature."

If, as Norman suggests, Merrick had located his manliness in his body's ability to labor, for Treves, Merrick's body could not be read as masculine in any way. Treves concluded his reminiscences by claiming that Merrick's spirit, were it visible, would "assume the figure of an upstanding and heroic man, smooth browed and clean of limb, and with eyes that flashed undaunted courage."[79] This emphasis on strength of character and the ability to overcome adversity was central to Victorian understandings of manliness. By the last decades of the nineteenth century, however, manliness was also increasingly becoming wedded to physical fitness, bodily integrity, and athleticism. The late Victorian middle and upper classes in particular emphasized the importance of sport and games to the development of a manly physique, and to the health and strength of the nation. In the age of muscular Christianity, character was thought best developed through training and disciplining the body.[80] Although this emphasis on physical vigor was merely one of many different styles of manliness available in this period—one often associated with the elite culture of the public school[81]—it was nevertheless central to Treves's understanding of masculinity.

Wilfred Grenfell and D. G. Halsted, the two men primarily responsible for Merrick's care while he resided at the hospital, were typical muscular Christians: involved in medico-missionary work, they taught boxing, gymnastics, and sailing to poor boys.[82] Treves, an especially athletic man, promoted their activities. He himself wrote treatises on physical education and considered that "the athlete, so far as his body and his personal equation are concerned, has reached the full and perfect stature of a man." Englishmen, he claimed, justifiably have "contempt for what is effeminate and feeble."[83] Despite his manly spirit, then, Merrick could not measure up to Treves's standards of masculinity, which emphasized bodily symmetry, strength, and physical perfection. Indeed, despite the "normal" aspects of his left side, of which Merrick was apparently "pathetically proud,"[84] Treves denied that Merrick's body had any masculine aspects whatsoever. While Merrick's right hand and arm were, according to Treves, monstrous and vegetable-like, his left arm was "a delicately shaped limb covered with fine skin and provided with a beautiful hand which any woman might have envied."[85] That which was normal about Merrick's body, Treves insisted, had no trace of manhood about it.

Despite the fact that Merrick appeared in his *carte de visite* photograph in a fitted three-piece suit (the marker of the modern man),[86] complete with collar, tie, handkerchief, and pocket watch and chain, Treves insisted that Merrick could not "adapt his body" to a "trimly cut coat." "His deformity was such," Treves claimed, "that he could wear neither collar nor tie, while in association with his bulbous feet the young blood's patent leather shoe was unthinkable." The dressing bag appeared to Treves to be part of an elaborate dress-up game, and Treves dwelled on Merrick's inability to use it for its intended purpose: to groom the male body. Merrick had no hair to brush nor beard to shave; "his monstrous lips could not hold a cigarette"; the shoehorn could not help him with his "ungainly slippers"; and the hat brush was unsuited to his cap and visor. "Merrick the Elephant Man," Treves declared ironically, became the "gallant" in the "seclusion" of his chamber.[87] By naming Merrick "the Elephant Man" in this context, using his show title rather than his proper name, Treves challenged any claim to normalcy that Merrick might have been making by attempting to adopt the trappings of middle-class masculinity that Treves had himself, at least implicitly, encouraged by purchasing the dressing bag.[88]

SCIENTIFIC SPECTACLE

By figuring Merrick as dependent, childish, and womanish, Treves undermined Merrick's masculine independence and, in the process, his ability to care for himself and make decisions governing his own body. Although admitting Merrick to the London Hospital as a permanent resident was certainly a benevolent act, as the hospital did not ordinarily accept incurable patients, it ensured that Treves would have unlimited access to Merrick's body, something he had been denied two years earlier. Indeed, Norman maintains that negotiations among Treves, Merrick, and himself in the winter of 1884 over access to Merrick's body were highly charged. According to Norman's memoirs, after Treves's initial examination of Merrick in November of 1884 Treves brought him over to the hospital two or three more times before Merrick refused to go again. A week later Treves arrived at the show shop with several people who wanted to see "the Elephant Man." "The doctor appeared almost desperate," Norman recalled, "afraid, I imagine of 'losing face' among his colleagues." When Merrick declined to be displayed to these "distinguished visitors," reported Norman, Treves "could hardly control his rage . . . especially when I said that in future he and his colleagues could only see Joseph as paying customers."[89] While Treves clearly felt that his professional status entitled him to unlimited free access to "the Elephant Man," Norman found the "visitors from the London Hospital" "a bit of a nuisance," as their constant questions "were holding up the business" and interfering with his own professional pursuits.[90] But by according Treves and his colleagues no privileged position vis-à-vis his spectacle of monstrosity, Norman was not only protecting his own business interests. He was also, like Merrick himself, challenging the medical profession's presumption of authority over the deformed body.

Merrick's refusal to submit to further scientific scrutiny is telling. He chose to exhibit himself in what he considered "a decent manner" and get paid for doing so, but he objected, he apparently told Norman, to being "stripped naked" and made to feel "like an animal at the cattle market."[91] Merrick asserted that he was not property but his own man, and as a man he had sole control over who saw and touched his body. Although he may have profited from his body, it was not like the bodies of cattle, literally for sale. As a freeborn Englishman he alone governed the use of his body, Merrick suggested, and he would not be treated as a scientific specimen, a position that was not only dehumanizing but also distinctly emasculating, as it rendered him a passive object of the medical gaze. By resisting examination and hospitalization, submitting to it only as a last resort, Merrick asserted not only manly self-control over his person but also his humanity, issuing a denial that he was first and foremost a medical monstrosity.

While Treves argued that Merrick's public exhibition was exploitative and "transgressed the limits of decency,"[92] the young doctor nevertheless staked his own claim to control over the exhibition of Merrick's deformities by placing him under his care at the hospital and thus controlling access to his person. In a letter to the *Times,* Carr Gomm announced that the London Hospital sought to prevent Merrick's "deformity being made anything of a show, except for purely scientific purposes."[93] This suggests that he felt that Merrick's exhibition was justified, but only in the context of medical research. Treves, in fact, not only repeatedly photographed Merrick naked but also brought a variety of medical practitioners to see him in the flesh. One of the hospital porters reported to Norman that Merrick was "constantly seen and examined" by a "never-ending stream of surgeons, doctors and Dr. Treve's [sic] friends."[94] In an article published in the *British Journal of Dermatology* in 1909, F. Parkes Weber diagnosed Merrick, whom he referred to only as "the famous 'elephant man,'" with Recklinghausen's disease, otherwise known as neurofibromatosis. "Many" people, stated Parkes Weber, "must have seen [this case] when he was at the London Hospital."[95] Since his article clearly addressed his professional colleagues, it suggests that medical men regularly visited Merrick for professional reasons. Norman insisted that Merrick was "keenly conscious of the indignity of having to appear undressed" before this "never-ending stream" of visitors who did not pay him for his services.[96] Grenfell confirmed Merrick's discomfort with having to exhibit himself in the hospital, writing in his own memoirs that "the poor fellow was really exceedingly sensitive about his most extraordinary appearance."[97]

Although Treves allowed Merrick to be seen and examined by medical professionals, he repeatedly emphasized the importance of keeping him out of the public eye. Hospital officials, Carr Gomm asserted, had strict "instructions to secure for him as far as possible immunity from the gaze of the curious."[98] Those who responded to Carr Gomm's letter proposed sending him either to a lighthouse, that most remote and solitary of places, or to an asylum for the blind.[99] Although neither of these suggestions was pursued, Carr Gomm insisted that this type of invisibility was essential to the preservation of Merrick's dignity. In fact, however, "the Elephant Man" was regularly put on public display in his private rooms, known to the hospital population as "the elephant house."[100]

Treves duly chastised the "thoughtless porter" or wardmaid who let "curious friends have a peep at the Elephant Man."[101] But he frequently exposed Merrick to a range of people outside the medical field who had no professional stake in Merrick's case. Merrick's story, Treves remembered, attracted attention in the papers, which meant that he had a "constant succession of visitors. Everybody wanted to see him. He must have been visited by almost every lady of note in the social world."[102] The only difference between the porter or wardmaid's friends and these curious members of the public was their social class, for the visitors who were admitted to Merrick's rooms came from high society and included William Gladstone and the Princess of Wales, as well as "half the celebrities in London." John Bland Sutton reported that "it became a cult among the personal friends of the Princess to visit the Elephant-Man in the London Hospital."[103]

Although Treves suggests that these high-society callers were *visitors,* he also indicates they "wanted *to see* him" (emphasis mine), and in some ways they had paid to do so. Since the London Hospital was a charitable institution that did not accept chronic cases, Merrick could only be housed as a permanent resident if his care was funded separately from the hospital's operating budget. Carr Gomm raised more than £230 on Merrick's behalf after his initial plea to readers of the *Times* in 1886. He also secured an annual donation of £50 from a Mr. Singer.[104] These visits to see "the Elephant Man," then, were not commercial transactions in that no one purchased a ticket. However, they still existed within a cash nexus, as it was only the elite, whose philanthropy paid for Merrick's upkeep, who were entitled to see him in the hospital. As Ann Featherstone has argued, Treves's relationship to Merrick was thus framed not only by the discourses of healing and compassion, as he and those who have embraced his narrative have claimed, but also by those of "ownership, commercialisation, and control."[105]

Treves's biographer rightly maintains that the steady stream of society visitors rendered "the elephant house" no more or less than a "genteel freak show."[106] In a reversal of the events of 1884, Norman applied to the hospital to visit Merrick (at Merrick's own request, he implied) but was turned away. He did not attempt to visit again. Who, then, "really exploited poor Joseph?" Norman asked. For, although "the eminent surgeon" "received the publicity and the praise" for rescuing Merrick from the freak show, Norman insisted that Treves was "also a Showman, but on a rather higher social scale."[107] Merrick's sojourn in "the elephant house," where he was examined, photographed, and stared at by curious visitors, thus appears little different from his days as a freak exhibit, except in one crucial way. As a freak Merrick had largely been in control over his own bodily display and had used that control to assert himself as a respectable working man. As a permanent resident of the hospital, however, he was entirely reliant on the goodwill of Treves and his patrons. In return for this care and support he was required to surrender his right as an independent man to govern his body and to determine its uses.

LAST RITES/LAST RIGHTS

After almost five years in the workhouse, Merrick checked himself out to begin life as a freak. After four years in "the elephant house" he chose another means of escape. Merrick had been forced to sleep in a seated position with his head resting on his knees in order to prevent asphyxiation. Norman had tried to help make Merrick more comfortable by having a padded yoke fitted to his shoulders to keep his head upright during the night,[108] but this device clearly did not accompany him to the London Hospital. When Merrick's dead body was found lying across his bed at 3:30 in the afternoon on 11 April 1890, the coroner's report concluded that he had died of natural causes: the weight of his head apparently "overcame him" during sleep and caused him to suffocate.[109] Treves believed that Merrick had tried to sleep horizontally and in the process had dislocated his neck. His death, Treves theorized, resulted from his "pathetic but hopeless desire to be 'like other people.'"[110]

Treves implied but avoided explicitly claiming that Merrick had committed suicide. He preferred to see Merrick's death as the result of his striving for, but inevitably failing to achieve, normalcy, and he continued to insist that Merrick was "happy every hour of the day." Halsted, however, maintained that he regularly had to "cheer him up if he felt depressed."[111] Norman interpreted Merrick's death—which occurred in the middle of the day and not during a "natural sleep," as reported by the press—in much more sinister terms.[112] Suicide, he suggested, was Merrick's only way out of being constantly interrogated by the medical gaze. Norman surmised that Merrick, in a "'what the Hell' frame of mind, quite conscious of the risk, lay full length on the bed and never woke up. Perhaps that is what he wanted."[113] According to Norman, Merrick's suicide was not the result of his failure to measure up to "the norm." It was instead his last expression of bodily control, an act of manly defiance that was ultimately an explicit refusal to be further objectified and pathologized by medical science.

If "the Elephant Man" could no longer be scrutinized by doctors, his body nevertheless remained the property of the hospital. Merrick had clearly understood that this would be the case: as Grenfell recalled, he "used to talk freely of how he would look in a huge bottle of alcohol—an end to which in his imagination he was fated to come."[114] Merrick's estranged father came to collect his effects, which included valuable gifts from his patrons, and indeed he would have been well within his rights to ask for the body should he have wanted to bury it whole himself. Although the hospital decided that no postmortem was to be performed, it did take tissue samples and made body casts, presenting one to the Royal College of Surgeons, presumably for installation in the Hunterian Museum alongside the remains of "the Irish Giant" and "the Sicilian Fairy." Thomas

Horrocks Openshaw, the pathological specimens curator at the London Medical College's Pathological Museum, then stripped the body of its flesh and boiled down the bones for articulation, as the House Committee had "decided that the skeleton should be set up in the College Museum." An undertaker removed his other remains, which included flesh and internal organs, and after they were buried in an unmarked grave, the hospital held a memorial service for Merrick in their chapel.[115]

Joseph Merrick's skeleton and body casts remain on display in the London Medical College's Pathological Museum alongside other relics of his residence at the hospital. Access to them is strictly limited to medical professionals and legitimate researchers who must apply to the curator of the museum.[116] Today Merrick's body can only be consumed as part of the advancement of scientific knowledge, for it is only medical professionals who continue to be entrusted with interpreting the meaning of his deformity. That Merrick's final resting place is in a pathological museum off-limits to the general public represents the ultimate triumph of Treves's narrative, which has proliferated in a popular culture that has largely embraced the medical model of bodily difference, with its firm belief in "the normal" and its concomitant desire to classify and correct "the deviant." Indeed, the stories that circulate today about Joseph Merrick build on Treves's account of his case and consistently seek to diagnose his condition—most recently as Proteus syndrome—underscoring the pathological nature of Merrick and his social value as a rare medical monstrosity.[117]

But "the Elephant Man" also had an afterlife in the show world. Like Treves, Tom Norman continued to commercialize Merrick's freakish body long after his death, displaying a bust of him in his waxworks, which operated in various venues through the First World War. When Norman sold the exhibit after the war the bust was deliberately left behind and stored away in a packing case.[118] That "the Elephant Man" continued to be exhibited even after his death in both of the venues that made him famous should come as no surprise. Significantly, however, it was the sideshow rather than the scientific institution that finally laid his body and his memory to rest.

Two Bodies, Two Selves, Two Sexes

Conjoined Twins and "the Double-Bodied Hindoo Boy"

AT THE SAME MOMENT THAT "the Elephant Man" was admitted to the London Hospital in the summer of 1886, "Lalloo the Double-Bodied Hindoo Boy" began to exhibit himself across the United Kingdom. The following year, like Merrick, he appeared before the Pathological Society of London as a case of "parasitic foetus." Lalloo was what was frequently referred to in the medical literature as a "double monstrosity," the scientific term then used for what are now called conjoined twins. But rather than being attached to a fully grown brother, Lalloo had a much smaller sibling growing out of his chest. This "parasitic twin," which had no head and no heart, was described throughout the act's twenty-year span as Lala, a little sister. Lalloo (sometimes spelled Laloo or Lalou) was thus a particularly fascinating "human oddity," as he embodied two characters that were frequently associated with the freak show: he was both conjoined twin and hermaphrodite. Not only was he attached to another body, but that body was apparently female.

This chapter argues that as both a spectacular entertainment and a pathological exhibit, Lalloo's double body generated popular and professional debate about the boundary between the self and the other, and the distinction between male and female. However, his act also raised concerns about the sexual potential of a double-sexed body. Although they never explicitly addressed the sexual relationship between Lalloo and Lala, the promotional materials that accompanied the exhibition and the medical case reports that circulated in professional journals suggested that this body was intriguing because of the ways in which it exploited late Victorian anxieties about masturbation, incest, pedophilia, and child marriage.

TWO BODIES, ONE HEAD

Although he was not first and foremost an exotic freak—his racial otherness was not his primary feature on display—Lalloo was always advertised in the United Kingdom as the double-bodied "Hindoo" boy. By the late nineteenth century the British public were well aware of the distinctions between the religious traditions of the Hindu and Muslim communities in South Asia. In this context, however, the term "Hindoo" was used to evoke Lalloo's racial, ethnic, and thus colonial status rather than his religious affiliation. Marlene Tromp has argued that Lalloo's double body, with its underdeveloped twin, could be read as a metaphor for the colonial relationship between England and India, the latter merely an excess appendage or parasite dependent upon the body of the host.[1] This interpretation of Lalloo as a specifically Indian exhibit that embodied and enacted an imperial relationship was enhanced by the fact that "the Double-Bodied Hindoo Boy" first appeared in the United Kingdom in the spring of 1886 at the "India in London" exhibition. This was a private venture that had been staged to capitalize on the high-profile Indian and Colonial Exhibition that had opened that May. Here Lalloo performed alongside a troupe of Parsi actors and musicians, ivory and sandalwood carvers, a reenactment of a durbar, and shops staffed by "authentic" Indians. He was thus initially positioned by his managers not necessarily as a "freak of nature" but as part and parcel of the cultural life of the subcontinent, a component of the colorful landscape of a fantastical India that had been carefully crafted for British pleasure seekers.[2]

But however much Lalloo might have been marketed originally as an explicitly Indian or colonial exhibit—which, as we shall see, had implications for understandings of his sexuality—once he hit the freak show circuit in 1887 his primary mode of display was as a version of the archetypal sideshow act, "the Siamese twins." A staple of the modern freak show, many "double monsters" made the rounds in the Victorian and Edwardian periods. These acts all followed upon the success of Chang and Eng, the original "Siamese twins," who first took the stage in 1829. Although they had adopted a moniker that stressed their status as "Orientals"—highlighting their national origin rather than the precise nature of their spectacular bodies—the term "Siamese twins" rapidly entered into the popular lexicon, shedding its geographical specificity and coming to mean any set of conjoined twins regardless of their place of origin.[3] As in the case of Lalloo, Chang and Eng's racial exoticism was clearly part of the attraction of the exhibition, but what the public had principally paid to see with their own eyes was the spectacle of a two-in-one person whose complex corporeality challenged modern understandings of the self.

Chang and Eng's promotional material, the media coverage of their appearances, and medical reports on their case all focused on the physical place of conjoining, obsessing about where one body began and another ended. Countless descriptions of the cartilaginous band that joined Chang to Eng circulated in the popular and medical press. When George Buckley Bolton, member of the Royal College of Surgeons, published his medical report on the twins in 1830 he included three different close-up views of the band, which appeared to float, disembodied, on the page. James Young Simpson's 1869 reports in the *British Medical Journal*, which coincided with Chang and Eng's return to London, included both a woodcut of the twins with their band exposed and a close-up of the band itself.[4] When they died in 1874, Drs. Harrison Allen and William Pancoast, members of the College of Physicians in Philadelphia, performed an autopsy. They then made a plaster cast of their torsos, the central feature of which was the band that joined the bodies (the cast remains on display in the College's Mütter Museum). When Millie-Christine, Radica and Doodica, Tocci-Giovanni, Rosa and Josepha, and other double bodies toured the United Kingdom in the late nineteenth and early twentieth centuries, they also exposed their bodily unions. For what curious audiences had come to witness for themselves was the place where two people became one.

Lalloo's promotional materials similarly focused intently on the peculiarity and specificity of the attachment of the bodies. The souvenir pamphlet that accompanied his 1886 London debut maintained that Lalloo was "a phenomenon without parallel in the world's history," typical sideshow puff. It was, however, structured as a medical case report and used Latinate scientific language throughout to describe the anatomical irregularity of the bodies. Aside from naming Lalloo "the marvelous Indian boy," the pamphlet uses medical explanations for his deformity rather than discourses of wonder and amazement, and it gives an extremely detailed description, using sophisticated and specialized medical terminology, of the manner in which the bodies were united by two bony "pedicles."[5]

Those who didn't invest in the purchase of this pamphlet or didn't understand its scientific language were nevertheless also schooled in how to read Lalloo's unusual body. The posters and leaflets that accompanied the show proclaimed that the "Double Bodied Hindoo Boy" had "TWO BODIES, ONE HEAD, FOUR PERFECT ARMS, FOUR PERFECT HANDS, FOUR PERFECT LEGS, FOUR PERFECT FEET," but only "ONE PERFECT HEAD." Indeed, one can infer that audiences were attracted as much to the novelty of seeing conjoined bodies as they were to the double-sexed nature of this body, for that this was a "Boy and a Girl Joined together" appeared almost as an afterthought at the bottom of the promotional materials and, tellingly, not in all capital letters.[6]

When Lalloo appeared with the Barnum and Bailey Circus in London at the turn of the century, the *Wonder Book of Freaks and Animals,* a publication describing the sideshow acts, devoted seven sentences to the intricacies of the attachment of the bodies. The official guide to the show was similarly focused less on the marvel of the double-sexed body and much more on the relationship between the parasite and the autosite. Although it described a body in which there was a "mingling of the sexes," the detailed description that followed focused much more on how and where the bodies were joined. "The second body, which is headless, and is attached by the middle of its back bone to the lower end of his sternum or breast bone, does not incommode his movements in any way, and he is a very happy and active person," it maintained. "There is a free rotary movement of the imperfect body about the point of attachment, and the arms and shoulders are almost independent of the body and legs. The attached body is fed from his own circulatory system, and has no free movement of its own, though fully equipped with sensory nerves communicating with his own nervous centres."[7] This promotional material thus encouraged audiences to see Lalloo and Lala first and foremost as a case of conjoined twins, and only secondarily as a male-female pair.

The publicity photographs that accompanied the show also drew the eye to the place of attachment, emphasizing the double body rather than its double sex. These photographs reveal that Lalloo wore silk or velvet breeches with a matching jacket. Although the *Lancet* reported that the parasite wore a "wrapper," a woman's robe, in these photographs Lala is always dressed in an outfit similar to Lalloo's, although "her" trousers are slightly longer than his knee breeches. While Lala's costume is not typical male attire, neither is it more feminine than Lalloo's outfit, which contemporaries considered "showy."[8] To have costumed Lala in a dress or skirt would have meant concealing more of its little body, and thus would have minimized the inherent interest of the act, which resided in Lala's status as a living being attached to another. Indeed, it was this attachment that was

Figure 5. Souvenir photograph of Lalloo, the Double-Bodied Hindoo Boy, Barnum and Bailey Circus, 1898. National Archives, COPY 1/439.

emphasized: in both photographs Lalloo holds Lala's arms away from his body to reveal that they are indeed physically joined. What drove audiences to see the act, then, was clearly the appeal of the double body itself and the philosophical and social problems it posed.

While Lalloo's publicity materials took great care to describe the characteristics of his double body, the mode of attachment, and the physical relationship between the autosite and the parasite—in part to convince the audience that this was no fake—his publicity materials, like that of other conjoined twins, also piqued the public's interest by complicating rather than clarifying the implications of being attached to another. Indeed, conjoined twins inspired intriguing but troubling questions about what constituted the self.[9] As Allison Pingree has argued, conjoined twins confounded the "mathematics of personhood," for they are "more than one yet not quite two."[10] A favorite story repeated frequently in the press involved the dilemma that "Siamese twins" posed for railway conductors: could they travel on just one ticket, or were they obliged to purchase two?[11] In Lalloo's case, it was suggested that Lala might be considered an infant in arms for the purposes of railway travel, a point I will return to later. While the train ticket story was meant to be comic, it was not *merely* comic, for it reveals a profound discomfort with the ways in which these two-in-one people proved difficult to discipline and regulate and, perhaps even more troubling, ultimately challenged the presumption that there existed a clear boundary between self and other.

The very first page of the promotional pamphlet that accompanied Chang and Eng's 1869 London show raised the question of their individuality:

TWO BODIES: ARE THEY TWO MEN? Numerically they are two; but with men of science it is a disputed point, if there is more than one *person!* Is it one *man* in two bodies, with a double set of limbs and organs?. Is there but one life, one responsible will, one accountable being, only with double bodies, double heads, and a double set of arms and legs? Or, are they really two men—each distinct from the other as Smith from Brown, with the exception of that one mysterious bond?[12]

The pamphlet, though primarily intended to draw the public into the show and serve as a souvenir of the visit, in fact questioned what made someone a person. Was the nature of individuality rooted in the integrity of the bounded body, or was it based on the will and the conscience, which make one an "accountable being"? In relation to Chang and Eng this was particularly difficult to answer, for while each responded only to his own name when called, they always wrote in the first person singular, signing themselves "Chang Eng, Siamese Twins."[13]

Promotional materials for conjoined twins tended to be deliberately contradictory, maintaining on the one hand that these were separate individuals and on the other that they were one person. A handbill for Millie-Christine, "the two-headed nightingale," advertised that "she . . . talks with two persons on different subjects at the same time," indicating by the use of the pronoun "she" that this was one person, while at the same time suggesting that the ability to carry on different conversations revealed that she was two people. Another handbill maintained that the twins would sing a duet "arising from Two Voices, but originating in the direction of One Mind," intimating that they shared a consciousness.[14] The name "Millie-Christine" invoked a compound individual, but the alternate name "Miss Millie Christine," as the twins were sometimes known, instead invoked a singular person.

When "the Pygopagi Twins," Rosa and Josepha Blažek, first appeared in Britain in 1880 as small children, the *Court Journal* maintained that it was "difficult to know whether they represent one or two persons."[15] Other publications that covered the act, however, frequently noted that the girls had "contrary emotions," "inclinations," and "desires." One, apparently, always wanted to sit while the other was "on the move."[16] *Pearson's Weekly* raised similar issues when it reported on another famous conjoined pair who were linked at the ribs; they had two heads and two hearts but shared their limbs. The magazine maintained that "Tocci Giovanni is usually considered as one person—because he has only one body." "I suppose, though," it continued, "it seems perhaps almost more reasonable that he should count as two persons, for he possesses two heads, and the identity of a human being is undoubtedly centred rather in the head and brain, which in this case are duplicated, than in the body and legs."[17] Here, the reporter concluded that the person was lodged in the mind rather than in the body, that identity and even humanity had little to do with the integrity of the body but rather was rooted in a consciousness of self. Although Lala clearly could not have a consciousness of self, having no head and thus no mind, doctors prodded and poked both autosite and parasite to try to unravel the question of where one body began and another ended, and to determine whether Lala was part of Lalloo, merely an appendage, or a separate individual.[18] The multiple ways in which con-joined twins were theorized thus reveals considerable interest in what con-stituted a person, the boundary between the self and the other, and the relationship between the mind and the body.

Much of the coverage of these types of acts focused on whether or not they could be separated. Doctors who examined Chang and Eng came to rather different conclusions about the viability of their separation, some theorizing that it would present little problem, others believing that it would likely be fatal.[19] The popular press was equally fascinated with the possibility that they could be separated. In 1868 the *Illustrated Times* main-tained that after an ongoing argument the twins had consulted a French surgeon with the hopes of being severed from each other. The *Illustrated Weekly News* similarly reported that they were making a return visit to Europe specifically to be surgically divided.[20] When they did appear in London a few months later, sixty years old and down on their luck after losing land and slaves during the Civil War, their souvenir pamphlet made much of the issue of separation. It highlighted the possibility that they might soon die and referred to the horror of "a living man" finding "him-self linked to a lifeless body." If their separation was indeed possible, the pamphlet declared, "its much longer postponement would be a disgrace to the College of Surgeons," revealing an assumption that separation, and thus the triumph of individuality, was always a preferable condition.[21] The naturalist Francis Buckland, who knew the twins well, reported that this was merely advance publicity, a "Yankee 'flam'" to attract the attention of the show-going public.[22]

The story of their impending separation was central to the marketing of "the Siamese Twins" in Britain, as it preyed on the public's curiosity about the nature of being conjoined, tapping into the fears and fantasies of audi-ence members for whom physical attachment to another person could only have been considered unbearable because it compromised the integrity of the self. But only one set of freak show performers—Radica and Doodica, "the Orissa Twins," who toured Britain in the 1890s as an independent act before joining the Barnum and Bailey Circus—actually attempted separation surgery. In 1902 Doodica fell ill and they were taken to France for a separation surgery by the famous Parisian surgeon Eugène-Louis Doyen. Doyen was known for filming his procedures so that he would be able to evaluate his performance and use the films for teaching purposes. Although the surgical separation was pronounced "entirely successful," Doodica died within a week, Radica two years later.[23] The film of the surgery was shown not only in medical contexts, however, but also on the fairgrounds. It was, in fact, the earliest incidence of transforming this type of separation surgery into a form of popular entertainment, a trend that has continued into the twenty-first century.[24]

This fixation on the possibility of separation—and public interest in actually seeing the surgery itself—reveals a growing concern with individuality and the autonomy of the self. Even when doctors knew that surgery would be dangerous to one or both twins, it was highly recommended.[25] When John Bland Sutton initially examined Lalloo in 1888, he argued that any "attempt to amputate the parasite, or even a part of the parasite, would clearly be dangerous; surgery of this kind is known to be highly unsatisfactory."[26] However, in a 1928 article on parasitic twins (a subject he seemed to find particularly intriguing) Bland Sutton recommended separation whenever possible. This would spare the autosite a "dreadful life of bondage," he remarked, as well as "the disgust and ignominy of being exhibited for gain in public shows."[27] Although surgical techniques may have advanced in the forty years between these reports, in the 1920s separation surgery remained a risky procedure, as it does to this day. What his insistence on separation reveals is not so much an advancement in medical technology, but rather a deep-seated cultural concern with the boundary between the self and the other that only intensified with the advancement of modernity, predicated as it was on a vision of the self as highly individualized. Although there is no evidence that any pair of conjoined twins wished to be separated until Laleh and Ladan Bijani requested this in 2003,[28] Bland Sutton insisted that to be attached to another could only be considered a form of "bondage," presumably because it violated the integrity of the person as a unique, autonomous, and possessive individual, who owned, rather than shared, his body. Conjoined twins were highly intriguing and disturbing, therefore, precisely because they challenged individualism, so central to modern understandings of the self.

A BOY AND A GIRL JOINED TOGETHER

If conjoined twins in general posed crucial questions about subjectivity and what it meant to be a person, Lalloo provoked further concerns about the divide between male and female bodies. Lalloo was unlike other "Siamese twins" in that his double body was marketed by his promoters as double-sexed: for almost twenty years Lalloo's parasitical twin was advertised as

"Lala," a little sister.[29] "The Double-Bodied Hindoo Boy" thus forced a reevaluation of not only the nature of the boundary between self and other, but also what distinguished the male body from the female.

When Lalloo first appeared in England in 1886, his parasitic twin was not yet being marketed as female. His souvenir pamphlet instead identified "the Half Body" as male. But if Lalloo was not in this instance framed as sexually ambiguous, the pamphlet did raise questions about the gendered relationship between the two bodies, and thus by implication called the sex of these bodies into question. The pamphlet used the metaphor of a mother nursing her infant to describe the pair: "When the Boy is in a sitting posture," the pamphlet maintained, "the Half Body lies in such a manner as to give the appearance of a mother holding her babe for the purpose of suckling." It is not merely the positioning of the parasite in relation to the autosite, but the fact that Lalloo nourishes "the half-body" through his own blood (which the pamphlet describes in great detail) that renders Lalloo's body femalelike, for this implied that Lalloo's body kept the parasite alive in the same way that a pregnant woman's body nourished her fetus. Both the image of a mother suckling her infant and that of a pregnant woman sustaining a fetus through her own circulatory system implicitly cast Lalloo in a female role in relation to his twin. Thus even before his promoters seized on the idea of a male-female pair of twins, Lalloo's publicity materials raised questions about the gendered relationship between these bodies and thus, by implication, their sexed status.

By 1887, when Lalloo appeared at Nottingham Goose Fair, one of the highlights of the festival calendar, "the Half-Body" had become "Lala," a little sister.[30] This appears to have remained part of the marketing of the act until Lalloo's death in a train crash in Mexico in 1905. Framing this act as Lalloo and Lala heightened interest in the act, as all other conjoined twins on the Victorian freak show circuit were of the same sex. A similar Indian act who toured the United States in the early twentieth century capitalized on Lalloo and Lala's success by borrowing this clearly marketable convention, advertising under the name "Piramal and Sami, Brother and Sister, Double-Bodied Hindoo Enigma."

While the posters and leaflets produced after 1887 specified that "the second, or smaller, body is that of a girl" and thus that in this body there was "a mingling of the sexes," the visual materials that accompanied the show were much more ambiguous about the parasite's sex. The photographs that accompanied Lalloo's exhibition reveal that his managers often chose to emphasize the oddity of the conjoined bodies rather than their double sex. Instead of being costumed in clothing that constructed Lala as a female, the parasite was often androgynously clothed in order to reveal as much of its body as possible. In a poster that circulated in 1887 (but may, indeed, have been produced before the decision had been made to market the parasite as female), Lala is not only *not* depicted as a female but is, in fact, constructed as an extension of the maleness of Lalloo's body. Here Lalloo is depicted naked except for cotton drawers, holding an ambiguously positioned set of arms in his left hand. The parasite's legs, also clothed in drawers, stick out of the front of Lalloo's underwear and rest, as if standing, on a chair. The awkward and unusual position of the legs, which emerge directly from his groin, suggest that Lala is in fact a version of a penis, that the parasite is not only an extension of the male body but is that which makes the body definitively male. A leaflet, also in circulation in 1887, however, explicitly constructed Lala as female. Here Lalloo is drawn seated in a chair, his hands resting on his thighs, while Lala's arms encircle his neck. Lala's undergarments are very fitted, hugging "her" shapely buttocks and upper thighs, which appear decidedly feminine. These visual materials were both used to advertise Lalloo's appearance at Nottingham Goose Fair, suggesting that even after the parasite had been constructed as Lalloo's little sister, there remained a degree of flexibility in the manner in which Lalloo and Lala were represented. It was thus precisely the sexual ambiguity of the parasite, which could not be comfortably contained under the sign of either male or female, that made this act so intriguing.

The sexual indeterminacy of Lala's body was compelling in part because it evoked that of the hermaphrodite. The hermaphrodite's essential defining characteristic was understood in this period to be either a doubling of the sex organs in extreme or "true" cases, or, more commonly, any manifestation of "double, doubtful, or mistaken sex" rooted in ambiguous genitalia.[31] Hermaphrodites were so challenging to both the medical profession and the public because they undermined the male/female binary that was so central to late nineteenth-century culture, for Victorians were heavily invested in sexual difference and its concomitant—and, as they understood it, natural—expression in gender roles. As the medical men who increasingly began to examine and report on these troubling cases in the last decades of the nineteenth century discovered, s/he could have testes and even a rudimentary penis but live as a highly feminine woman. Challenging the notion that the world must be divided into male and female persons who must then conform to expectations of masculine and

Figure 6. Poster for Lalloo, the Double-Bodied Hindoo Boy, first tour in Great Britain, 1887. ©British Library, Evanion Collection 461.

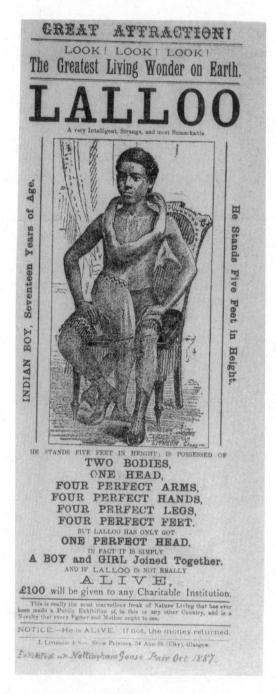

Figure 7. Leaflet for Lalloo, the Double-Bodied Hindoo Boy, at Nottingham Goose Fair, 1887. Guildhall Library, City of London.

feminine desires and behaviors, the hermaphrodite, like Lalloo, threatened deeply held beliefs about gender roles and hierarchies. Doctors thus argued that the hermaphrodite's "true sex" must be discovered in order to classify the individual and definitively place him or her within a prescribed gender role. The outer signs of "true sex" must be corrected, they theorized, in order that the anatomy resemble as much as possible the "normal" sexed body.[32]

Although cases of hermaphrodism were examined and discussed in professional medical circles (and circulated within Victorian pornography), the hermaphrodite, who had occasionally been on display during the early modern period,[33] did not become a stock character in the modern sideshow until well into the twentieth century. Nineteenth-century British freak shows did not actually feature hermaphrodites, for this would have required exposing the genitalia to a paying public, an act that would have been considered obscene. While many freak show acts occupied the margins of respectable entertainment, displaying genitalia marked the limit and would not have been tolerated by the police and other authorities in charge of licensing entertainment venues.

The public appearance, particularly in American shows, of hermaphrodites (more commonly called morphodites) in the 1920s emerged as the result of representational shifts that allowed for a different kind of portrayal of the double-sexed body. This portrayal, which did not involve the exhibition of genitalia, actually contained rather than provoked anxieties about gender. As Laurence Senelick has argued, the morphodite emerged in the early twentieth century as a staple of the American sideshow circuit in the new guise of the "half and half," a body bisected vertically so that the right side appeared masculine and the left feminine. This new way of imagining a double-sexed body as divided into two distinct sexes that were not intermingled or ambiguous marked a shift away from Victorian understandings of hermaphrodism. The early twentieth-century morphodite was imagined to be more clearly divided than the Victorian hermaphrodite, not only half male and half female but half masculine and half feminine. The "half and half" thus confirmed rather than challenged essential gender difference, for s/he represented not a blending of the sexes but rather their inability to intermingle.[34]

The "half and half" was still decades away when Lalloo and Lala were making the rounds of British freak shows. But because the division between male and female was in this period so "fraught with significance and anxiety," any violation of these distinctions garnered both public and professional attention and allowed the concept of hermaphrodism to be stretched to accommodate all cases of "gender confusion."[35] Thus, despite the fact that Lalloo's ambiguously sexed body was not truly hermaphroditic, it nevertheless raised similar concerns about the relationship between sex and gender and the distinction between male and female. This provoked the medical profession to examine the twins more closely in order to determine the "true" sex of the parasite. The medical profession's desire to proclaim the parasite to be male, despite obvious confusion about the precise markers of maleness, reveals its stake in asserting the incommensurability of sexes and the importance of reestablishing order in the face of a natural challenge to the organization of sexual difference.

PROFESSIONAL MEDICINE AND THE SEXED BODY

Although medical professionals could easily have distanced themselves from the sensationalism of "a boy and girl joined together," rejecting freak show exhibits as unworthy of their time and expertise, the medical elite were in fact much more invested in the question of the true sex of this double body than were the act's promoters. Indeed, Lalloo's case—even more so than that of Joseph Merrick, "the Elephant Man," who was also exhibited before the Pathological Society—stimulated intense debate within the medical community and led to a series of published case reports. These explored the relationship between the bodies and reported the results of tests designed to determine whether Lalloo felt pain when the parasite was pinched or pricked. But the doctors who examined Lalloo were fascinated not primarily by the relationship between the parasite and the autosite, but instead by the parasite's ambiguously sexed body.

The medical reports' lengthy descriptions of the size, shape, and smell of the parasite's sexual organs suggest the extent to which the profession was heavily invested in drawing boundaries between male and female bodies. But the confusion among members of the medical profession as to the sex of the parasite's body also reveals that, even in the 1880s, modern medicine was still relatively unclear as to the markers of "true" sex, and thus that doctors made decisions based as much on gendered assumptions about the body as on widely agreed upon scientific "facts." As Anne Fausto-Sterling has argued, "labeling someone a man or a woman is a social decision" that is informed by beliefs about gender. Debates, whether scientific or popular, over how to categorize an ambiguously sexed body thus provide important insight into the ways in which a culture organizes bodily difference and maps the relationship between the categories of sex and gender, which, as scholars have increasingly argued, are both socially constructed.[36]

The 1888 medical coverage of Lalloo focused on the parasite's male sex, in part as a response to the freak show's marketing of the act as a male-female pair. Had the parasite indeed been a girl, this would have been a remarkable medical case that required completely rethinking how conjoined twins were formed. Indeed, Bland Sutton seemed particularly eager to pronounce on the sex of Lala precisely in order to confirm his theory about the origins of conjoined twins. In the seventh edition of his text on tumors, he proclaimed that Lalloo was "exhibited as 'a boy and girl united together alive,' and this proved an attractive feature for many thousands of curious persons in Great Britain." He continued that since all "conjoined fetuses hitherto reported have been of the same sex," he had been "determined to settle this question." Verifying that Lala was actually male was necessary, he argued, to confirm his theory that conjoined twins were the result of a split ovum.[37]

When Lalloo's case was exhibited before the South Indian Branch of the British Medical Association in 1886, two theories had been advanced for the cause of his monstrosity: he was the product of a double-headed and double-tailed spermatozoa, or two fertilized eggs had become grafted onto each other. Both hypotheses left open the possibility that the parasite was indeed female.[38] Subsequent reporting in 1888, however, favored Bland Sutton's theory that Lalloo was the result of an "abnormal cleavage of a single ovum."[39] The fact that the twins were of the same sex lent credence to this theory, which seemed definitively proven by the time Bland Sutton revisited the subject in 1928.[40] His stake in settling the issue of the parasite's "true" sex was thus bound up in a desire to have his own theory corroborated.

But even the confident Bland Sutton betrayed some anxiety about Lala's sexual markers. When he returned to the case in 1922, Bland Sutton asserted that the "parasitic foetus had unusually large nipples, and that these were exhibited as proofs that the imperfect individual was a girl."[41] This is, however, the only mention of Lala's unusual nipples in the historical record; it appears in the seventh edition of Bland Sutton's book on tumors, but it is not mentioned in any of the previous or subsequent editions, in which he also described the case. His initial report on Lalloo in 1888 noted that the parasite had "two nipples on the skin over the scapulae, 6 cm. apart, and 3 cm. from the base of the pedicle," but made no mention that they were unusually large. Bland Sutton's account of Lala's nipples helped him to explain how a clearly male body might have been marketed as female. However, there is no evidence that Lala's naked torso was ever put on public display. But it also reveals that, even in the late nineteenth and early twentieth centuries, professional medicine was not always certain of the precise markers of maleness or femaleness, something that is evident in much of the medical reporting on Lalloo and Lala.

The medical coverage of Lalloo's case can be traced through the *British Medical Journal,* the *Lancet,* the *Transactions of the Pathological Society of London,* and the *Indian Medical Gazette,* all of which reported on him as a fascinating medical specimen.[42] He first appeared as a medical case study in the *BMJ* in the summer of 1885. A thirteen-year-old boy with what was initially labeled "posterior dichotomy" was reported to be exhibiting himself in Poona and Bombay to great success. The journal suggested that a report of this case "drawn by a competent anatomist, would be of great interest, the condition of the monstrosity being more extreme than in the Siamese twins or in Millie-Christine."[43] In December, C. W. Shirley Deakin, a surgeon in the Bengal Service best known for his vocal support of the regulation of prostitution in India, responded that he had seen what must have been the same boy exhibited opposite the Bombay railway station. In July of 1886 a similar report of a boy with a parasitic twin exhibiting in Hyderabad was reported in the *Indian Medical Gazette.* The case was then covered extensively in the *BMJ,* the *Lancet,* and the *Transactions of the Pathological Society* in 1888, for by this time Lalloo was a star freak show attraction in Britain and had been exhibited in front of both the London Pathological Society and the British Medical Association.[44] The case reoccurred in the medical press in 1898, when Lalloo was one of the highlights of Barnum and Bailey's sideshow in London.

The early medical coverage of the case, which was based on rather cursory examinations, identified Lalloo as clearly and distinctly male, but the articles' authors considered the parasite to be ambiguously sexed. Deakin's description begins with Lalloo's genitals, although he noted that the "lad was nervous and bashful at first when I asked to be allowed to examine him more closely." Nevertheless, he managed to ascertain that the "subject of the deformity was an up-country Hindoo lad, aged twelve, a bright intelligent boy of fair development for his age; his genital organs appeared to be well and normally formed, penis and scrotum." The parasite, however, appeared to Deakin to have "female genitals." Their female qualities are not, however, evident from his detailed description. There was, he reported, "a long foreskin attached to what were probably the corpora cavernosa at the upper end of a sulcus into which opened an urethra; there was no vaginal orifice, neither was there an anus."[45] What made these genitals appear to be female then? There was no vagina or ovaries, and the other parts identified, aside from the urethra, were clearly male organs: females have neither foreskins nor corpora cavernosa, both of which form part of a penis.

According to Mr. Browning, who examined Lalloo in Hyderabad and presented his case before the South Indian Branch of the British Medical Association, "when one first looked at the buttocks one was struck by the resemblance they bore to those of a female." Indeed, he argued, the general appearance in "this region is more that of a female than that of the opposite sex." But once again he provided little evidence to support this statement except for "the smell, which was very strong from the penis and surrounding integument," which, he maintained, was "similar to that of the female organs." Despite the female smell of the penis, it was nevertheless a penis. On separating the thighs, Browning maintained, "the penis, stunted, but otherwise perfectly formed and not circumcised, is visible." Although there was no scrotum and no testes, the penis was identifiable as such and passed urine. While Browning observed that there were "two rounded elevations like the labia majora" where the anus should be, he, like Deakin, described what most Victorian medical men would have identified as male genitalia, however incomplete.[46] Why, then, did they insist on the femaleness of the genitalia?

That the two physicians who initially wrote up the case history both referred to the parasite's genitalia as female in some way reveals that even in the 1880s there was a considerable amount of contention within the medical community about what constituted a male or female body. When Lalloo was exhibiting himself in India, where these two doctors examined him, he presumably was not marketing the parasite as female. This piece of showmanship seems to have been a distinctly British addition to the act. Lalloo's first promotional pamphlet, which dates from around 1886, clearly declares that the "Half Body" is male.[47] It was not until 1887 that the "Half Body" had become female in order to differentiate the act from other "Siamese twins." Unlike the medical professionals who examined the pair in 1888, then, these doctors were not influenced by freak show promotional materials that cast the parasite as female. As colonial medical men they had perhaps not had as much experience with anomalous bodies as the metropolitan elite who made up the membership of the prestigious London Pathological Society, a group that later identified the parasite as a male body. One could argue, however, that colonial doctors often had greater access to a wide variety of pathologies and deformities, as different geographical locations yielded genetic mutations that doctors based in Europe had not yet encountered. That they both independently saw these genitalia as female suggests that these medical men shared a belief in the relationship between completeness or perfection and maleness, implying that older ways of thinking about sexed bodies survived well into the modern period.

As Thomas Laqueur has expertly demonstrated, "sometime in the eighteenth century, sex as we know it was invented."[48] During the Enlightenment western European culture moved from the dominant one-sex model—according to which male and female bodies were understood to have essentially the same sexual organs, the female an inverted and imperfect version of the male—to a two-sex model. The two-sex model articulated the incommensurability of the sexes, provided the female genitalia with its own discrete names that were not feminine versions of terms applied to the male organs, and reimagined bodies as unambiguously sexed. In the age of the one-sex model gender did not necessarily adhere to the body; gender roles were clearly defined even when bodies were sexually unstable. It was only in the eighteenth century that gender came to be rooted in biological difference. Once previously unquestioned gender norms came to be interrogated in the Age of Reason, biology was produced to account for, and indeed justify, gender difference and inequalities. It was the politics of gender, Laqueur argues, that produced modern understandings of sexual difference, not sexual difference itself that gave rise to gender norms.

Laqueur's theory has recently been refined by historians who have argued that the shift from a one- to a two-sex model of the body was a much longer and more uneven process than his *Making Sex* suggests.[49] Many of the revisions to this narrative of change have been launched by early modernists who have sought to provide a more nuanced understanding of both scientific and cultural shifts in understandings of sexual difference. What has largely been left unexplored, however, are the ways in which older ways of thinking about sexed bodies survived well into the modern period, for historians have widely agreed that by the late eighteenth century there had occurred a paradigm shift that firmly articulated that male and female bodies were not only totally different, but that that difference permeated the body down to the bone.[50]

The attempt to classify the parasite in a fixed sexual category was a product of nineteenth-century medicine, which appeared to hold to the two-sex model of sexual difference: the belief that male and female bodies were not homologues, but incommensurably different biological entities. But the ways in which doctors managed their confusion over the parasite's sex reveals that the one-sex model could nevertheless rear its head. Both clothed and naked the parasite appears to the untrained eye to be neither particularly male nor evidently female. It has no head, and thus no facial features to help determine its sex, and, like all prepubescent children, its body appears androgynous. Despite the later handbills' insistence that the parasite's limbs were "perfect," Deakin maintained that they and the trunk were "much smaller [than the autosite's] and imperfectly developed." Indeed, medical men repeatedly described the entire body, including the genitals, as imperfect, undeveloped, and incomplete. This was a body that was obviously lacking, hence the freak show's initial use of the term "Half Body." Despite the presence of a functional penis, the parasite, the medical literature insisted, did not resemble a male body. The lack of scrotum and testes, the stunted penis, and the general incompleteness and imperfection of the parasite revealed that it was at best an ill-formed male and thus much more female than male in the final accounting.

The more extensive 1888 medical coverage of the case came as a result of Lalloo's exhibition in London both as a public entertainment and as a medical specimen. In February, Edmund Owen, Fellow of the Royal College of Surgeons and an expert on venereal diseases, exhibited the case of an "anomalous appendage" before the Pathological Society. In discussing the case John Bland Sutton diagnosed the eleven-week-old baby as having a parasitic twin. An "interesting specimen" of this kind could now be seen on exhibition in the Tottenham Court Road, Bland Sutton told his colleagues. Bland Sutton had examined him there and promptly gave a brief report of the case.[51] As I argued in the previous chapter, Bland Sutton was clearly accustomed to visiting cheap freak shows and had seen not only Lalloo but also "the Elephant Man." Although he condemned the shows as voyeuristic and degrading, Bland Sutton used them as a source of interesting pathologies and regularly exhibited the anomalous bodies he had discovered to other curious medical men. Two weeks later, in fact, he brought Lalloo to the Pathological Society meeting, evidently having collected him from the Tottenham Court Road exhibition site. A report of this meeting was published in the *Lancet* and the *BMJ*, as the Pathological Society reports generally were, but this case also received additional coverage in the *BMJ* and in the *Transactions of the Pathological Society of London*. This was a reflection of both Bland Sutton's professional status in the group (he was one of the most famous medical men of his day) and the inherent interest of the case.

The 1888 medical coverage of Lalloo also focused intently on the sex of the parasite, but here there was no mention of female genitalia. The parasite, concluded all the experts, was clearly a male. The medical press emphasized several elements of the parasite's anatomy that rendered it conclusively male, summarized by the *Lancet* as it "passed urine involuntarily, . . . possessed pubic hair, and the penis was capable of feeble independent erection."[52] The focus on pubic hair in all of the case reports—the pubes was always described as "hairy" or as "surrounded by pubic hair," which was variously described as "abundant" or "luxuriant"[53]—is telling, as its presence was used to support the contention that Lala was really a boy, since a prepubescent female was not supposed to have body hair. The repetition of this point and the specific language used illustrate the way in which journals and textbooks used and disseminated information from medical case reports; the text of these reports was frequently lifted verbatim, often without citing the original source. But its repeated appearance also indicates that abundant pubic hair was thought to be a particularly masculine trait. As we shall see in the next chapter, pubic hair was seen as a particularly erotic aspect of the female body precisely because it was so unfeminine; its sexual charge derived from its transgressive nature.

Alice Dreger, who has studied the medical examination and classification of hermaphrodites in nineteenth-century Britain and France, has argued that by the late nineteenth century doctors had agreed that correctly identifying the sex of a body was contingent on determining the presence of either testes or ovaries; she calls the period between 1870 and 1915 "the Age of the Gonads."[54] But all those who described this case agreed that the parasite had neither. This did not, however, interfere with the medical profession's ability clearly to identify the parasite in 1888 as "of the same sex" as the autosite and thus male.[55] Those who examined Lalloo and Lala repeatedly emphasized that the parasitic twin possessed what was clearly identified as a penis that could urinate and was capable of erection. They always described the penis as "well-formed" or "well-developed"; an illustration of the parasite's penis adapted from a photograph in fact accompanied the report in the *BMJ* to provide visual proof of this point.[56] The fact that the penis could pass urine and frequently urinated on an unsuspecting Lalloo suggested that not only were these indeed two separate bodies but that the organ was a functional penis. It did what a penis was supposed to do: urinate and, significantly, become erect. Indeed the parasite's penis, it was often noted, "was capable of erection," which occurred "at times," or "sometimes" "independent[ly]."[57] This discussion of urination and erection was part and parcel of identifying the parasite as having a penis that worked, and thus as classifying it as indisputably male. The functional penis—so critical to identifying a male body today, as Suzanne Kessler's work on intersexuality has demonstrated—was thus in the late nineteenth century clearly as important a marker of maleness as the gonads. This suggests a continuity between early modern and modern ideas about the sexed body: Ambroise Paré's 1573 treatise on monsters and prodigies similarly proclaimed that the presence of a penis of "the right size" that could become erect and ejaculate, as well as the presence of body hair in the groin, indicated that a seemingly hermaphroditic body was in fact male.[58]

By definitively identifying the parasite as a male body, Bland Sutton and his colleagues were able not only to corroborate his theory of the split ovum, but also to classify this body in its "true" sexual category and thus to assert the authority of the medical profession to interpret, and thus contain, ambiguous bodies that might at first seem to violate sexual boundaries. What they were not able to control, however, was the public's interpretation of this double-sexed body and the popular engagement with the parasite's sexual possibilities.

THE SEX LIVES OF SIAMESE TWINS

Although the medical accounts of the size, smell, shape, and sensation of Lalloo and Lala's genitals were much more voyeuristic than the freak show's halfhearted marketing of the act as a "boy and girl joined together," the medical profession condemned the show as indecent. In the encyclopedia *Anomalies and Curiosities of Medicine,* George Gould and Walter Pyle reproduced a souvenir postcard of Lalloo and described his case, criticizing his promoters for claiming this to be a double-sexed body. "To pander to the morbid curiosity of the curious," Gould and Pyle maintained, "the 'Dime Museum' managers at one time shrewdly clothed the parasite in female attire, calling the two brother and sister; but there is no doubt that all the traces of sex were of the male type." Similarly, Barton Cooke Hirst and George Piersol in their gruesome medical text *Human Monstrosities* explained the popularity of the act by insisting that the feminization of the parasite was intended "to arouse the prurient curiosity of the public."[59] The *BMJ* reported that Lalloo's exhibition had been deemed "indecent" and was officially forbidden. His manager, however, corrected this assumption, claiming that he had "never been forbidden to exhibit Laloo on the score that such an exhibition would be indecent," and that he had in fact exhibited him without any interference across the United Kingdom.[60] As Harriet Ritvo has argued, the readership of professional medical journals "shared the fascination with the lurid that inspired general interest in monstrosity."[61] They were nevertheless quick to denounce these shows as lewd. But what these medical men took for granted but did not explain is why a double-sexed body is more morbid or prurient than other same-sex conjoined twins, a plethora of which were also on display at freak shows in Britain and considered respectable entertainment.

To understand why an interest in Lalloo was considered by some to be prurient, his double body must be located within a wider discourse of "deviant" sexuality that was part and parcel of public and professional engagement with "Siamese twins" in general. The sexed bodies of conjoined twins and their sexualities were frequently the subject of both popular and medical interest. Indeed, the insistence that they be separated was clearly bound up in concerns about sexual behavior, a theme that remains central to the discourse of separation surgery today.[62] By describing freaks as happily married, promotional material and press coverage constructed them as little different from curious audience members. Souvenir photographs often included husbands, wives, and children as a normalizing device. Invoking the domestic arrangements and reproductive capacities of freaks, however, also directed public attention to their sexual lives.[63] In the case of conjoined twins, their sexuality was necessarily considered deviant: however much the public and medical professionals debated whether the twins were one or two individuals, when it came to sexual relations it was always implied that sex with "Siamese twins" necessarily involved more than two people.

From the moment Chang and Eng stepped onto British soil, their medical and popular coverage reflected widespread concern over their sexuality. In his case report on the twins George Buckley Bolton focused first not on the band that joined them, but instead on their genital organs, which he proclaimed were "regularly formed," as far as he could tell (the "youths are naturally modest, and evince a strong repugnance to any close investigation on this subject," he explained).[64] Bolton's assessment of the functionality of their genitalia underscored Chang and Eng's potential for sexual relations, something often noted or at least implied in other coverage of the act. An 1829 article in the *Times* drew attention to Chang and Eng's youthful sexuality by describing an incident with their chambermaid, a frequently eroticized figure in nineteenth-century culture. When the twins checked into their hotel and retired to their bedroom they encountered a chambermaid who "told them they should be her sweethearts, at which they laughed, and in a playful and boyish manner they at one and the same time kissed each side of her cheek." They then maintained coyly that it was "Mary that wanted to have them for a sweetheart, not they that wanted to have Mary."[65] Another writer maintained that they have taste enough "to be very partial to beauty in the other sex. They are much attached to the wife of Mr.____, one of the individuals who brought them to Europe."[66] Indeed, Bolton argued, although they might not wish separation at the moment, "some female attachment" may occur and induce them to seek surgical separation; they might later desire to sever their physical attachment to each other and replace it with an emotional bond to a member of the opposite sex.

Surgeons investigated the possibility of separating the twins—despite the fact that they were themselves resistant to any operation—precisely because, as sexually active men, they "shocked the moral sense of the community."[67] On their return visit to England in 1869 Sir James Young Simpson reported in the *BMJ* that their separation was not a matter of life and death but rather of "seemliness," since they both had wives.[68] The marriages of Chang and Eng, who took the last name Bunker, confirmed that conjoined twins could marry and produce children. The interest aroused by the living arrangements of the Bunker family, and in the number of children these marriages produced, suggests public interest in the sex lives of conjoined twins. Embedded within the descriptions of how the Bunkers split their time between wives and homes is a narrative of unorthodox sexuality in which more than one man and one woman share a bed and thus participate in a sexual relationship in some manner. When their marriages were reported in the *Times* in 1843, the article quoted the outrage expressed in the *New York Commercial* at the "unnatural things men and women will do": "What sort of women can they be who have entered into such a marriage? What sort of father to consent? What sort of clergyman he who performed the unnatural ceremony?" it demanded.[69] The unions were "unnatural" because, the newspaper implied, they were polygamous. A poster for their 1869 London show at the Egyptian Hall featured illustrations of their wives and children.[70] The pamphlet produced to accompany this show discussed their marriages. Although it refrained from accusing them outright of bigamy, it discussed the Siamese custom of taking plural wives. Some Siamese men, the pamphlet declared, have "a number that would make even Brigham Young," leader of the Mormon Church and the most famous nineteenth-century polygamist, "stare in wonder."[71] A newspaper report on their death in 1874 maintained that "they married—separate wives of course—and when we last saw them, they, or at any rate one of them, had a grown-up family," a sly suggestion that they might have shared wives and that exactly who fathered the children was open to question.[72]

After their death, one of their widows responded to the charge that "unnatural" sexual relationships were taking place within the Bunker family by declaring that as each man had been master in his own house, the other utterly subservient to his wills and desires, there "had never been any improper relations between the wives and brothers."[73] This understanding of "alternate mastery," reported the doctor who had done the autopsy on their bodies and who had clearly quite explicitly asked one of the wives about their sexual relationship, allowed the twins to "occupy the same marital couch with the wife of one," something that was clearly "immoral and shocking" to the wider world.[74]

Several sets of female conjoined twins found their sexual lives equally open to scrutiny, in part because their promotional materials encouraged it. When the "Orissa Twins" were exhibited at the Royal Aquarium in 1893, their publicity materials gestured to the fact that the girls "have already had their little romances."[75] Similarly, the souvenir pamphlet sold when Millie-Christine exhibited in London in 1885 underscored their sexuality:

> Girls in this city are divided into two classes—single-headed girls and doubled headed ditto. The single-headed ones are certainly the most numerous, but the double-headed ones appear to be the most attractive. This is evident from the fact, that while we can see a single-headed girl almost any time, we have to pay in order to be introduced to the maid with the duplex cranium. We say "maid," because the last double-headed girl we saw was not married. There was one man who courted her successfully, as he thought, for a time, but before popping the question he kissed one face first, and then could never get the consent of the other head. She is now waiting till a two-headed man comes along, and is gay with hope. This duplex girl, however, must be in every way a desirable match. Though the assurance given that she eats with both heads may tell against her with parsimonious wooers, yet the fact that she buys dresses for one only must be an immense advantage.[76]

This comic passage clearly suggested that Millie-Christine was an object of sexual attraction. It linked her to the prostitute by underscoring that one had to pay to visit her, but at the same time it firmly situated her within the economic and domestic accounting of the middle-class marriage market. The sexuality of "the maid with the duplex cranium" was also enhanced by the exhibition of her bare flesh, for the public was allowed to see the place where their bodies joined. While their pamphlet assured that this part of their back could be glimpsed "without any infringement of modesty," the medical profession was allowed more access not just to the exterior, but to the deepest recesses of their bodies.[77] Bland Sutton, who may or may not have personally examined the twins, maintained that the "anal orifice was single" and that while "the vulva appeared to be single," within it were "two vaginal and two urethral orifices."[78] This reveals that public and professional audiences were equally intrigued by the sexual possibilities of this unusual body.

The twins Rosa and Josepha Blažek—who, according to the *BMJ*, had "one vulva, but two vaginae"[79]—forced these issues of the privacy and sexuality of conjoined twins into the public sphere.[80] Rosa fell in love with their manager, married him, and conceived a child. When the twins returned to London in 1911, *World's Fair* reported that although they came with the nine-month-old baby, "the husband is now in Berlin," suggesting that he was not merely Rosa's husband but belonged to both of them. A publicity photograph showed the twins with the baby and an elaborate bassinette, catering to the public's fascination with their reproductive capacities and their sexual lives.[81] This situation forced the public to contemplate the fact that at the very least the unmarried twin would be a spectator to the intimacies of married life, a perpetual voyeur in the marriage bed. But it was equally possible that she might be the sexual partner of her brother-in-law, a participant in a bizarre ménage à trois. In order to normalize these complicated and disturbing sexual relationships for the show-going public, *World's Fair* noted that it "often happens that one is sleeping while the other lies awake reading."[82] This implied that sexual intercourse could take place while one of the twins was asleep. Describing the case years later, Bland Sutton maintained that the "sexual inclination of each differs," suggesting that although Rosa was sexually active, Josepha had no such desires, thus attempting to close down any suggestion that they had, in fact, shared "the husband."[83]

All double-bodied acts were sexually suggestive and deeply vexing, as they posed the problem of how to live a normal—in other words, heterosexual and monogamous—life while attached to another person. But Lalloo was particularly troubling precisely because of the nature of his double body, which combined elements of both the male and the female and thus opened up further questions about his, and her, sexuality. Lalloo's promotional materials played up his sexual attractiveness and suggested to the audience that he was in many respects a "normal" man, meaning both masculine and sexually active. Indeed, while Lalloo was in the United States a souvenir photograph was made of him that did not even include the parasite. A traditional portrait, this souvenir photograph featured only Lalloo's face and upper torso, completely effacing the presence of the twin and suggesting that, as an attractive young man, he was a draw regardless of his unusual body.[84] When Lalloo exhibited himself in the United Kingdom with the Barnum and Bailey Circus in 1898, their *Wonder Book of Freaks and Animals* maintained that "he is a very handsome fellow" and that he "seems to possess a great attraction for the fair sex, and he receives more love letters than are received by any two of the other members of the family of freaks. Whether it is his ready tongue, his shining black eyes, or his famous collection of fine diamonds that dazzles his feminine admirers, Lalloo's friends have not determined."[85] This sexualization of the freak, making him or her the object of marriage proposals and romantic attraction, was not uncommon in the promotional materials that accompanied these shows. Lalloo was repeatedly advertised as a "remarkably handsome and well-formed young man."[86] The use of the term *well-formed* here is significant, as it was also applied to Lalloo's penis in the medical literature. That he was a "well-formed young man," then, implied that he was virile.

But if Lalloo was seen as an object of sexual attraction, the perversity of this sexuality was bound up in the perceived intimate relationship between him and his twin. As Allison Pingree has argued, the marriages and reproduction of Chang and Eng were shocking to the public because they "presented prospects transgressive to the Victorian American culture in which they lived: homosexuality (because both were male), incest (because they were brothers), and adultery (because each would, in a sense, be sleeping with a woman not his wife)."[87] While Lalloo did not appear to provoke fears around either adultery or homosexuality, his double body did raise complicated issues around sexuality. The fact that the parasite's penis could become erect signaled that this was a body capable of sexual arousal. That it was attached to another body equally capable of sexual arousal may have stimulated concerns over "unnatural" sexual relations, specifically masturbation, incest, pedophilia, and child marriage, all of which were matters of moral, medical, governmental, and imperial concern in late Victorian Britain.

The ambiguity of the physical relationship between Lalloo and his twin—were they one body or two?—meant that concern over what might in this context be considered "solitary sex" was implicit in the act itself. As I have argued above, in at least one instance the parasite was visually constructed literally as Lalloo's penis. Any contact between Lalloo and Lala would therefore by definition be masturbatory. Indeed, the medical profession was intensely interested both in the genitalia of Lalloo and Lala and in the ways in which the bodies shared sensory perception. Whether the parasite felt pain—and by extension pleasure—when the autosite was touched and vice versa was highly intriguing to the medical men who examined this double body. "Light touches with the point of a quill pen are not felt; more sharply inflected ones are felt at all parts, and can be localized by the boy when blindfolded. The upper limbs are more sensitive than the lower," reported Bland Sutton and S. G. Shattock in their 1888 report. They noted the presence of old burn marks on the parasite's feet and buttocks, which suggested that at one point this test of sensation might in fact have been part of the exhibition. Each medical report on the case noted that the parasite passed urine "without the boy's cognizance" and that his penis independently became erect.[88] While the former fact also appeared in his souvenir pamphlet, the latter information was not deemed appropriate for a popular audience, as it made explicit what the other information only implied: the discussion of shared sensation, and of the capacity for both bodies to experience a form of sexual pleasure, suggested an autoerotic relationship between autosite and parasite.[89]

Equally troubling for late Victorian audiences was the issue of heterosexual incest. The leaflet shown in figure 7, at least two copies of which have survived, depicted the twins as lovers. Here Lala's left leg is slightly raised off the floor in a gesture of sexual surrender, "her" arms wrapped around his neck as if the two are in an amorous embrace. This leaflet clearly underscored the titillating nature of this anomalous body, making explicit not only the sexual potential of "the Double Bodied Hindoo Boy," but also the incestuous nature of this coupling. This might have been why the medical profession accused the act of being merely prurient and why some spectators might have been drawn to the show. For there is "no point on which men are so morbidly sensitive"—and thus, one could maintain, morbidly curious—than incest, remarked the *Westminster Review* in the 1860s.[90] Indeed, argues the literary critic James Twitchell, who uses a turn of phrase that anticipates my own analysis, the terms "horror" and "incest" have been linked "like Siamese twins in popular lexicon."[91]

In the mid-1880s, contemporaneous with Lalloo's British exhibitions, incest became a topic of social debate. The literature of social investigation, such as Andrew Mearns's *The Bitter Cry of Outcast London* and George Sims's *How the Poor Live,* revealed to the middle-class reading public the shocking state of the urban slums and fixated on the morality of the poor, charging that poverty led to debauchery. Living cheek by jowl, these social and religious reformers suggested, could lead even brother and sister to depraved sexual relations. The proximity of siblings, as well as parents and children, to each other, the sharing of beds, and inadequate clothing that left bodies partially exposed, these exposés warned, could lead directly to incest. These fears not only circulated in the popular press and pamphlet literature but also became central to government inquiries into the state of the urban slums, such as those conducted by the Royal Commission on the Housing of the Working Classes, which interviewed experts who testified to the frequency of incest among the urban poor.[92] Although it would be imprudent to take these middle-class readings of working-class sexuality at face value and assume that incest and urban squalor did, in fact, go hand in hand, as Louise Jackson has cautioned,[93] this focus on incest marked a new state and social concern with child abuse, and by extension child sexuality itself.

Although pedophilia dates back much further than the nineteenth century, it was in late Victorian Britain that the practice was identified as a social problem.[94] This relatively new anxiety was epitomized by the formation in 1884 of the Society for the Prevention of Cruelty to Children (SPCC)—which successfully lobbied for the passage of the 1889 Prevention of Cruelty to Children Act—and W. T. Stead's 1885 exposé of child prostitution, "The Maiden Tribute of Modern Babylon." This sensational piece of journalism led directly to the Criminal Law Amendment Act, which raised the age at which girls could consent to sexual relations to sixteen.[95] It was in the context of these new concerns over child abuse and child sexuality in the 1880s that British understandings of incest began to narrow, coming to refer specifically to sexual relations between an adult male and a young female relative, particularly between fathers and daughters and brothers and sisters. This new definition left aside questions of whether one could marry one's deceased wife's sister—an issue that had until this moment framed the public debate on incest—and instead focused on the figure of the vulnerable child victim.[96] Following the passage of the

1885 Criminal Law Amendment Act, feminist organizations mounted a campaign to criminalize incest. The Children Act of 1908 eventually cemented the crime as an offense specifically against children.[97]

The period from the mid-1880s until the early twentieth century was thus a moment in which cultural anxieties over sex with children, particularly within the family setting, intensified. It is significant that Lalloo's exhibition occurred right in the midst of these debates over incest among the urban poor, the refinement of the definition of incest (which underscored the brother-sister relationship), and new concern over child sexuality and sexual abuse. For if Victorian audiences feared that proximity and near nudity could lead to sexual relations between those who shared a bed, what about those who shared a body? These changes to the public discourse around incest and the new focus on the sexuality of young girls would have made Lalloo particularly susceptible to these charges, for the act was constructed as a brother-sister pair, with Lalloo as the dominant male twin and Lala as a childlike female sibling, and thus exactly the kind of victim that "The Maiden Tribute of Modern Babylon," and the SPCC had identified as particularly vulnerable to sexual exploitation.

That Lalloo was Indian could only have intensified these concerns, for the late 1880s and early 1890s were a time of increased public debate over Indian sexuality in particular. When Lalloo appeared at the "India in London" exhibition, he was one of many types of entertainer. The group included not only acrobats and snake charmers but also nautch girls, dancers whom British audiences considered highly erotic because they were frequently, though incorrectly, conflated with temple prostitutes.[98] Lalloo himself was repeatedly framed as sexually attractive precisely because of his Asian identity: his "shining black eyes" were often suggested as the root of his romantic attraction. In his promotional photograph for the Barnum and Bailey Circus (see figure 5) he is seen seated in front a Chinese screen and on top of an Oriental rug, symbols in Victorian culture of the luxury and sensuousness of the East.[99]

In fact, Lalloo's relationship to a seemingly perverse "Oriental" sexuality was also used to account for his deformity. When Bland Sutton and Shattock originally described the case they suggested that "early Oriental marriages" might be the cause of his monstrous parasite, thus situating Lalloo within the heated debate of the time over Indian child marriage. Around the same time that the British Criminal Law Amendment Act was passed in 1885, concerns about child sexuality also emerged in debates about child marriage in India. Following on the highly publicized case of

Rukhmabai, who was married at age eleven to a much older man, debates over child marriage, and in particular the consummation of these marriages, erupted in Britain and in Bengal (Rukhmabai had refused to live with her husband, and he subsequently filed for the "restitution of his conjugal rights").[100] This eventually led to the 1891 Indian Age of Consent Act, which set the age at which a girl could consent to sexual relations (and thus consummate a marriage) at twelve as opposed to ten, significantly lower than the age that had been established for British girls a mere six years earlier.[101] While Bland Sutton and Shattock eventually rejected their theory that "early Oriental marriage" had led to his deformity, this was only because Lalloo was the second child of a twenty-five-year-old mother.[102] That they had raised these concerns at all suggests the ways in which Lalloo's anomalous body was interpreted from within these colonial discourses of "sexual perversion" that circulated in the decades around the turn of the century.

Lalloo "the Double-Bodied Hindoo Boy" was thus a particularly fraught act. He was popular and troubling because as both conjoined twin and a type of hermaphrodite he confounded the division between self and other as well as male and female. Although this act was never explicitly advertised as sexually transgressive, the ways in which he was marketed to the public and was read by medical professionals suggest that Lalloo's body might well have provoked a range of anxieties over non-normative sexuality and "Oriental" perversity at a moment when these types of sexual behaviors were increasingly pathologized. The significant public and professional attention that Lalloo's act garnered and the vague sense of discomfort that this particular double body evoked reveal the freak show's central place in modern debates over subjectivity, the production of sexual difference, and the construction of normative sexuality.

THREE

The Missing Link and the Hairy Belle

Evolution, Imperialism, and "Primitive" Sexuality

IF "THE DOUBLE-BODIED HINDOO BOY" elicited concerns about colonial sexuality, similar debates about the erotics of the imperial—and thus non-normative—body were playing out in the 1880s on the stage of the Westminster Aquarium in London. In 1883 the great Canadian impresario G. A. Farini unveiled his latest discovery: "Krao, the Missing Link." Krao was a seven-year-old girl from what Victorians called "Indochina"[1] whose small, dark-skinned body was covered in soft brown hair. Farini exhibited her in the United Kingdom for seven months as "A Living Proof of Darwin's Theory of the Descent of Man," the missing link between man and monkey.[2] She then appeared in France, Germany, and the United States. Indeed, Krao was a staple of the late nineteenth- and early twentieth-century international freak show circuit, performing with Barnum and Bailey, then Ringling Brothers, and later their combined circuses, until her death in 1926 from influenza. This chapter argues that Krao was an extremely popular freak show act because her exhibition capitalized on late nineteenth-century preoccupations with the interrelationships among Darwinism, imperialism, and the sexuality of the "primitive" body.

Krao made her public debut in January of 1883 at the Westminster Aquarium, although she had been shown to members of the press during the 1882 Christmas season. "The Aq," as it was affectionately known, had been built in 1876 as part of London's expanding entertainment industry.

A pleasure palace within easy reach of Charing Cross, the aquarium boasted a theater, concerts, variety shows, freak acts, and temporary exhibits of extraordinary marine animals, including a beluga whale, a walrus, and a manatee, the last of which Farini advertised as a "mermaid."[3] Despite the venue's name, the fish exhibits were clearly an afterthought: they were few in number and apparently far from the main attraction. According to one contemporary, the fish were "on view for some time; in fact, I think that one or two lingered on to the very end twenty-seven years later." "I have always wondered," he continued, "whether anyone went to look at them and if the water was ever changed!"[4]

Despite the lack of fish, "the attractions of the place soon began to be very 'fishy' indeed," as the aquarium became known as a promenade for prostitutes. It was, recalled one contemporary, "one of the favourite resorts of ladies of easy virtue."[5] In 1889 the London County Council's Theatre and Music Hall Licensing Committee debated denying the venue an operating license precisely because of numerous complaints that it was little more than a convenient location for the soliciting of sex.[6] The following year it was involved in a scandal over sexually provocative posters advertising the scantily clad gymnast Zaeo.[7] The aquarium was thus a pleasure palace masquerading as a site of scientific and educational interest. It was, therefore, the perfect place for Krao, a sideshow freak whose appeal stemmed both from her claim to be "a perfect specimen of the step between man and monkey"[8] and from the erotics of her hairy, "primitive" body.

DARWIN'S MISSING LINK

As Kathryn Hoffman has demonstrated, "monkey-girls" circulated in textual, visual, and material form in European culture throughout the early modern period. The figure of the hairy girl appeared in fairytales, medical literature, academic art, and cabinets of curiosities and had been exhibited in the flesh on fairgrounds since at least the seventeenth century.[9] But the meanings generated around the body of the monkey-girl were profoundly reworked in the context of the popularization of Darwinian theories of evolution.

Throughout the latter half of the nineteenth century, popular understandings of evolutionary theory structured audiences' approach to the freak show, as the anomalous bodies on display were often interpreted as "steps on the evolutionary ladder" or "throwbacks" to earlier forms.[10] The liminal being that bridged the animal and human worlds was a trope of the display of human oddities in the eighteenth and nineteenth centuries, as "the Bear Lady," "the Tiger Lady," and "the Elephant Man"—all popular acts—make clear. After the publication of *Origin of Species* in 1859, these half-animal, half-human characters "became easily defined as 'missing links'" in an "increasingly fluid chain of being."[11] Farini's use of the scientific discourse of evolution to frame his exhibition of Krao was only the most explicit attempt by a variety of freak show entrepreneurs to capitalize on widespread interest in Darwinian theory. But, significantly, it also served to legitimize Krao's exhibition and to attract audience members who might not otherwise attend the freak show.

The use of scientific language enabled both Farini and the popular press that reported on this attraction to distance themselves from the charge increasingly lodged by middle-class moralists that exhibitions of bearded ladies and the like were vulgar forms of entertainment. In order to attract the widest audience with the deepest pockets possible, Farini stressed that this was no freak of nature and encouraged the press to promote her as an educational exhibit in much the same way that "ethnological types" were advertised, particularly in the latter half of the nineteenth century.[12] "There are many who condemn, perhaps with justice, the taste which takes the form of looking upon 'freaks of nature,'" reported the *Morning Post,* but Krao "does not come within that unwholesome category, because her peculiarities are hereditary."[13] Indeed, the press and the showman repeatedly stressed that Krao was not "offensive" or "repulsive," but instead a "fascinating" "specimen" of interest to the "ethnologist" and "naturalist" alike, and thus not only an acceptable, but even an edifying, form of entertainment.

While a scientific discourse was strategically employed to circumvent accusations of impropriety, the hirsute child also served as a focal point for public discussions of Darwinian theory, revealing that the freak show operated as an important space for the popularization of scientific debates. Whether Krao was more human than monkey, a member of a separate race, a member of a transitional species, or merely a true "freak of nature" preoccupied accounts of her exhibition in the 1880s. Indeed, Farini structured the show as a scientific demonstration, the "Living Proof of Darwin's Theory of the Descent of Man." Throughout the promotional pamphlet that accompanied her exhibition, Farini held up Krao as a scientific "specimen." Krao, Farini argued, "transcends in scientific importance and general interest any creature that has yet been seen in Europe."[14] He maintained that the Siamese monarchy had eventually allowed her to leave the country in order to assist "Europeans in their researches in connection with the theory of the Descent of Man."[15] Krao, he claimed, was the "key-stone to the arch" that the many builders of evolutionary theory had labored to construct, explicitly placing himself in the illustrious company of evolutionary theorists such as Ernst Haeckel, Alfred Russel Wallace, and Charles Darwin.[16] Many years later Farini told a reporter that he had "saturated" himself with Darwin in order to be able to "talk to the most learned scientist of them all."[17]

The Sporting and Dramatic News further aggrandized Farini's self-proclaimed scientific achievements: "There stood the great Farini," it maintained, "he who had done with a Cook's tourist ticket and an agent, in a few months, more than poor Darwin had achieved with the aid of all the animal world in a lifetime."[18] Farini did not fail to capitalize on this quote, placing a version of it on the back of the pamphlet. He also issued a *carte de visite* produced by the fashionable photography firm W. & D. Downey, which the *Penny Illustrated Paper* noted was a highly appropriate choice: the hairy girl, it joked, "naturally has a Downey photographer."[19] Borrowing from the conventions of spirit photography, this souvenir photograph featured an apparition of Darwin, who had died scarcely a year previous, floating above an especially simian depiction of Krao.[20] Darwin himself, this publicity photograph implied, bore witness to this great discovery and marveled at Farini's scientific achievement even from beyond the grave.

Darwin's *Origin of Species* merely alluded to the application of the principle of natural selection to the study of human evolution. "Darwin's Bulldog," Thomas Huxley, however, had by the 1860s fully expanded the theory to situate man's place in nature nearer the apes than the angels. By the time of the publication of *The Descent of Man* in 1871, Darwin's name was indelibly associated with "the ape theory."[21] Caricatures of Darwin-as-monkey proliferated in the popular press as scientific debates quickly found currency within the wider cultural milieu.[22] One of the key ways in which Darwinian principles were more broadly understood was through the concept of the missing link. Critiques of Darwinian evolution had centered on the fact that no species between man and monkey had been identified. In the popular imagination this missing link would be proof of the theory of human evolution. In the second half of the nineteenth century the missing link began to appear as a whimsical and comic character in popular fiction, satires, and burlesque.[23] Beginning in the 1860s, P. T. Barnum exhibited an African-American man in a fur suit as the "missing link" or "Man Monkey." "Zip," as he was later known, however, received greatest fame not primarily as a missing link but as a "nondescript"—a phrase that denoted animals not yet classified by science—as Barnum marketed the act under the title "What is It?"[24] In the 1870s, a hairy fourteen-year-old microcephalic girl was also exhibited in France as "Darwin's Missing Link."[25] It was Farini, however, who most successfully capitalized on popular interpretations of Darwinian theory by promoting Krao as half-human and half-monkey. Indeed, she continued to market herself as "the original missing link" throughout her career, suggesting both that she was the first widely popular act of this nature, and that others had piggybacked on her success.[26]

Krao's pamphlet advertised her as the crucial, but heretofore elusive, piece of the evolutionary puzzle. It began: "The usual argument against the truth of the Darwinian theory, that Man and Monkey had a common origin, has always been that no animal has hitherto been discovered in the transition state between 'Monkey' and 'Man.' This 'Missing Link' is now supplied in the person of KRAO, a perfect specimen of the step between man and monkey."[27] In order to accentuate Krao's status as missing link, Farini underscored her simian characteristics: her nose was level with the rest of her face, her cheeks contained pouches in which she could store food, she shot out her lip like a chimpanzee when pouty, her joints were flexible, she turned the soles of her feet up when sitting down, she had the rudiments of a tail, and of course she was covered in hair. Farini excerpted quotes from the popular press that stressed these monkeylike attributes, such as the *Standard*'s report that "she has a double row of teeth on the upper jaw; that she can, in the hollow of her cheeks, stow away food to be eaten when required as the monkey does in his 'pouches,' and that the fingers and toes bend backwards and forwards to the same extent and with equal ease."[28]

Farini had clearly delivered a lecture to the press on Krao's simian qualities at a special viewing. He then deliberately chose quotations for the front and back of Krao's promotional pamphlet that parroted his contention that Krao was half human, half monkey, although which half was which was clearly a matter of debate. "The lower portion of the body is more like that of a monkey," maintained the *Daily Chronicle,* while the *Evening News* reported that her "face presents an aspect singularly akin to that of the gorilla, but with a humanised expression."[29] Other reports drew attention to her resemblance to Pongo, a gorilla that Farini had exhibited at the aquarium in 1877, and gestured to her similarities to the "lower order of animals whose pranks are a never failing source of delight to visitors at the Zoological Gardens."[30]

The images that accompanied Krao's 1883 exhibition stressed her simian characteristics. The illustration that adorned the cover of her souvenir pamphlet represented Krao as a small monkeylike child, naked except for copious amounts of body hair, indeed, much more hair than contemporary photographs of her indicate that she actually possessed. Another promotional photograph showed her clinging, naked, to her adoptive father, arms and legs wrapped around him in a simian embrace. A cartoon of this photograph was reproduced in the *Sporting News* with the caption "Linked Sweetness," a caption that stressed Krao's "winsome ways" but also implied that she was as much animal as human. Beside this cartoon appeared another that depicted Krao in her "bib and tucker." Here the artist exaggerated her lips to stress her status as a "talking monkey," accentuating her racial otherness and—unlike the "Linked Sweetness" image—rendering Krao grotesque.[31] As Z. S. Strother has argued in relationship to the representation of Sara Baartman, the "Hottentot Venus," Krao's body clearly "did not speak for itself," and thus her souvenir pamphlet guided the eye to seek out her simian qualities. The unofficial images that surrounded her appearance at the aquarium thus also helped to structure the public's consumption of Krao as "the missing link."[32]

Krao's reputation, like that of many other freaks, rested on her authenticity, and thus it was essential for Farini to engage with scientific "experts," although how much of their interest in her was purely scientific, and the precise nature of their expertise in the authentication of missing links, is open to question. Farini commenced Krao's souvenir pamphlet with a conversation between himself and Francis Buckland, a well-known naturalist and a personal friend. Unabashedly interested in "curiosities of natural history," Buckland was nonetheless a respected scientist.[33] Although he had died in 1880, his presence in the narrative helped to position Krao as a legitimate subject of scientific study. During a visit to Dublin in 1883, Farini arranged for Krao to be exhibited at a private gathering of local intellectuals, including Trinity College professors, doctors, veterinarians, members of the Royal Society, and select representatives of the press. She was presented in her undergarments and examined and touched by the audience, who were encouraged to verify her status as missing link. Well trained by Farini, she greeted each visitor with a "How d'you do, Sir?"[34] By conducting these private viewings for select distinguished guests, Farini sought to construct Krao as "worthy of [both] public attention and careful scientific examination."[35]

Much of the "scientific" discussion of Krao focused on the proposition that she came from a hairy family, and indeed a hairy species. She was not a freak, the press reported, no "*lusus naturae* such as bearded women, spotted dogs, or giantesses." Rather, "she is a regular production in the regular order of Nature."[36] This narrative was part of an attempt not merely to distance her from the freak show, which for many people occupied the moral borderlands of popular entertainment, but also to emphasize her scientific importance. If she were a freak, a true anomaly, then she could not be considered a missing link, which by definition was a member of a transitional species. Accentuating her hairy family, therefore, was essential to protecting her status. Krao's pamphlet dwelled on her capture and on the hairiness of her parents, who did not accompany her to England. Krao's father had apparently died of cholera two weeks before Krao left her home in Laos, but as a woodcut that also appeared in the pamphlet revealed, his "whole body was completely covered with a thick hairy coat, exactly like that of the anthropoid apes."[37] By constructing Krao as the missing link, with a hereditary condition common not only to her family but to an entire tribe, and indeed a species, Farini suggested that she was not a subject for pathologists and teratologists, who were concerned with diseases or congenital anomalies, but rather for the anthropologist.

In an article entitled "Krao, The 'Human Monkey,'" which appeared in the scientific journal *Nature* in January of 1883, the English popular anthropologist and professor of Hindustani A. H. Keane reported on Farini's discovery. Eager to find the "missing link" (he would later endorse Eugène Dubois's 1892 proclamation that his "Java Man" was "the missing link"), Keane underscored Krao's "prognathism," her protruding lips, and her other apparently apelike characteristics. Although he did not entirely endorse the showman's claims, Keane proclaimed that "apart from her history," one might feel inclined to regard "this specimen merely as a 'sport' or *lusus naturae,* possessed rather of a pathological than of a strictly anthropological interest." But if the pamphlet about her is indeed true, Keane continued enthusiastically, then she is of "exceptional scientific importance."[38] A few months later, however, *Nature* published a letter from a resident of Bangkok that shed light on Krao's personal history. Krao, the author declared, was a Siamese child who came from ordinary parents. "Krao" was not the sound her parents made when calling her, as Farini had claimed, but rather meant "whiskers," her nickname. She was no more flexible than any other Siamese person, the letter writer maintained, and "beyond her abnormal hairiness presents no peculiarity." The child was looked upon at home "as even a greater natural curiosity than she is considered to be in England," declared the correspondent; in fact, her parents had also exhibited her to paying customers before selling her outright.[39]

While Keane corroborated these particulars, Farini of course ignored and suppressed them, continuing to quote Keane's original observations on the back of Krao's pamphlet. Indeed, as was to be expected, he only included quotes that emphasized her monkeylike nature, conveniently expunging material that clearly indicated that neither the scientific community nor the popular press was convinced of her authenticity. The *Medical Press and Circular,* the *British Medical Journal,* and *the Journal of the Anthropological Institute* concluded that she was merely a case of hypertrichosis, the scientific name for a superabundance of hair.[40] Indeed, the *BMJ* noted that all her physical peculiarities were common "amongst the yellow coloured races found inhabiting the eastern parts of India."[41] The *Daily News* maintained that "anatomists and anthropologists must decide whether Krao is in any degree structurally allied to the ape. The ordinary observer is not likely to discover that she is."[42] She shows "far too much intelligence to please the out-and-out Darwinite," suggested the *London Figaro,* while the *Morning Advertiser* maintained that the true link that needed to be found was the one that connected Krao "with the monkey-world."[43] A journalist for the *Penny Illustrated Paper* satirically "confess[ed]" that after a careful study of "Miss Krao and her hirsute showman," who sported a full beard and moustache, he could only say: "The Missing Link! Which is it?"[44] In fact, while Krao was certainly a curiosity, some were clearly disappointed with the exhibition. "I had steeled myself to behold something very Darwinian," reported *Land and Water,* Francis Buckland's own weekly journal, "picturing a gorilla-like half-animal being," but instead found "a bright little girl."[45] Indeed, declared the *Illustrated London News,* "there is many an English child more deserving to be called a monkey" than Krao.[46] She should, therefore, proclaimed the *Medical Press and Circular* in a tone that was decidedly unironic, sue for libel those claiming that she is more monkey than human.[47]

Despite the doubts raised about her authenticity, Krao's exhibit was undoubtedly a popular and financial success. She was, according to another performer, "immensely popular for years."[48] A contemporary showman recalled that Krao "was showing at the time when Darwin's theory was in the news so enormous crowds for a long time [were] the order of the day."[49] Whether or not freak show audiences were convinced of Farini's claims about Krao, they were nevertheless attracted by the link to Darwinian theory. Krao's exhibition was successful, therefore, because, whether she was "real" or not, she literally embodied popular interpretations of evolutionary theory, reflecting back to the freak show audience its own understanding of the processes of human evolution and encouraging them to participate in the advancement of scientific knowledge. At the same time, as we shall see, Krao reinforced British beliefs about the distance between their own civilized and evolved bodies and "primitive" Others.[50]

CIVILIZING THE SAVAGE

If the pamphlet sold at Krao's exhibition framed the show as scientific and educational, capable of leading one to a better understanding of evolutionary theory, it also situated Krao as part of a triumphant narrative of British imperialism. Evolutionary theory and imperialism were linked by what Anne McClintock has called "anachronistic space." Colonized people were, according to this trope, mired in "a permanently anterior time within the geographic space of the modern empire as anachronistic humans, atavistic . . . the living embodiment of the archaic 'primitive.'"[51] Less evolved both physically and culturally, colonial subjects thus represented lower branches of the monogenetic family tree. The imperial element of Krao's story enhanced the scientific positioning of her as an intermediary life form, for where else would the missing link be found but in the under-explored and undeveloped regions on the edges of empire.

The dramatic tale of Krao's capture was part of a pervasive late nineteenth-century narrative that figured imperialism as an adventure that tested men's mettle. Although this part of Southeast Asia was not yet part of the British empire, Krao's capture in Laos and the complex negotiations with the Laotian, Burmese, and Siamese monarchies over her removal reads like an imperial adventure novel, a genre that was about to reach its apotheosis with H. Rider Haggard's *King Solomon's Mines* (1885) and *She* (1887).[52] While Krao was likely born in Siam, she was, according to her souvenir pamphlet, captured in Laos. Farini's freak hunters had been dispatched to Southeast Asia, for rumors abounded that hairy men with tails could be found in the region. John Crawfurd's *Journal of an Embassy from the Governor-General of India to the Court of Ava in the Year 1827* described a man named Shwe-Maong, whose body and face were covered in long silky hair, and who, having been trained to "imitate the antics of a monkey," attended the king.[53] Shwe-Maong's daughter, Maphoon, and one of her sons had inherited her father's hirsuteness and were described by Captain Henry Yule twenty-eight years later in "A Narrative of the Mission sent by the Governor-General of India to the Court of Ava in 1855." The existence of this hairy family was widely known. Charles Darwin mentioned them in a discussion of "abnormally redundant hair" in *The Variation of Animals and Plants Under Domestication,* and the British naturalist Reverend William Houghton, had presented the case to the Ethnological Society in 1868.[54] Barnum had in fact apparently offered King Theebaw a large sum of money for his "Sacred Burmese Hairy Family," but Theebaw had refused, "declaring that if he parted with them, the downfall of his throne would soon follow."[55] It was, in fact, photographs of the "'Hairy Family' living at Mandalay" that Farini claimed had sent him in search of the missing link.[56]

Southeast Asia, or Indochina as it was commonly called in the late nineteenth century, sat at the edge of empire. The British, contesting French colonial expansion in the region, had been actively encroaching into this territory since the first Anglo-Burmese war of 1823–26. Britain annexed the port of Rangoon in 1852, converted the Straits Settlement into a crown colony in 1867, and began to absorb Upper Burma into the British Empire in late 1885.[57] While India had been effectively domesticated by the 1880s, Indochina still figured in the British imagination as a mysterious and savage outpost of empire that few could actually locate on a map; indeed, the press coverage of Krao suggests widespread confusion about exactly where Laos lay.[58] By the early 1880s, a tense moment in British-Burmese relations over the balance of power in the region, the Victorian press had begun to depict the Burmese as uncivilized, corrupt, and barbaric.[59] Krao's pamphlet contributed to this rhetoric. It was into this "country of bribery and corruption" ruled by a "bloodthirsty and treacherous sovereign," home to "wild tribes" of "robbers and murderers," that Farini plunged his audience.[60]

Strand Magazine noted in 1897 that a "whole library of entertaining facts might be written about the romance of freak-hunting and curiosity-finding for the side-shows of the world." Farini's "costly expedition to Northern Siam in search of 'Krao, the Missing Link,'" it continued, "reads like one of Jules Vernes's wildest flights."[61] Even years after her debut, Krao was clearly still selling the same souvenir pamphlet at her shows. The narrative of her capture was so appealing to freak show audiences and survived for at least two decades because it tapped into the late nineteenth-century taste for imperial adventures. Indeed, Farini clearly modeled Krao's pamphlet not only on imperial fiction, but also on the story of "The Wild Men of Borneo." From the 1850s the diminutive Barney and Hiram Davis toured the United States and Europe as Waino and Plutano, "The Wild Men of Borneo." When P. T. Barnum exhibited them in the 1870s he sold a pamphlet at the show that detailed their exciting capture off the "rocky coast of the Island of Borneo." It theorized that these "savage" brothers came from Siam or Burma and were "hardly more elevated in social standing than ourang-outangs."[62] These freak show "true life histories" were thus highly formulaic and both borrowed from and informed not only each other, but also fictional and nonfictional imperial adventure stories that circulated widely throughout Victorian culture.

Like Haggard's exotic tales, the story of Krao's capture is rife with adventure. Edward Sachs, the first of Farini's explorers, is bound hand and foot by his guides and left hanging upside down from a tree to be "torn to pieces by wild beasts." He outwits the natives by "extending his powerful muscles to their fullest extent" before he is bound, so that the ropes loosened as his muscles relaxed. By the "superhuman effort of his powerful muscles," he escapes and returns to Mandalay to surprise his betrayers. Sachs, however, like many an imperial explorer, contracts both smallpox and dysentery and is forced to give up the search. The quest for the missing link is then taken up by Carl Bock, who had already procured for Farini a walrus and a group of Laplanders in the Arctic, another site of nineteenth-century adventure stories. Bock was already engaged in an equally "onerous journey" through "some of the most difficult regions of Borneo, amid the 'head hunters,' and the cannibals" (which resulted in his sensational book *The Head-Hunters of Borneo*), when he agreed to take up the search for the missing link. The "dangerous journey" into Laos "surrounded by tigers and bears, by leopards and panthers, by elephants and rhinoceri, by snakes and crocodiles," results in the successful capture of Krao and her parents (and, incidentally, the fodder for another book, *Temples and Elephants*). But when he tries to leave Laos with his treasure, the king detains him. Bock is held as a "virtual prisoner" for months until he threatens the Laotian monarch with the wrath of the King of Siam, who had, apparently, sanctioned the search for the missing link.[63]

The trials and tribulations of Sachs and Bock are typical of the imperial adventure genre. They penetrate the dark jungles of distant conquerable lands, survive the attacks of savage tribes, suffer tropical diseases, hunt for treasure, and outwit foreign rulers. Their superior physical strength and European intellect and rationality trump the weak and superstitious natives, and in the end their courage and persistence is rewarded.

Krao's appeal was thus due in part to her pamphlet's success in catering to the desires of the audience for these tales from dark continents.

Not only did the story of her capture fit perfectly into the genre of imperial fiction, but Krao also served as a human trophy of imperial expansion, a synecdoche of Indochina, parts of which were on the verge of being absorbed into the British Empire. Like the "Burmese Imperial State Carriage and Throne Studded with 20,000 precious stones Captured in the Present Indian War," which was exhibited at the Egyptian Hall in 1825 in the midst of the first Anglo-Burmese war, the British public could consume Krao as a prize, a souvenir of imperial conquest.[64] This was equally true of the Burmese "Sacred Hairy Family" itself for, according to one commentator, what "Barnum was unable to accomplish" was "eventually brought about by the British troops."[65] After the annexation of Upper Burma in November of 1885, the Hairy Family also hit the freak show circuit, appearing first at the Egyptian Hall and then at the Piccadilly Hall in London in 1886 as "King Theebaw's Sacred Hairy Family." Their exhibition underscored that, like Burma itself, what had once been a private possession of the Burmese monarch was now available to be consumed by the British public.

With their hairy and thus primitive bodies on public display, both the "Sacred Hairy Family" and Krao were emblematic of all that was wild, lawless, and savage but ultimately conquerable in the lands at the edge of empire.[66] To emphasize her savagery Farini circulated portraits of Krao that underscored not only her simian characteristics but also her essential primitiveness. Even when clothed in the trappings of middle-class respectability, Krao was placed in a natural and explicitly savage environment, either leaning against rocks or perched on the stump of a tree. The image of her that most explicitly cast her as a "wild child" was made around 1884. This souvenir *carte de visite* produced in Liverpool depicts Krao in a jungle setting. Here she is completely naked, which accentuates her hairy body. Her hair surrounds her face like a lion's mane (a trope of other hirsute freak performers), and her right leg is raised to rest upon a rock in order to better expose her flat, hairy, and thus primitive feet. This image was reproduced as a woodcut, likely around 1885, and was used as part of the promotional materials for her 1887 reappearance at the aquarium. But here, significantly, the artist introduced a small beaded loincloth for the sake of modesty.

If Krao epitomized the primitive nature of colonial subjects, so too was she quickly domesticated by the media, which underscored how easily she had been civilized since her arrival in Britain. Her pamphlet and the press reports of her exhibition return repeatedly to the success of the civilizing

Figure 8. Handbill for Krao, the Missing Link, Westminster Aquarium, 1887. The Bodleian Library, University of Oxford, John Johnson Collection, Human Freaks Box 4.

process, for this wild monkey-child was regularly held up as a charming, well-behaved little girl. Krao's pamphlet figured the Indochinese as wild and savage: the tribe of hairy people to which Krao supposedly belonged lived in a state "as low and as bestial as the beasts of the field."[67] Her capture was therefore construed as a rescue, for she was saved from this savage life and civilized. When Bock declared to Prince Kromolat of Burma that Krao would be "far better cared for in Europe [by Farini] than she possibly could in the wild country" that was her home, the prince apparently replied that he had indeed heard of "the Great Showman" and at once acquiesced to her removal "on condition that she should be formally adopted by Mr. Bock, on behalf of Mr. Farini, as his adopted daughter."[68] While the prince's admiration for Farini was inserted into the story to aggrandize the showman, it also served to underscore the dominant imperial ideology that figured colonial peoples as grateful recipients of Western culture.

The final phrase of Krao's pamphlet asserted that this "daughter of a tribe of hairy men and women, now makes her appearance before the civilised world."[69] But much of the press coverage of her exhibition focused on the success of Krao's civilization. Her ability to speak English was often noted, as were her good manners. Like an appropriately grateful immigrant, Krao was apparently so taken with her new home that she announced her "intention of residing in England."[70] Argued A. H. Keane, Krao recognized her own good fortune and had "so far adapted herself to civilised ways, that the mere threat to be sent back to her own people is always sufficient to suppress any symptoms of unruly conduct."[71] Similarly, her parents had, according to her souvenir pamphlet, been equally "anxious" to leave their native land and accompany Bock back to England.[72] Ironically, the freak show, seen by many as voyeuristic, prurient, and immoral, was in this context cast as a civilizing force. As Rosemarie Garland Thomson has similarly argued in relationship to the "nondescript" hirsute attraction Julia Pastrana, her "exploitation becomes a salvation; her colonization becomes a conversion; and her display becomes a testimony."[73]

Krao's formal adoption by Farini confirmed that she could not only be successfully transplanted but also transformed into a little English girl. Krao's adoption officially anglicized and domesticated her, and her adaptability to her new surroundings was often noted. She appears "to be happy enough in her new position," remarked the *Daily News*, "and to regard her papa, as she calls Mr. Farini, with feelings of affection."[74] Other journalists maintained that she appeared "much attached" to Farini, "her kind foster parent,"[75] and indeed she bore the surname Farini throughout her life.

Not only did her adoption normalize and westernize Krao by locating her within a Victorian family unit (making her, as one newspaper noted, not only "hair apparent, but heir apparent"),[76] but several newspaper reports highlighted the fact that she had been vaccinated.[77] By the 1880s all British children were not only required by the state to be vaccinated, but they were also obliged to be educated. *The London Figaro* noted that before long the "Board School officers will be looking up Miss Krao" and will likely "insist [on] her passing her standard like any other young lady of colour located in this country."[78] By advertising her vaccination and the possibility that she might be educated, Farini accentuated Krao's admittance into British society though the rites and rituals of Western childhood.

As part of this discourse of successful civilization, Farini often clothed Krao in the dress and elegant black boots of a middle-class girl, although her costume always left her hairy arms and legs exposed. In one souvenir photograph she is garbed in an elaborate hat and ruffled dress that resemble the clothes of a Victorian fashion doll.[79] These "civilized" images of Krao served as the basis of an illustration that appeared in American newspapers when she first crossed the Atlantic. In the Peru, Indiana, *Republican* in 1885 a well-groomed and neatly dressed Krao was depicted sitting beside a younger and decidedly more simian version of herself, adapted from the image that first appeared on her promotional pamphlet.[80] The illustration suggests the distance she had traveled from savage to civilized in the space of a mere two years. If Krao was a trophy of empire, she was therefore also an object lesson in imperial relations. Her representation as a charming child, happily adapting to English life, underscored Britain's role as a civilizing force and its ability to turn even the most primitive peoples into good British subjects. At the same time, as Peter Stallybrass and Allon White have suggested, her "mimicry of the polite" was ultimately absurd and thus reassured Krao's audiences that civilization was the "essential and unchanging possession which distinguishes the European citizen" not only from animals, but from all Others.[81]

THE EROTICS OF THE "PRIMITIVE" BODY

The Darwinian and social Darwinian messages of Krao's exhibition are clear; indeed, her success stemmed in large part from Farini's ability to cast Krao as an educational act rather than as a freak. However, it is hard to ignore that at least part of Krao's appeal, particularly in the decades around the turn of the century, derived from the implicit sexuality of her partially exposed hirsute body. Although she was not primarily an erotic performer,

Krao's body could be, and clearly was, read as sexually available. The very act of displaying one's body publicly rendered the female performer, regardless of the content and nature of the performance, a sexual object. Krao's costume, a version of which she wore throughout her adult career, promoted this reading of her body. It was similar to those preferred by female acrobats (like the scandalous Zaeo), whose performances were structured to allow male viewers to see as much of the female body as possible, and whose aerial feats permitted the audience to look up at their spread legs from below. By the end of the nineteenth century Krao, like other hirsute acts, was also regularly depicted reclining on her side in a jungle setting. This was a recognizably erotic pose that evoked Titian's *Venus d'Urbino,* Manet's controversial *Olympia,* and countless Orientalist paintings of the highly fetishized odalisque. This particular languid and alluring stance was also adopted by actresses, who were widely believed to be little more than prostitutes, in their publicity materials; indeed, Victorian pornography often featured naked women lounging in a similar position.[82] By evoking these cultural fantasies of sexually submissive and sexually available women, Krao's promoters used sex to sell her act.

It was not merely the erotic poses and skimpy costumes that suggested Krao's sexual precocity, but in fact the hairiness of her body itself. The hairy woman was eroticized in part because female body hair typically emerges during puberty, thus serving as a sign of sexual maturity. A woman's body hair is thus directly linked to her fertility and thus her availability for sexual relations.[83] But since at least the Renaissance, the hairy female body had also been associated with animalistic lust.[84] Late nineteenth-century sexologists in fact theorized that prostitutes could be identified by their abnormal amounts of pubic, body, and facial hair.[85] By exposing her female body and facial hair for all to see, Krao thus signaled both her sexual maturity and her own unnatural desire. She also made visible that which generally went unseen: her body hair, and later her beard, evoked pubic hair, a preoccupation of erotica and pornography since at least the eighteenth century. In fact, the term "beard" was often used as slang for the pubes.[86] By exhibiting rather than hiding her hair, Krao thus allowed audience members access to an erotic, if not necessarily feminine, aspect of the female body.

This reading of her hirsuteness, however, also had an important imperial component that linked her sexuality to her racial otherness. Krao was, significantly, not marketed as a bearded lady, the most common hirsute female act on the Victorian stage. Indeed, Farini declared in Krao's souvenir pamphlet that she was "an entirely different being from the 'bearded women'" typically on view in London.[87] Historians have argued that bearded women, staples of the nineteenth-century freak show, evoked anxieties about "maintaining proper gender roles" at a moment in which women were increasingly beginning to demand the same rights as men.[88] But publicity materials suggest that bearded women actually attempted to underscore their femininity and thus to contain their sexuality by promoting themselves as wives and mothers—models of heterosexual, procreative, middle-class domesticity. Miss Annie Jones, a Virginian who regularly appeared in Britain with Barnum's circus, was described as "a Southern lady" who, except for her "unladylike appendage," was "a very handsome woman" and a talented musician. *The Era* took pains to note that she was married, reinforcing her normative sexuality.[89] In 1909 a veteran showman remembered Miss Jones as a "pretty woman" with a "sweet voice," "beautiful tresses," and a "dark Spanish beauty" that made her "a most attractive freak."[90] Indeed, her British promotional material declared that even her facial hair was "not quite a masculine beard" and emphasized that despite its prominence, it "does not hide the femininely attractive features" of "Miss Jones [who] is the very impersonation of daintiness, with a pretty little foot, neatly turned ankle, and shapely, delicate hands that proclaim her to be of good birth." She was, the guide to her exhibition proclaimed, "devoted to that dearest indulgence of feminine fingers, fine embroidery." In case the copy did not make the point, her publicity photograph depicted her in a modest high-necked gown that emphasized her respectable middle-class femininity.[91]

Madame Clofullia's handbills similarly claimed that her "beauty" was unimpaired by her bushy black beard. Her "bust," the most distinctive outward sign of womanhood that could be shown on a Victorian stage, was "finely formed," leaving "not the least doubt as to her Sex," her publicity materials declared. She was extremely accomplished, spoke "French fluently," was well educated, and was in every way an ideal woman, the advertisements suggested. That she was later advertised as having given birth to a child—a fact that her handbill stated could be verified by the attending surgeon—and that she often exhibited herself with her daughter served to confirm her sexual and gender identity as a model heterosexual, maternal, and thus feminine lady.[92] Similarly, Madame Polonawsky's 1886 handbill drew attention to this bearded lady's feminine breasts and shapely behind by depicting her in a dress that sported a plunging neckline and an ample bustle. Her buttocks are further accentuated in the illustration by the strategic placement of her fan, which appears to extend the bustle even further.

Figure 9. Handbill for Madame Polonawsky, Albert Palace, 1886. Guildhall Library, City of London.

The bearded women on display in the nineteenth and early twentieth centuries could easily be constructed as models of middle-class, and thus normative, sexuality because they were without exception white Europeans or Americans. Madame Clofullia's handbill described her as fair-skinned; indeed, her face was apparently of an "extraordinary whiteness." Krao, on the other hand—"a dusky little hairy Asian girl"[93] and a potential colonial subject—was never marketed as a bearded lady despite the beard and moustache she sported as a young woman. Instead, her appeal stemmed from a different articulation of the sexual connotations of body hair that had a distinctly racial component. For, although not a hard and fast rule, nonwhite hairy women tended to be promoted as hybrids—part human, part animal—and thus were associated with a more base, primitive carnality.

Perhaps the best-known non-European female hirsute act of the nineteenth century was Julia Pastrana, who was generally exhibited as "the Nondescript" but sometimes advertised as "the Baboon Lady," "the Bear Lady," or "the Gorilla Woman."[94] Her advertising copy, although often pointing out the feminine qualities that made her similar to European bearded ladies, nevertheless also underscored both her racial difference and her relationship to brute creation. Pastrana's handbills and posters maintained that she came from the tribe of "Root-Digger Indians" that inhabited the mountains of Mexico and "live[d] in caves of animals of different descriptions, such as Bears, Monkeys, Squirrels." These "Indians," it continued, "are very much of the monkey order, very spiteful and hard to govern."[95] Her souvenir pamphlet similarly declared that Pastrana and her mother were discovered living "only with Baboons, Bears, and Monkeys."[96]

While the medical and scientific literature on her case described her as a "bearded and hairy female," thus allying her to other bearded women, it also accentuated her bestial qualities. The Russian scientist who embalmed her body after she died from complications following childbirth maintained in the *Lancet* that the "protruberance" of her "frontal bones [was] not more than normal," that "Camper's facial line retained an almost vertical direction," and thus that her "facial angle had an inclination of from 90 to 95 degrees," which was typical of most Europeans.[97] However, another article in the *Lancet* declared that her head was a perfect "facsimile of that of the gorilla."[98] Darwin himself similarly remarked that because of "the redundancy of the teeth her mouth projected, and her face had a gorilla-like appearance."[99] A poster advertising her exhibition at the Regent Gallery in 1857 exaggerated her racial otherness by portraying her in profile with large red lips and a big nose, typical of the racialized images of African-Americans that circulated at this time, despite the fact that scientists declared that her "physiognomy is not that of the negro."[100]

Julia Pastrana was unique in that she made the rounds of the freak show circuit both alive and dead: after her death in Moscow in 1860 her embalmed body, dressed in her own homemade costume "and placed in the attitude of a *danseuse*," was exhibited alongside that of her dead child, to great acclaim.[101] But she was also typical of the ways in which excessively hairy women who were not white Europeans were constructed as animal-human hybrids rather than as bearded ladies. This was particularly the case in the 1880s. The hairy Senorita Anita from Paraguay, who appeared in London with her brother Robinson, "the Bear Boy," in 1886, was not exhibited as a bearded lady, although she could easily have fit into this genre, but rather as a "Tiger Lady." The image on her poster, though it depicted only her brother, suggested a very primitive member of an indigenous South American tribe.[102]

Similarly, Madame Howard—who was exhibited in a Lambeth show shop in 1883, at Mitcham Fair in 1885, and on the Borough High Street in South London many years later—could have been advertised as a bearded woman. Instead she was billed as "the African Lion-faced Lady." Although born to English parents, her pregnant mother, her leaflet claimed, had watched her husband being torn to pieces by lions while stationed with the army in Sierra Leone. As a result, the child had been born with the face of a lion. Although her parents were clearly white English citizens, their child, who was born on African soil, had "dark brown mottled skin" on her face, "drooping eyebrows," and "broad distended nostrils." With her "wavy flowing mane" she resembled, her handbills clearly indicated, both the human and animal inhabitants of the "dark Continent."[103] Her ambiguous racial identity encouraged her promoters to market her as a cross between human and animal. By the early 1900s, "Leonine, The Lion Faced Lady," who was on exhibit at Pickard's Museum in Glasgow, was using a story identical to that of Madame Howard, but she added that she had been raised by an "old coloured nurse," accentuating the relationship between her animalistic qualities and her racial difference.[104]

This construction of nonwhite hirsute women as animalistic allowed spectators to associate them with a primitive, excessive sexuality. While civilized humans practiced self-control, Victorians theorized that animals were driven by instinct and could not contain their drives. The primitive

Figure 10. Leaflet for Madame Howard, the African Lion-Faced Lady, Mitcham Fair, 1885. Guildhall Library, City of London.

or savage body, whose defining characteristic in the nineteenth century was its hirsuteness, was thus widely associated with unbridled, perverse, and pathological sexual drives.[105] Madame Howard's pavilion at Mitcham Fair offered young men and women the opportunity not only of gazing on a "Lion-faced lady," but also of going through a process that would reveal their future husband or wife, thus explicitly linking the hairy savage woman to future romantic and sexual fulfillment. That Julia Pastrana was said to have been discovered as an infant suckling at the breast of her mother, who had been living with animals, suggested that she was the product of interspecies breeding.[106] As the hairiest of these nonwhite hirsute acts, Krao embodied these fantasies about the sexuality of the primitive other. Thus even as a small child, Krao could be, and clearly was, read as an erotic object.

The eroticization of Krao found its earliest expression in France in 1886. The French media transformed the previously innocuous representation of an eight- or nine-year-old Krao in her jungle setting into an image of a considerably older, sexually aggressive, and sexually available young woman. This illustration, which appeared on a poster advertising her exhibition in a private room at the café-concert the Alcazar d'Eté (a competitor of the Folies-Bergère where King Theebaw's "Sacred Hairy Family" would be exhibited the following year), had clearly been adapted from the British woodcut, but its tone and meaning had changed. Instead of confronting the viewer with a direct and passive stare, more animal than human, Krao looks over her left shoulder and grins suggestively at her viewers in a coquettish come-on. Her legs and thighs are considerably more curvaceous and she rises up on her toes to exaggerate the curved arches of her feet. Similarly, a picture of a nude Krao seated on the lap of a scientist was significantly altered in a French cartoon to emphasize the lasciviousness of the scientist, and the sexual maturity of what was now clearly a young woman.[107]

That the French interpreted Krao as a sexual object even at this very early stage of her career indicates heightened anxieties, as Diana Snigurowicz has argued, over the sexual connotations of female hirsuteness, which suggested bestiality, zoophilia, and interspecies breeding.[108] For the British, the erotic nature of Krao's act seems to have been more implicit. The media coverage of Krao's exhibition in Britain, in contrast to her publicity materials, often emphasized not her bestial qualities but her humanity and even her femininity. There was little question that Krao was, in fact, a young girl with more human than simian characteristics. Most

Figure 11. Poster for Krao, the Missing Link, Alcazar d'Eté, by Jules Cheret, 1886. Deutsches Historisches Museum.

newspapers reported that she had "lovely" or "lustrous" eyes. Even her own pamphlet drew attention to what was obviously seen as her best feature: "How many a fair lady will envy Krao those full and sparkling eyes! How their dark luster would be set off on a fair skin!"[109] This remark implied that despite the existence of "several British subjects who are uglier than Krao,"[110] she could never be truly beautiful, as her dark skin (hairy or not), the clearest marker of her racial difference, precluded this. Nonetheless, as the newspapers all indicated, she showed "truly feminine delight" in the clothes, jewelry, and satin slippers she was provided with.[111] This feminization of Krao, however, suggested that she was not only flirtatious but possibly available. Maintained one reporter, this "pretty little girl" exhibited "the elementary coquettishness of her sex," asserting her "fair sex through and through her hirsute appearance."[112] She is, remarked the *Morning Post,* "a rather forward young person."[113] Indeed, *Punch* suggested knowingly that she was ready to receive company: "Entrance without knocking, ask for the Hairy Belle," a sentiment that Farini clearly endorsed as he placed this quote on the promotional pamphlet itself.[114]

Krao's evening appearances at The Star of Erin music hall in Dublin in 1883, even more than her daytime exhibition to learned professionals in her underclothes, underscored the erotic readings of her body. According to Shane Peacock, Farini's biographer, "Each night the lights were dimmed, primitive music played and she slowly emerged onto the stage . . . in a short blue dress with red stockings and shoes, her side turned to the crowd and her face partially covered. . . . [W]hen she came fully into the footlights and dramatically lifted her head to the audience there was always an audible gasp. . . . But once again her most striking characteristic was her personality—she was a charming, charismatic performer who enjoyed being on stage."[115] The music hall setting, unlike the pseudoscientific setting of the Westminster Aquarium, encouraged Krao to perform her freakish bodily difference in dramatic and sexually provocative ways that explicitly located her as a "primitive" Other. Her performance, complete with music, lighting, and a costume, prefigured that of Josephine Baker, who self-consciously manipulated the discourses of primitive sexuality to market herself as an exotic, and therefore erotic, act.

When Krao returned to Britain in 1887 the aquarium program maintained that "old friends will be astonished at her development,"[116] hinting at her body's maturity. Seven years later *The English Mechanic* reported that while on exhibit in Germany, Krao had received a marriage proposal, a not uncommon phenomenon for sideshow freaks, but that she had refused her suitor because "she had learned too much independence during her wild life in the woods."[117] The press thus advertised her sexual maturity. When she was in her early twenties Krao accentuated her hairiness by sporting a full beard and moustache and by cultivating a great mane of hair, which, like "the African Lion-faced Lady," she wore loose. By letting her long hair cascade over her shoulders or down her back rather than wearing it up in the neat coiffure of the respectable Victorian lady, Krao signaled her sexual availability. For loose and flowing hair, as the pre-Raphaelite paintings of the period suggest, was "a sign of women's sexuality."[118] Indeed, for Victorians luxuriant hair was an "index of vigorous sexuality, even of wantonness."[119]

However, it was not until the turn of the century that Krao's sexuality explicitly generated concern in Britain. When Krao reappeared at the aquarium in 1899 an irate member of the public wrote to the London County Council to complain about her exhibition. The shocked correspondent maintained that in the "interest of decency" the act should be withdrawn. "The revolting inference in the attraction" is that the public should "behold the result of copulation between a woman and one of the most filthy beasts." Such an exhibition, the letter continued, might lead to the logical next step: an exhibition of the woman and the monkey, the "authors of the horror exhibited."[120] This letter writer interpreted Krao's claim to be "half-woman, half-monkey"—a phrase that the aquarium used in its advertisements and that appeared on promotional posters—as a declaration that she was the product of interspecies breeding.[121] While Krao continued throughout her adult career to promote herself as "the missing link," an evolutionary adaptation, not a product of sexual union between man and monkey, she clearly elicited concern over bestiality. While the London County Council investigated and found "nothing whatever in the exhibition or the costume of the woman that could call for any remark whatever,"[122] Krao nevertheless both generated and preyed on cultural anxieties over the nature of both evolution and imperial relations. As historians have demonstrated, sexual unions between man and monkey were both implicit in Darwin's theory, and part of "porno-tropic" fantasies dating back to the early modern period.[123]

Krao's sexuality, although not the primary focus of the act, thus served to enhance the dominant imperial and socio-biological message of her exhibition. For in the late nineteenth century the discourses of evolution, imperialism, and primitive sexuality were mutually reinforcing, as Britain justified colonialism by promoting it as a civilizing mission. Krao's long-term success, evidenced by the fact that she was one of the highest-paid freaks in the Ringling Brothers lineup,[124] was thus due to her ability literally to embody the relationship among primitive sexuality, imperial ideology, and Darwinian theory. For by displaying her hairy body, Krao reinforced the profound difference between evolved British bodies and "primitive" Others. Her hirsuteness, and thus essential savagery, reassured British spectators across the class spectrum of their racial, national, and imperial superiority. At the same time she continued to serve as proof of the success of the civilizing process. As "the best-liked of freaks" who "never complained," Krao was, according to "the fat lady," her longtime friend, destined for the ultimate rewards of Christian civilization: "If any one has gone to heaven," she proclaimed, "that woman has."[125] Audiences across the United Kingdom thus swarmed to see "Krao, the Missing Link" because she provided the British public with perfect proof of their supreme status on what her pamphlet called "the Darwinian chain of evolution" that joined "molecule to man."[126]

FOUR

Aztecs and Earthmen

Declining Civilizations and Dying Races

THE DISCOURSE OF CIVILIZATION THAT was so central to Krao's exhibition also featured prominently in a variety of other performances in the late nineteenth century. When "the Last of the Mysterious Aztecs" were exhibited in London in the late 1880s and early 1890s, contemporaneously with Krao, their publicity materials emphasized that they were the only remaining members of a once great civilization that had over time become degenerate and thus died off. Although this act was on its last legs by the turn of the century, at midcentury it had been a smash success. This chapter argues that "the Aztecs" were exceptionally popular in the 1850s—a crucial and triumphant moment in Britain's imperial self-fashioning—because they had helped to instruct the British public exactly how to imagine their place in the hierarchy of civilizations and empires. As the last specimens of a now-extinct nation, "the Aztecs" functioned as a warning of the decline and fall of even complex civilizations. At the height of Britain's industrial and imperial ascendancy, however, this performance also encouraged spectators to construct themselves as members of a historically unparalleled and uniquely advanced culture that would not only survive, but expand, progress, and inevitably dominate the globe.

If the year 1851 was distinguished by the meeting of the "inhabitants of nearly all the civilised countries in the world," who came to marvel at the Crystal Palace, then 1853 was, according to the *Illustrated Magazine of Art,* remarkable for the numerous visits made to the United Kingdom by members of the "families of men" from the "uncivilised parts of the earth."[1] Although the article mentioned the large number of African peoples then on display in London, it was referring primarily to a new act that had recently appeared on the freak show circuit under the title "the Aztecs," or sometimes "the Aztec Children" or "the Aztec Lilliputians." The Aztecs, a brother-and-sister pair named Maximo and Bartola, were advertised as "Descendants and Specimens of the Sacerdotal Caste, (now nearly extinct), of the Ancient Aztec Founders of the Ruined Temples" of Central America. They were exhibited across the United Kingdom in the mid-1850s, returned to London in 1867, 1870, and 1876, and then reappeared in the late 1880s and early '90s at the Barnum and Bailey Circus and the Westminster Aquarium before finally disappearing off the British freak show circuit in 1893.

The Aztecs' souvenir pamphlet, a long, romantic adventure story entitled *Illustrated Memoir of an Eventful Expedition into Central America,* claimed that Maximo and Bartola were the last of the ancient Aztec race. It recounted the journey of three travelers to the long-lost "Idolatrous City of Iximaya," where they discovered the children being worshiped as idols by the Iximayan Indians. "Forbidden, by inviolably sacred laws, from intermarrying with any persons but those of their own caste," the pamphlet explained, the Aztecs had "dwindled down, in the course of many centuries, to a few insignificant individuals, diminutive in stature, and imbecile in intellect." The *Illustrated Memoir* claimed that the Aztecs had been saved from utter extinction by Pedro Velasquez, the only surviving member of the expedition, who fled the city with the children in tow. He then arranged for them to be exhibited in the United States and the United Kingdom as "the greatest ethnological curiosities in living form that ever appeared among civilized men."[2] This souvenir pamphlet, which sold for one shilling at the show, framed the Aztecs as degenerate members of an almost extinct race who had founded a mighty civilization that had been destined for decline. The Aztecs' exhibition thus contained a comforting object lesson: that those who live in isolation, who have "no intercourse whatever with the rest of mankind," and are forbidden from associating with others outside their caste can only be inbred, and thus degenerate.[3] Maximo and Bartola thus stood in marked contrast to the cosmopolitan and expansionist, though certainly not miscegenational, citizens of the United Kingdom who visited their show.

When the Aztecs made their London debut in July of 1853, after docking in Liverpool on June 18, they were the toast of the town, attracting curious crowds to their exhibition rooms.[4] According to their publicity materials they reeled in almost 400,000 visitors in London, 18,109 in Liverpool, and 3,031 in York.[5] These figures are likely inflated, but their marketing technique assured that they would draw customers from across the economic spectrum: during their 1853–55 tour of the United Kingdom, the Aztecs' managers charged a wide range of fees—ranging from a whopping five shillings down to a mere penny—in order to entice as many people to their show as possible.[6] As a result, Maximo and Bartola were seen not merely by curious commoners but also by so many notables (including Queen Victoria herself) who bestowed lavish gifts on them that the *Morning Advertiser* facetiously asked, "Who would not be an Aztec?"[7] Their astounding success led to many imitations: "Aztecs" or "Estics" (who much later would be labeled "pinheads") could be seen at sideshows well into the twentieth century. Perhaps the final act in this genre, "Maggie, the Last of the Aztecs," appeared in Tod Browning's 1932 film *Freaks.*[8]

During the mid-1850s the original Aztecs were continuously on display in popular entertainment venues, in the drawing rooms of those who could afford a private viewing, and in places such as the Adelaide Gallery, which billed itself as "the National Gallery of Practical Science" and offered its customers "a carefully contrived blend of entertainment and edification."[9] But they were also exhibited in the more elite scientific spaces of the capital. Maximo and Bartola were presented to the Ethnological Society, examined by medical professionals, and invited to visit the Royal College of Surgeons, provoking lively debate in British, American, and European scientific circles for forty years.[10] In fact, the comparative anatomist Richard Owen, the first British scientist to examine them, was so intrigued by their unusual appearance that he collected photographs of Maximo and Bartola throughout their half-century career.[11] The Aztecs, as their promoters had hoped, clearly claimed the attention not merely of pleasure seekers but also of "European men of science, ethnologists, physiologists, philosophers, and physicians," who were encouraged to interpret the Aztecs as members of "a race kept preserved in rocky fastnesses, and now discovered on the eve of physical decline and disappearance."[12]

The Aztecs sparked considerable interest among both scientists and the lay public, in particular in the 1850s, because they served as an exemplar of the decline of civilizations and the extinction of inferior races. The act offered visible proof of the fate of primitive peoples who lived mired in the past, did not evolve, and thus degenerated as a civilization and died off as a race. Maximo and Bartola, their souvenir pamphlet declared, were "living specimens of a *sui generis* race of beings . . . which are at once its melancholy trophies and its physiological attestors."[13] The Aztecs thus helped to articulate mid-Victorian Britain's understanding of its own position vis-à-vis other empires, peoples, and civilizations. For the Aztecs were exhibited just two years after the Great Exhibition promoted Britain to itself and to the world as the pinnacle of industrial prowess, modern civilization, and imperial might, and during the 1853 Great Industrial Exhibition in Dublin, which had sought to keep this triumphant spirit alive throughout the United Kingdom. Their first tour of the major cities of the British Isles also coincided with the Crimean War, which was fought, at least in part, to demonstrate Britain's military and naval superiority, and to assert its position as the world's new imperial superpower rather than one of many nations working to retain a balance of power in Europe. As the last remnants of a vanished people, then, the Aztecs served as a cautionary tale of degeneracy, decline, and the end of civilization. At the same time, however, they threw into stark relief the many reasons why Britain—which saw itself as the epitome of modern civilization and successful empire building—was destined to evolve, expand, and ultimately endure.

DISPLAYING DEGENERACY

The spectators who came to see the Aztecs were offered first and foremost a glimpse of a degenerate people. The narrative that framed the Aztecs' performance maintained that they came from a priestly "caste" that had been forbidden from marrying outside their order. As such they had not only failed to reproduce themselves, but their intermarriage had rendered them "diminutive in stature, and imbecile in intellect."[14] This explanation was perpetuated by the press, which reported that their "degeneracy" was the product of a "prohibition against marriage with strangers, or members of an inferior caste." This strict law against exogamous marriage was similar, both the *Times* and the *Illustrated London News* pointed out, to the customs of the Brahmins, the priestly caste of India, suggesting that the Brahmins would meet a similar fate, that they were destined for degeneracy.[15] Even after the exhibition had faded from the limelight, a correspondent to *Notes and Queries* used the Aztecs as an example of the dangers of marriage among first cousins. Citing Jews and Egyptians as examples of peoples who mingled family blood, he compared the Aztecs to these other "comparatively feebled and emasculated race[s]."[16]

The Aztecs' diminutive stature functioned as evidence of their degeneracy. Owen recorded Maximo's height as thirty-four inches and Bartola's as thirty inches.[17] Their publicity materials underscored their smallness, claiming that they were "about the length of a man's arm," or "about 2 1/2 feet high."[18] A handbill claimed that these "little creatures" were "extraordinary in their size and dimensions."[19] Many of the images used to promote the act portrayed the Aztecs as much tinier than they actually were. A poster for a Boxing Day appearance depicted them as able to fit inside a top hat and as the size of a violin. The proportions implied by the drawings suggested that the Aztecs were half the size of a little girl and measured only as high as a gentleman's knee.[20] A lithograph of Maximo and Bartola that was used on souvenirs depicted the pair as tiny individuals able to stand on their manager's palm. Although John Conolly, then president of the Ethnological Society, reported in 1855 that he had, in fact, seen Maximo stand somewhat precariously on his exhibitor's hand, the picture clearly exaggerated their dimensions in order to promote them as having physically deteriorated to such an extent that they had significantly shrunk.[21]

Although their promotional materials repeatedly claimed that the Aztecs were in "every way beautifully proportioned," in fact they had very small heads, "the size of your fist," which gave them a "birdlike appearance." A handbill published shortly after the act opened maintained that although the "first impression of the spectator is that they are dwarfs," a "second glance" revealed that the "head of the dwarf is invariably larger in proportion than the body—the heads of these children are smaller." They were thus often described as having greatly diminished intelligence, another sign of their degeneracy.[22] When the race scientist Robert Knox examined them, he concluded that each of their heads resembled "a form of idiotic head."[23] Owen noted that their skulls seemed arrested in their development and explicitly compared Maximo's head to that of an "idiot" whose skull was preserved at St. Bartholomew's Hospital. To emphasize this point, he included a drawing in his report comparing the two cranial structures.[24] The *Athenaeum* reported on the 1851 findings of the Boston Society of Natural History, which had also found the children possessed of "a very low degree of mental and physical organization," although they were, apparently, not "idiots of the lowest grade."[25] A phrenologist writing in the *Illustrated London News* similarly declared that their "mental constitution" was "extremely defective." The *Dublin Medical Press,* claiming to quote Conolly, proclaimed them to be "squeezed and mutilated idiots."[26]

Owen initially identified them as a case of "arrest of development," claiming they had the appearance of "hemi-cephalous monsters." But at an 1863 meeting of the Anthropological Society, he and others discussed the Aztecs as an example of "microcephaly."[27] The word *microcephaly*, which first came into use in professional circles in the late 1850s, was a relatively new scientific term for those having an abnormally small cranial capacity. In Carl Vogt's treatise "On Microcephali; or Human-Ape Organisms," which was translated from German into English and reprinted in the *Anthropological Review* in 1867, he catalogued Maximo and Bartola among several examples of microcephalics.[28] Here the freak show, as in the case of "the Elephant Man" and Lalloo, provided medical professionals with examples of physical and mental abnormalities that could serve as specimens or case studies. Indeed, the Aztecs continued to be referenced in medical literature on "mental retardation" through the end of the nineteenth century, serving as a prime example of microcephaly.[29] When they debuted in 1853, however, this scientific terminology was not yet available. Their mental deficiencies, therefore, served not to undermine their story, but rather to support the contention that they were members of a once mighty civilization that had dwindled down to a few imbecilic individuals.

Further evidence of their degeneration, and thus their civilization's decline, emerged in the course of a debate over whether the Aztecs could, in fact, speak, whether they had language, a key element of culture. A souvenir ticket for the act declared that the Aztecs had no language.[30] Newspaper coverage of Maximo and Bartola repeatedly asserted that they had "no means of communicating with each other by language," one article declaring that the "only vocal noise they emit is a short indefinite grunt."[31] This suggested that the Aztecs were extremely primitive beings whose civilization had deteriorated to such an extent that even its language had disappeared. A phrenologist theorized that it was not merely the case that they were unable to speak, but also that they had no ideas to communicate, no powers of reasoning. They might be able to "utter a few words in a parrot-like manner," but they were too deficient in mental abilities to be able really to converse.[32] In a letter to the *Leeds Intelligencer* reprinted in the *Times,* Charles Waterton, the naturalist, traveler, and author of *Wanderings in South America* (1825) declared that the children did, in fact, understand some English, which they had clearly only recently learned. He thus disputed that it was possible that they could have no language of their own. If that story about them were true, he argued, they would surely have heard and learned the language of their priestly guardians. "One would surmise," he maintained, "that the faculty which enables them to understand a language would enable them to speak one."[33]

A paragraph in the *Illustrated London News* offered a rebuttal of Waterton's analysis. Under the heading "Can the Aztecs Speak?" the writer maintained that, although not dumb, the Aztecs did indeed lack a "vernacular language." They apparently did not speak to each other, he declared, and explained that while under the care of the Iximayan priests they had been kept in utter seclusion, "adored in silence, and prevented intercourse with other human beings." "The worship of silence," he continued, "appears to be the description of worship which the Mayan Indians pay to these Aztec divinities."[34] Whatever explanations were offered, the fact that the Aztecs could not (or at least did not) speak served as prime evidence of their degeneracy and thus contributed to the narrative of the decline of their civilization that framed the act.[35]

That the Aztecs were cast as degenerate mute "imbeciles" did not, apparently, diminish their appeal. Despite the fact that some people found them "stunted," malformed, and "wretched little dwarfs,"[36] the public tended to agree with the *Illustrated London News*'s phrenologist-reporter who maintained that "the extremely defective condition of their mental constitution does not entail upon them any of the distressing and repulsive states, usually seen in persons of very weak minds." Even the "most sensitive person," he continued, "can experience no painful emotions on beholding these mentally infantile creatures."[37] The *Freeman's Journal* similarly reported that unlike the other "diminutive races" previously exhibited in the United Kingdom, who were "revoltingly ugly," the Aztecs were of "perfect and slender proportion" and even considered by some to be "beautiful." The girl, it declared, is "a really pretty little creature."[38]

That many members of the public found the Aztecs adorable despite the fact that they were degenerates is evident in *Household Words'* coverage of the show, which proclaimed that visitors to the exhibition constantly desired to kiss them and to feel their heads. "They are like dolls' heads," it reported, "and so of course it is agreeable to feel them."[39] When the British clown Whimsical Walker, who worked for P. T. Barnum, was sent back to England in the early 1880s to secure both Jumbo the elephant and the Aztecs for Barnum's "Greatest Show on Earth," he found them on display in a show shop in South London. Walker recalled in his memoirs that the public clustered around the Aztecs, "the ladies especially," because they were "anxious to shake them by the hand," despite the fact, he added, that "their palms were generally moist and dirty and very disagreeable to the touch."[40]

These audience members were responding to the allure of cuteness. The term "cute" emerged in the middle of the nineteenth century in the United States and was used to refer to small and lovable objects that appealed primarily to women because they evoked a maternal response.[41] Although the word was not widely used in Britain at this time, Robert Aguirre has argued that the concept at least was clearly evident in the marketing of the Aztecs.[42] Working against the rhetoric of monstrosity, the Aztecs' exhibitors insisted that instead of horrifying audiences, Maximo and Bartola were charming and delightful. "You cannot witness their walk, jump, or skip across the platform without laughing!" proclaimed a handbill. They are "so extraordinary in their gambols; so funny in their pranks; so bewitching in their smiles," it continued, that they never failed to "keep their visitors in a continual titter and laugh."[43] This marketing of the Aztecs as endearing was a strategic move. It allowed the narrative of degeneracy to remain at the forefront of the exhibition, but at the same time it removed Maximo and Bartola from the sphere of the grotesque and rendered them sympathetic, respectable, and distinctly nonthreatening.[44]

DECLINING CIVILIZATIONS

That the Aztecs were mere "pocket editions of humanity,"[45] and therefore "insignificant" members of mankind, meant that their once mighty civilization was equally unable to challenge the greatness of Great Britain, which each year was spreading its modern civilization further around the globe. It was only in the early decades of the nineteenth century that the British began to become interested in the Mayan and Aztec civilizations that had dominated Central America until the arrival of Europeans in the sixteenth century. Londoners had been exposed to Aztec culture through exhibitions at William Bullock's Egyptian Hall in the 1820s, through displays of artifacts at museums, and through travel narratives in the 1840s.[46] But in many respects Mexico and its neighboring nations were still blank spaces on the British world map, as they were not part of the formal empire and not necessarily rich in potential resources. As Aztecs, Maximo and Bartola were thus considered much odder and more intriguing in Britain than they had been when they were exhibited in the United States, whose population was more familiar with the peoples on its southern border, having just fought them in the 1846–48 Mexican-American War.

If the British public was unfamiliar with these New World cultures, they nevertheless quickly assimilated them into a familiar Orientalist imaginary. The narrative that accompanied the show owed much to John Lloyd Stephens's immensely popular 1841 travelogue, *Incidents of Travel in Central America, Chiapas, and Yucatan,* which was illustrated by the British artist and architect Frederick Catherwood, who was well known for his drawings and panoramas of Egypt and the Holy Land.[47] This creative borrowing from Stephens's text was duly noted by British audiences, but the narrative was also read in England as an Orientalist traveler's tale. Describing the arrival of Hernán Cortés in the New World, the *Illustrated Memoir* declared that he "found himself like Sindbad of the Oriental romance, in the midst of the valley of diamonds."[48] One of the things that fascinated British audiences most about the exhibition was Iximaya's relationship to old-world civilizations. The *Illustrated Memoir* recounted that the adventurers had reached Iximaya by "travelling due east" and that the city's "domes and turrets" had an "emphatically oriental aspect." Its inhabitants were said to wear "turbans" and "tunics."[49] Maximo and Bartola were thus often exhibited in Britain wearing "short robes," "golden dresses," and sometimes sandals, which suggested the garb of ancient but unspecific easterners.[50] Press coverage of Iximaya emphasized the "Oriental aspect of its architecture" and drew attention to the similarities between the "Oriental" tradition of keeping cocks underground to prevent their crowing from alerting outsiders to the presence of the city, and comparable practices of the Iximayan Indians.[51] Even those who dismissed the story interpreted it through an Oriental lens, maintaining it was merely "a tale of the Thousand-and-One Nights."[52] Knowing little about the cultures and people of South and Central America, British audiences constructed the Aztecs as Easterners.

The authors of the *Illustrated Memoir* shrewdly preyed on these Orientalist fantasies and, hoping to cash in on recent interest in a particular archaeological discovery, also linked the Aztecs to the Assyrians, the remains of whose civilization were at that moment being excavated to great interest. The original version of the pamphlet was published in the United States in 1850, a year after the British explorer Austen Henry Layard published his first book on his excavations at what he declared to be Nineveh, the ancient Assyrian capital, a book that soon became a best seller in both its original and popular editions.[53] The British pamphlet, published in 1853, included a preface that maintained that "the Iximayans claim descent from an ancient Assyrian colony, a claim somewhat affirmed by the existing analogy, between the monuments of Nineveh, and those of Central America."[54] When the Aztecs' promoters constructed their own narratives about Iximaya, they thus drew on these recent discoveries of Assyrian grandeur to cast this civilization as an equally astonishing vestige of past glory that had nevertheless been similarly doomed.

The narrative of the "eventful expedition" to the "Idolatrous City of Iximaya" was said to have been written by Pedro Velasquez, who had made this pilgrimage in the company of Mr. Hammond, a Canadian, and Mr. Huertis, a Cuban-American. Hammond was a civil engineer, while Huertis, who "had travelled much in Egypt, Persia, and Syria, for the personal inspection of ancient monuments," functioned in the story as an expert in ancient civilizations.[55] The *Illustrated Memoir* maintained that once inside the city's walls the travelers soon found that a series of "colossal statues" glimpsed from afar were actually "statues of the ancient kings of Assyria, from before the foundation of Babylon, and of their descendants in the Aztec empires of this continent." Later it explained that the Aztecs had in fact migrated from the "Assyrian plains."[56] The promotional material for the act thus established the Aztec people as descendants of the Assyrians, promoting the diffusionist anthropological theory that maintained that New World civilizations could not have developed independently but must have been outgrowths of old-world cultures. Instead of positing an Egyptian or Phoenician origin for the Aztecs, as had been typical in the eighteenth and early nineteenth centuries, the *Illustrated Memoir* and press coverage of the act capitalized on this recent interest in Mesopotamia and proclaimed Maximo and Bartola to be descendants of Assyrian migrants to Central America.[57]

Although the Assyrian connection was certainly not the major theme of either the *Illustrated Memoir* or the Aztecs' performance, British audiences seized upon it. The Aztecs arrived in London the same year that Layard, by now a British hero, released his report of further excavations and explorations, *Discoveries in the Ruins of Nineveh and Babylon.*[58] Assyria was thus all the rage during the Aztecs' 1853–55 tour of the United Kingdom. Both a panorama and a diorama of Nineveh could be viewed in central London in the early 1850s. *Sardanapalus, King of Assyria,* loosely based on Byron's play *Sardanapalus,* played at the Princess Theatre between June and September of 1853 using sets drawn from Layard's lithographs. Its success spurred a knock-off burlesque at the Theatre Royal, Adelphi that attracted crowds from July to October.[59] In 1854 the Assyrian Court, a replica of Nineveh based on Layard's illustrations, was erected as part of the

Sydenham Crystal Palace. Complete with copies of some of the treasures Layard had deposited in the British Museum, the display was hastily introduced at the last minute precisely because of public demand for all things Assyrian.[60] Assyria was thus at the very forefront of the public imagination during the Aztecs' sojourn in the British Isles, and their promoters capitalized on this interest to attract a steady stream of visitors.

Another 1853 London edition of the Aztecs' pamphlet contained illustrations taken from Layard's book on Nineveh in order to draw unambiguous comparisons between the Aztecs and the Assyrians.[61] A promotional poster for the show featured the statement "'How like the Nineveh marbles!' exclaimed the great LAYARD, while gazing upon the Aztecs."[62] Similarly, an 1853 advertisement for the act declared that the Aztecs were allied to "the ancient races whose portraitures are found on the antique Sculptured Obelisks and Hieroglyphical Pictures brought from the ruins of Nineveh, Egypt, and Central America," explicitly drawing these civilizations together.[63] The popular press picked up on this alleged relationship and repeated the tale of the "Assyrian magnificence" of Iximaya and its inhabitants, even while often challenging the pamphlet's veracity.[64] Even the *Illustrated Magazine of Art,* which suggested that Maximo and Bartola's story was merely "apocryphal," noted the resemblance between Aztec architecture and the structures of "Egypt, Babylon, and Assyria."[65] Knox uncritically reproduced these fabulous accounts, maintaining that the Aztec people "bore a distant resemblance in many circumstances of their lives to the ancient Copts, Assyrians, and Babylonians."[66]

The *Freeman's Journal* was one of many papers that perpetuated the idea that Maximo and Bartola were "living types of an antique race of priesthood, nearly extinct, who had accompanied the first migration of the people from the Assyrian plains."[67] The *Illustrated London Magazine,* which reported on the act as part of a longer disquisition on the "Aztecque" race, also claimed a physiognomical relationship between the Aztec Lilliputians and "Coptic or Assyrian" peoples.[68] Similarly, an Edinburgh dentist named Robert Reid, who had examined the children's teeth, wrote that "Assyrian lineaments" marked "the upper portion of Maximo's face."[69] The *Illustrated London News,* which had fully documented the installation of the Assyrian artifacts in the British Museum, enhanced this description, arguing that Maximo's hair fell in small, black, glossy ringlets that reminded one of "sculptured Assyrian hair."[70]

Although this construction of the Aztecs as similar to the Assyrians was timely, it was not actually novel. The sixteenth-century Franciscan missionary Toribio de Benavente Motolinía was the first to compare the Aztecs to the Assyrians, figuring the conquest of the Aztec empire by the Spanish as divine punishment for the sins of its similarly despotic leadership.[71] Three centuries later this analogy structured British audiences' reception of the Aztec Lilliputians, whose relationship to Assyria served as part of a larger narrative of the inevitable decline and fall of decadent empires, which were destined to be replaced by more modern, progressive civilizations. The souvenir pamphlet described Central America as "rich in vestiges of a civilization which bear a parallel of comparison with the classic grounds of Memphis, Thebes, Baalbec, and Nineveh; and could each monument which now stands [like] a moss-covered sphinx, be read through its hieroglyphics, we should have doubtless a history of empire as varied and remarkable as that which has made Greece and Rome the Mecca of all pilgrims of antiquarian lore."[72] The Aztec empire, the *Illustrated Memoir* implied, had once been as mighty as that of Greece, Rome, and Assyria. But at midcentury Assyria in particular was emblematic of powerful civilizations toppled not just by foreign invaders but by their own sloth and vice. Assyria, however great its past, was now a wasteland, Victorian commentators argued. Assyria thus functioned in the Victorian imagination as "a moralizing and cautionary tale and counter example to Western 'progress.'"[73] It stood both for ancient grandeur and for decay, and its narrative of decline could easily be mapped onto the Aztec empire.

The *Illustrated Memoir* stressed that Iximaya's grandeur was evident from its sculptures and temples but that it was a "*ruined* city": "passing ages had corroded rough crevices between the layers, and the once perfect cornices had become indented by the tooth of time."[74] The moral of the Aztecs Lilliputians' act thus appeared to be that the Aztecs had "founded an extensive, and in the main a civilized empire," but one that had eventually and inevitably been destroyed both because of internal decadence and because of external conquest by a more advanced people.[75] The Aztec Lilliputians, the only survivors of this culture, were "a debased specimen of this once great people and their once mighty King Montezuma," who was renowned, like the Assyrian king Sardanapalus, for his life of "highest luxury and magnificence" and his tyranny.[76] According to the catalogue of Reimer's Anatomical Museum, where models of Maximo and Bartola were also on display in 1853, "these diminutive and dwarf-like creatures, whose intellects are but slightly advanced above the beasts of the field, speechless, and almost void of those nobler sentiments of the human mind, may have been one of the wisest and most illustrious of the ancient Assyrian nations," suggesting that this "lilliputian race" was the last chapter in the story of the decline and fall of the Assyrian empire.[77]

The Aztecs, like the Assyrians, then, served as an object lesson in over-expansion and overindulgence, a warning to imperial Britain: while the Assyrian excavations served to confirm a "cultural continuum" of great imperial civilizations, "crowned by Great Britain," they also raised the specter of the decline even of Britain and its vast empire. If Nineveh was "firmly entrenched in Britain's own mythology," so too was its downfall.[78] An 1851 article in *Household Words* on the installation of the Nineveh winged bull in the British Museum—an article that was written as a solil-oquy from the bull's perspective—ended with its prediction that it would survive and outlive one more "mighty kingdom."[79]

Interest in the decline and fall of former empires and civilizations, and the lessons such decline offered to even the most advanced societies, had been a part of British culture since at least the eighteenth century. The conjectural historians of the Scottish Enlightenment had theorized that commercial societies might enter a stage of decline if they succumbed to luxury and decadence, as had happened, at least according to this theory, to the Romans and the Chinese. Indeed, David Hume and Adam Smith had both worried that their own civilization had entered such a phase.[80] Building on the work of the conjectural historians, Edward Gibbon had underscored this threat of cultural decay in his *Decline and Fall of the Roman Empire,* the first volume of which was published in 1776, the same year that Britain's empire first began to crumble as the American colonies declared their independence. The Romanticists' interest in ruins carried these themes of decay and decline into the early nineteenth century, when they clashed head on with the emerging Victorian ideal of progress. Into the 1850s and beyond, debates raged on both sides of the English Channel over whether great civilizations could progress indefinitely or were doomed eventually to deteriorate.[81] This led to a wealth of literature on "lost tribes" (such as the Lost Tribes of Israel), "lost continents," and "lost civilizations" (such as Atlantis and Lemuria, its Indian Ocean counterpart), a preoccu-pation that reached its peak in the period between the 1880s and 1920s.[82] The Aztec Lilliputians, then, were an early chapter in the history of this modern fascination with vanishing worlds and disappearing peoples

But however much the Aztecs or the Assyrians provoked anxieties about civilizational decline or imperial decay, at this triumphant moment in Britain's history the Aztec Lilliputians served primarily as a foil against which Britain could read itself as a modern, progressive, and enduring civilization and empire. As a contributor to the *Illustrated London News* declared, "it is impossible," both "physically, as well as morally," that "after any lapse of ages five times as numerous as those which separate the present era from the era of Ninus, the same shadows should develop *[sic]* the memory of Victoria."[83]

At midcentury Britain was at the height of its industrial and imperial optimism. The Great Exhibition of 1851 was a paean to progress, clear and visible proof of Britain's industrial, and thus also scientific and technological, prowess, and therefore its material and cultural progressiveness. When the Crystal Palace was erected in Hyde Park that year, it became the first structure to exceed the Roman Coliseum in volume. Indeed, in 1851 London, with its population of almost two and a half million people, was the only European city that could confidently claim to rival Rome in its imperial heyday.[84] Britain was not subject to the upheavals that disrupted much of Europe in 1848. In the 1850s—at a moment when it was fighting to thwart Russia's own imperial aspirations and to protect Christians in Jerusalem (or so it claimed)—Britain could thus champion itself as a stable, progressive nation, the guardian of Western civilization, and destined to rule not only the waves but the entire world.

It is no coincidence, then, that in 1853 the Aztecs were taken to Dublin, where they were brought to admire the Great Industrial Exhibition, organized as an attempt to capitalize on the success of the 1851 Crystal Palace. Although it focused as much on fine art as on industry, this exhibition had been mounted to reinvigorate Ireland's economy after the famine. It was also intended to perpetuate the triumphant and progressive spirit of 1851, which had celebrated the successful spread of British civilization throughout the world, and thus to include Ireland within this imperial imaginary. The *Times* noted in May of 1853 that at the Dublin exhibition we "have found in the arts of industry and in the departments of trade a glorious embodiment of the spirit of modern civilization."[85]

This juxtaposition of modern and ancient civilizations was central to the success of the Aztecs' act. In Dublin, Maximo and Bartola were on display not at the Great Exhibition but in the Rotunda, a popular concert and variety venue. They were nevertheless taken to see the wonders of the Great Exhibition, although an initial visit had to be rescheduled when the Aztecs were mobbed by crowds more eager to see them than what was on display at the exposition itself.[86] When they returned a few days later, not only were they afforded a more peaceful opportunity to view the marvels

of the fair, but the other visitors were treated to a spontaneous performance of the Aztecs' otherness. When they entered the Medieval Court,
Maximo immediately "seated himself in idol posture before one of the
altars and became apparently deeply engaged in his devotions."[87] The
adoption of this attitude was central to their own performances; it was part
of their show at the Rotunda and often appeared on their publicity materials, as it demonstrated the manner in which the Iximayan Indians had
worshiped them.[88] In this context, Maximo's apparently spontaneous
assumption of his priestly pose in a room dedicated to Britain's past brilliantly illustrated the distance between this ancient culture, which had not
advanced and was still idolatrous, and the modernity of the peoples of the
United Kingdom.

Other spectators, however, preferred to assimilate the Aztecs into a narrative of progress, an imperial articulation of the benefits of British civilization. Reporting on their original exhibition in the summer of 1853 for
Charles Dickens's *Household Words,* Henry Morley and W. H. Wills noted
that "many ladies come repeatedly to observe whether the children make
any progress as the days roll on." One such lady, their article "Lilliput in
London" maintained, declared to her friend that Maximo was "very much
improved" since her last visit. Prompting Maximo to speak, she asked him
to identify a squeaking toy in the shape of a cat: " 'What's that,' asked the
lady. 'Isn't it a cat? Say cat. Say cat, de-ar!' " "Maximo at last was persuaded
to obey," recounted Morley and Wills. " 'It's the first time,' said the lecturer, in an interested way, 'that I have heard him pronounce the word—
cat.' " "We were all, of course," the article snidely remarked, having found
the act distasteful, to say the least, "thrilled with interest."[89] That the
Aztecs were acquiring some English suggested to some members of the
audience that although their civilization had disappeared, and they had no
language of their own, they could nevertheless learn to adapt to a new civilization and adopt the language that was clearly on its way to becoming
the world's vernacular, a theme that, as we have seen, was also central to
the exhibition of "Krao, the Missing Link" thirty years later.

The Aztecs' exhibitors responded to this desire of the spectators to see
the children advance. When the act reappeared in London in 1854 their
advertisement proclaimed that they were "greatly improved in every way,"
now able not only to spell some English words, but also to "walk upright,"
as if they were ancient, apelike human ancestors who were only now
becoming bipedal.[90] Racial scientists, however, fiercely resisted this idea.
John Conolly remarked on their 1855 reappearance, claiming that "the

Aztec children have not advanced at all" and noting that they were not capable of "erect walking," the most basic characteristic of the modern human. They cannot dress or feed themselves, he argued, implying that left to their own devices they could not survive.[91] While no single interpretation could entirely structure audiences' reading of the Aztec Lilliputians, and the idea of improvement continued to rear its head throughout their half-century career,[92] Conolly's insistence that Maximo and Bartola had not advanced supported the theory, widespread amongst anthropologists and crucial to the popularity of the act, that some races were indeed mired in the past and could never become more civilized.

DYING RACES

Britain could be certain that its civilization would endure because the cultural argument—that Britain was a more technologically advanced nation and thus culturally superior—was gradually being undergirded by a biological determinism that focused on the survival of the fittest races. The Enlightenment narrative of progress from savage to civilized was challenged in the 1840s and '50s by new racial theories, some distinctly polygenesist, that identified racial types as fixed, immutable, and distinctly different from each other. Alongside these ideas emerged a discourse of dying races, which posited that certain groups of people were doomed to extinction while others would inevitably not only survive but flourish and dominate the earth. By the middle of the nineteenth century, many ethnologists were theorizing not that all peoples advanced at different paces along the savage-civilized continuum, but rather that the darker races were mired in the past, could not progress, and thus would necessarily become extinct. The founding of the Ethnological Society in 1842—which severed itself from the Aborigines Protection Society in order to examine scientifically human physical and cultural difference—marked an important step away from humanitarian efforts to rescue "primitive" races and toward scientific explanations for racial inequality. This "scientific" theory of the inevitability of dying races and the ultimate triumph of the "Caucasian" circulated widely even before Darwin explained the process of natural selection. It gained in popularity throughout the nineteenth century because it allowed Britain, as a highly successful imperial nation, to justify its conquest of other countries and the subsequent deaths of indigenous populations that rapidly followed the colonization of both Southern Africa and Australia, to say nothing of Ireland.[93]

The Aztec Lilliputians offered perfect proof of this theory, popularizing it for a mass public, for key to the act was the idea that Maximo and Bartola were the last of a dying race. These children, their pamphlet declared, were "living specimens of an antique race so nearly extinct." A letter sent to the *Times* by their exhibitors Anderson and Morris drew upon the twin discourses of declining civilizations and dying races, arguing that the Aztecs were descendants of "a race which in past ages had held a high position among mankind, and the members of which have rivalled in civilization the Assyrian, the Theban, and the Hindoo; but a race now becoming extinct, and which unless Christianity step in to their rescue, will soon—'Upon the living earth have left no living trace.'"[94] Elsewhere Anderson compared them to the recently unearthed mastodon, which served as undeniable proof of species extinction.[95] An early handbill, though it cast them more as pigmies than as Aztecs, similarly portrayed them as presumed to be "extinct."[96] The claim on numerous handbills and advertisements that the Aztecs were alive, then, was not merely part of the typical sideshow assurance that spectators would not be shown wax figurines or bottled specimens. It was also part and parcel, as Robert Aguirre has argued, of the act itself, which fulfilled the popular and professional desire to see living examples of vanishing peoples.[97]

The message that the darker races were doomed to extinction in the face of white biological superiority was enhanced in the Aztecs' act by their pairing with the Earthmen. In the mid-1840s San peoples from Southern African began to be exhibited in England as "Bushmen" or "Bosjesmen." The appeal of the Bushmen was that they were living examples of "Stone Age" peoples, "the lowest grade" of mankind, "sunk in the scale of humanity to the level almost of the beasts of the forest," and thus destined to disappear.[98] Lecturing on the troupe of Bushmen he was exhibiting across Britain in 1847, J. S. Tyler maintained that it was inevitable that the Bushmen would soon be "exterminated." "Even now, London and Paris, in their museums, have stuffed skins of these people," he declared. "A short time, alas! and such will be the only relics left of them."[99] An advertisement for a different troupe of Bushmen who appeared the same year maintained that "they are of a race sentenced to speedy extinction."[100] In his memorable 1853 essay on the Zulu and Bushmen exhibitions in London ironically titled "The Noble Savage," Charles Dickens encouraged this impending disappearance, proclaiming that it was "highly desirable" for these "savages" to be "civilised off the face of the earth."[101]

Capitalizing on the success of these Bushmen acts, but at the same time in an attempt to present something truly novel, two San children were exhibited in 1852 as Martinus (or sometimes Martini) and Flora, "the Earthmen" or "Erdmanniges." Just over three feet tall, with "skins of a bright bronze hue," the children sang and danced for the spectators clothed in nothing but animal hides.[102] Their repertoire featured the popular minstrel songs "Buffalo Gals" and "I'm Going to Alabama." Ironically, these authentic Africans were mimicking the performance of imitation African-Americans, a subject I return to in chapter 5. Perhaps even more jarring, at least in retrospect, "the Earthmen" also performed "Rule Britannia," with its memorable last line "Britons never shall be slaves," thus highlighting the difference between the free white Englishman and the only recently liberated black African.[103] A notice in the *Times,* borrowing from their promotional pamphlet, declared that "the Earthmen" were "the last link in the human chain," below even the Bushmen.[104] Ethnologists maintained, however, that the Earthmen were not an entirely novel and separate race but actually members of the "Saab (Bushmen)" people, which, they argued, differed "more than any other anatomically, from the other races of men."[105]

In December of 1854, the Earthmen were paired with the Aztecs for an appearance at the Queen's Concert Rooms, Hanover Square in the fashionable London neighborhood of Mayfair, and they continued to tour with the Aztecs until Barnum took over both acts in 1860 for his American Museum in New York City.[106] John Conolly argued that exhibiting these two groups together did nothing for either of them, for the Earthmen (whom he had also seen exhibited before the Ethnological Society) were "perfect in their kind," lively, witty, and clearly intelligent, while the Aztecs, he declared, were "arrested in their growth," both mentally and physically.[107] As Bernth Lindfors has argued, when they were exhibited on their own, the Earthmen were a great success precisely because they charmed their audiences, demonstrated that they were "acquiring the rudiments of European civilization," and even provided, according to one contemporary account, "a direct Contradiction to the Theory lately set forth, of the Impossibility of Rendering the Savage a Thinking, Feeling Being."[108] Once exhibited with the Aztecs, however, their promotional materials ceased to underscore their lively, intelligent natures and instead emphasized the similarities between the two groups, not as representatives of ancient civilizations, but rather as "Two New Races of People, the First of either Race ever discovered."[109]

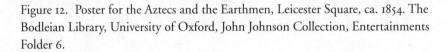

Figure 12. Poster for the Aztecs and the Earthmen, Leicester Square, ca. 1854. The Bodleian Library, University of Oxford, John Johnson Collection, Entertainments Folder 6.

These newly discovered people, their publicity materials maintained, were extremely primitive. The Earthmen, like the Aztecs, a souvenir ticket maintained, could not speak. They "burrow under the earth in South Africa," it recounted, "subsisting upon insects and reptiles."[110] Indeed, even before they were joined on stage, the Earthmen and the Aztecs were seen as analogously primitive peoples equally incapable of advanced civilization. A contributor to *Blackwood's Magazine* declared that he was astonished to learn of the ability of underwater coral polyps to produce magnificent structures. This was much the same sort of surprise one would express, he maintained, upon discovering "that the pyramids and temples of antiquity had not been constructed by Egyptians or Romans, but by a race like the Earthmen of Africa, or by a set of pigmies like the Aztecs now exhibiting in London."[111] While Jane Goodall has argued that exhibiting the acts together reinforced the Aztecs' racial exoticism,[112] the more specific message of the pairing was that racial inferiority, and thus lack of an advanced civilization, led to the inevitable disappearance of nonwhite peoples. Britain, as a racially superior nation, the exhibition implied, had nothing to fear. It would not only survive but would spread its civilization.

This fascination with the Aztecs as not only examples of a declined civilization but as a more primitive racial type permeated the coverage of the act, particularly in the 1850s and '60s. Joseph Morris and John Henry Anderson declared in a letter to the *Times* that the Aztecs were not being exhibited to the public "as dwarfs, hunchbacks, Tom Thumbs, Siamese Twins, or other distorted curiosities," but rather as a separate race.[113] As in Farini's marketing of Krao, this was a means of distinguishing them from the plethora of other freak performers and placing them in the more respectable category of ethnological exhibition, although the distinction between the two was largely a rhetorical move that had little to do with what was actually presented on stage. In this context their diminutive stature was recast as a racial trait. According to their souvenir pamphlet, the bodily differences that Maximo and Bartola exhibited were "plainly the peculiarities of race" rather than a congenital anomaly.[114] This was accentuated by their pairing with the Earthmen, whose appeal rested almost entirely on their small size, their defining racial characteristic. In their promotional material the Aztecs, like the Earthmen and other small African people, were often marketed as "Pigmies." This connoted anything tiny, but since antiquity had also referred to a race of people of very small stature. This language was picked up by the popular press, which referred to Maximo and Bartola in both senses of the term, at times as "little pigmies," at others as "pigmy in race."[115]

The first medical report on the case, published in the United States, in fact maintained that not only were the Aztecs a more primitive race, but that at first glance it appeared that they did not "belong to the human species." It was only after the eye adjusted to their odd appearance, it continued, that one could discern that they indeed belonged to the "brotherhood" of man.[116] This discourse was picked up by British commentators. The Aztecs seem, declared *Blackwood's Magazine,* "hardly allied to the human family."[117] Conolly compared them to "domestic animals," while Morley and Wills maintained that they were little different from trained monkeys "who played monkey tricks for the amusement of the public, which assembled round them very much as it collects about the monkeys at Regent's Park."[118] Others went further. A report in the *Illustrated London News* maintained that their brains were similar in size and shape to those of "the Simial genus." Their heads are "identical with the cast of the head of an oran-outan," declared the columnist, "identical in form and size with the heads of the more gentle and intelligent of the monkey genus."[119] Questioning the humanity of other races and assessing their closeness to primates was part and parcel of the newly emerging anthropological discourse and central to Victorian racial science more generally, even before Darwin's startling declaration that man and ape had a common ancestor. Owen, a religious, conservative monogenesist who was uncomfortable with evolutionary theories that explicitly linked man to monkey, attempted to lay these accusations to rest, however. He declared that "in all the essential characters derived from the dentition and the structure of the upper and lower limbs they are strictly human, and make no nearer approach to the brute than other well-formed individuals of the genus *homo.*"[120]

Despite the fact that into the 1860s some scientists continued to theorize that the Aztecs were a human-animal "hybrid,"[121] public and professional spectators seemed generally to agree with Owen that however strange they were, Maximo and Bartola were nevertheless members of the human family. Yet exactly which racial type they belonged to was never self-evident and widely debated. Newspapers, publicity materials, and scientific reports routinely noted the Aztecs' "olive" complexion and dark eyes. The *Illustrated London News,* however, suggested that their skin was not olive but rather "dark, similar to that of a Hindoo," while the *Illustrated London Magazine* insisted that their skin was of a "deep bronze or copper-colour."[122] Their skin color, which was an important but in no ways definitive marker of racial type at midcentury, thus proved a contentious sign of difference, not easily deciphered even by those claiming to be experts in racial classification.[123]

The Aztecs' promotional pamphlet, however, structured how audiences were supposed to interpret their physiognomies. Their "lineaments" were "peculiar and strongly distinctive," the pamphlet argued, a legacy of their Assyrian heritage, which could also be discerned on the sculpted monuments found throughout Central America. Advertisements in newspapers and handbills reinforced this supposed resemblance to ancient statues.[124] Richard Cull, secretary of the Ethnological Society, picked up on this suggestion, maintaining that the Aztecs' heads resembled the sculptures made known to British audiences through the 1822 English translation of Antonio del Rio's *Descriptions of the Ruins of an Ancient City, Discovered near Palenque* and Stephens's 1841 travelogue. More specifically, he argued, they resembled the bas-reliefs typical of Toltec sculpture. The children, he argued, appeared to be similar to the Toltecs, "so far as physiognomy is concerned."[125] Many of the visual representations of the Aztecs accentuated their similarity to ancient Central American monuments by depicting the children as having extremely sloped foreheads, typical of these carved figures. The souvenir pamphlet made this connection explicit by including drawings of Central American bas-reliefs and directing the reader to the similarities between the Aztec Lilliputians and these sculptures. "The accompanying engravings, sketched from the ruins of Central America," it insisted, "bear both in features and in position of the head, a resemblance all will readily detect to the Aztec children, found in the same country."[126]

In order to accentuate their resemblance to the images on Central American monuments, the Aztecs were regularly depicted in profile. The measurement of the facial angle, which could only be seen in a profile view, was crucial to mid-Victorian racial theories, as it was used to categorize humans on a scale from primitive to civilized. Scientists and the popular press alike seized on this indicator to provide insight into the ancestry and racial classification of the Aztecs, whose facial angle was extreme. Many years later the angle was estimated to be forty-five degrees, a sign of primitive origins that in Pieter Camper's original scheme would have situated the Aztecs well below the "Negro" and somewhere between the monkey and the orangutan.[127] As Aguirre has argued, the Aztecs' facial angle was exaggerated in the popular press, in which their sloping profiles were juxtaposed to the nearly vertical forehead of an implicitly "normal" middle-class European male.[128] On the cover of W. West's version of "The Aztec Polka," sheet music that was sold as a souvenir of the show, Maximo—depicted facing sideways—holds what appears to be his own sketch of his exhibitor's perfect classical profile, underscoring the difference between his own sloping forehead and that of his English manager.[129] Robert Reid emphasized the extremity of the angle and argued that Maximo's profile resembled that of a hawk, employing a frequently used comparison. He suspected, in fact, that the children were of different races precisely because Bartola's "facial angle was entirely different" from Maximo's.[130] Although Owen eventually concluded that the children were not "representatives of any peculiar human race," he nevertheless reinforced the importance of the facial angle by comparing Maximo's profile to that of an idiot's skull, using a technique straight out of craniometry's visual lexicon.[131] If the grinning skull that towers over Maximo's diminutive head suggests, as Aguirre has posited, the "symbolic annihilation of his subject-hood,"[132] it also acts as a memento mori of his allegedly soon-to-be-extinct race, whatever that race might be.

If the facial angle provided clues to their primitive origins, their hair—another key factor in Victorian racial classification—was also often noted, although it proved puzzling as an indicator of their ancestry. A handbill maintained that it was "raven black and flowing."[133] The *Times* and *Illustrated London News* both repeated this assertion, claiming that their hair was "black and glossy" and fell in small ringlets. A highly romanticized drawing of the children that accompanied this latter report (and that bears no resemblance to any other image of the Aztecs) depicted them with elegantly curled hair.[134] Later coverage of the act noted that they had "a thick crop" of hair, groomed so that it stood "erect nearly a foot high."[135] When they reappeared in less exoticized form in 1867, their hair remained a telling marker of their otherness. The *Times* reported that year that the "only way in which the Aztecs seek externally to distinguish themselves from ordinary folk, is a strange method of dressing the hair. This is very long, and instead of hanging down, stands upright, approaching the dimensions of a grenadier's cap, and what is singular enough, instead of being of a wiry texture, it is extremely soft to the touch."[136]

The Aztecs' strange hair led to great confusion among scientists over their racial categorization. Reid noted that Bartola's hair was "crisp" when not looked carefully after, unlike Maximo's, which was "silky," suggesting an African origin for the girl but not the boy.[137] R. G. Latham, a medical doctor and member of the Ethnological Society who trained as a philologist under

Figure 13. Cover illustration for sheet music of "The Aztec Polka," composed by W. West, ca. 1853. ©British Library, Music Collection, H.724.o(14).

James Cowles Prichard, indicated in his 1856 report to the Ethnological Society that he believed the Aztecs' hair to be similar to that of "the Spaniard" or "the Jew."[138] Owen argued that their hair was not characteristic of the aboriginal peoples of the Americas, which is "straight, coarse, or lanky." Rather, he noted, it was "smooth" and fell in "graceful curls" more typical of the "southern Europeans" who colonized Central and South America. Their hair was so unusually wavy that at first he imagined it had been artificially curled. But having visited the Aztecs at their residence and examined them before they had left their beds, Owen was satisfied that the "close wavy curls" were in fact natural.[139] The *Illustrated London Magazine* concluded that because their hair was not "lank" or "straight" like that of American Indians, the Aztecs must have had "a mixture of blood in their composition."[140] Luke Burke, a phrenologist who joined the Ethnological Society in 1861 and was a founding member of the Anthropological Institute, declared that their hair was "wholly un-American." Maximo's hair indicated a western Asian origin, he proclaimed, while Bartola's "is precisely that of *Mulattoes* and other half casts of Negro race."[141] In 1863 he asserted at a meeting of the Anthropological Society that the "negro blood in the Aztec children might easily have been known by the curly hair."[142] Their hair, one of the more intriguing aspects of their physical appearance, thus suggested to experts a mixed racial origin for the children.

What was both compelling and disturbing about the Aztecs, as the debate over their skin and hair reveals, was that they were hard to identify racially. If they were not Aztecs, nor were they clearly something else. Although models of them had been built for the ethnological department of the Crystal Palace at Sydenham, which opened in 1854, they were never displayed there, as experts had concluded that whatever they actually were, Maximo and Bartola were not "types of any race."[143] Other wax models of the children were, however, exhibited at three different anatomical museums in London. Reimer's boasted a "Gallery of All Nations" in which the Aztecs appeared as a specimen of their supposedly pure racial type. At the other museums they were catalogued as a novelty but identified as most likely an elaborate fraud.[144]

Many commentators who sought to debunk the authenticity of the Aztecs identified them as impure specimens of the human family. Reid, in fact, argued that Maximo and Bartola were not even of the same race.[145] Knox maintained that South and Central Americans were all of mixed ancestry, combining "European, Negro, Indian" blood in their veins along with that of the ancient Aztecs. Anyone from this region, he suggested, would therefore necessarily be of an impure race, exhibiting more or less marked traits of their ancestors in accord with "the law of 'interrupted descent,'" whereby certain features could appear in an individual long after the mingling of blood had occurred.[146] While, as Evelleen Richards has argued, Knox was making a particular point about evolutionary laws that explicitly challenged Owen's ideas about the extinction of species, he was also contributing to the discourse of the inherent impurity of Central American peoples in general and the Aztecs in particular.[147]

A letter to the *Times* had similarly argued that when Cortés conquered Mexico, "the inhabitants of that region were most probably a mixed race," whom he argued might be termed "Aztecs or Mexicans" but were often grouped "under the general name of Indians."[148] The Aztec Lilliputians, these commentators suggested, were thus not members of a pure race but rather merely the mestizos "so common in Mexico."[149] The Aztecs, declared the *Lancet,* the voice of orthodox medical authority, are "merely *cretins* of a mixed Spanish and Indian breed."[150] Indeed, by insisting they were members of a "caste," the *Illustrated Memoir,* supposedly written by the Spaniard Pedro Velasquez, had suggested that they were of mixed race. When the Spanish applied this term to South and Central American peoples, it referred specifically to those of mixed European, Indian, and African descent.[151]

The idea that the Aztecs were a hybrid—some form of intermixture of the indigenous peoples of Central America and other so-called "degenerate" races—emerged consistently in both the public and the professional debate surrounding the exhibition. Owen's initial conjecture was that they were descendants of southern Europeans who had settled in "tropical or warm latitudes of Asia or America."[152] When his report was paraphrased in the *Athenaeum,* the journal maintained that Owen had also declared the children to have "some mixture of Indian blood."[153] In 1863 he did, in fact, finally conclude that they were "hybrid Spanish and Indian children from San Salvador."[154] Latham also maintained that they were probably from South America and that they were "Indians" who had "an intermixture of Spanish (or other) blood."[155]

While it was often theorized that Spanish and American Indian blood coursed through the Aztecs' veins, other commentators drew attention to their physical resemblance to races widely believed to be either degenerate or brutish, particularly "the Jew" and "the Negro." Reid maintained that Bartola seemed "African" in origin because her dental arch resembled that of the "Negro."[156] Morley and Wills married these theories by proposing that the Aztecs were as "likely as not" to be "the abnormal offspring of a Hebrew father and a mulatto mother."[157] A few days later Luke Burke asserted in *The Leader* that it was plain that "the father of these children was a *Jew,* the mother a *Mulatto*—the offspring of a Negress and a Spaniard, or of a Negress and a Jew."[158] The *Dublin Evening Post* reported that they appeared to be a cross between "the Indian" and "the Israelite."[159]

Although this theory was far-fetched, it was not an entirely novel conjecture, as many theories proposing that the Aztec and Mayan peoples were in fact descendants of the "Lost Tribes of Israel" who had found their way to the New World via Persia, China, and then across the Bering Strait had circulated since the sixteenth century. In the 1830s Edward King,

Viscount Kingsborough, had expended more than £32,000 attempting to prove his theory that the Mexicans were one of the lost tribes of Israel and thus Jews. Although they eventually dismissed it, Mariano Edward Rivero and John James von Tschudi, in a book on Peruvian antiquities published the very same year that Maximo and Bartola first arrived in England, again raised and debated "the Israelite theory."[160]

Although the Aztecs were clearly not thought to be of pure Jewish stock, let alone descendants of one of the "Lost Tribes of Israel," commentators were repeatedly struck by what they identified as the Aztecs' Jewish appearance and physiognomy. Early news coverage of the act in the *Times* reported that the girl's "aspect is more Jewish than that of her companion." Two days later the *Illustrated London News* similarly maintained, using almost identical language, that "her features are more of the Jewish cast than are those of her companion."[161] Writing in *Notes and Queries*, George Sexton, a medical doctor, argued that the "Jewish characteristics" of the Aztecs were "very distinct, and cannot fail to strike every observer."[162] This suggests that the Aztecs' promoters fed the press this copy, circulating publicity that pointed to, among other things, the "Jewish physiognomy" of the children.[163] But the repetition of this point also indicates that the press did not consider this an outlandish theory.

What was "decidedly Jewish" about their "countenances" was, apparently, not merely their olive skin and dark eyes but also their prominent noses.[164] In 1861, in a book recounting his travels in Mexico, the anthropologist E. B. Tylor noted that the Aztec nose tended to be "Jewish" in type.[165] When the popular press reported on Maximo and Bartola's physiognomies, a great deal of emphasis was often placed on the Aztecs' "Hebraic development of nose."[166] This was part of the discourse of the facial angle, which was so crucial to the new science of anthropometrics, which, as we have seen, sought to distinguish racial types scientifically through bodily measurements. But it was also key to identifying the Aztecs as having a Jewish appearance, as the prominent hooked nose was in the nineteenth century a particularly important marker of the Jewish "type."[167] The nose in both cases, reported Richard Owen, was "large and prominent," and in the boy exposed "more of the aperture of the nostril than is common in European children."[168] The nose, declared *Bell's Life in London,* was of "exaggerated Hebrew proportions," which made the "expression of the face" appear "strongly Jewish."[169] Similarly, the *Standard* reported that in both children "the strongly-delineated Jewish nose" was prominent.[170] Indeed, one of the few things that Walker recalled about the Aztecs, whom he escorted from England to America on behalf of P. T. Barnum, was their "big hook noses."[171]

Racial scientists perpetuated the popular perception that the Aztecs looked like Jews. Burke declared in 1853 that in the "cast of features, and especially in *expression,* they are pre-eminently Jewish." The Aztecs, he continued, represent an "extreme type" of Jew, "an ultra ideal to which all true Jews more less approximate." In fact, he maintained, "they are a caricature of the ordinary Jew."[172] Knox suggested that the "Jewish blood" that was evident in the Aztecs probably came not directly from a parent, but rather from an occurrence of the "law of 'interrupted descent.'" For, he argued, "Jewish, Negro, or Gipsy blood, once mingled with another race, seems never to disappear."[173] Although in the end there was little evidence for the Aztecs' supposed Jewish ancestry, this comparison stuck. It was repeated ad nauseam precisely because in the nineteenth century the Jew served as the paradigm of degeneracy.[174] If many saw the characteristics of the Jewish "type" so indelibly marked on Maximo and Bartola's bodies, this was largely because of the connection to the discourse of degeneracy so central both to this act and to the Victorian perception of the Jew.

It was not long before the true history of the Aztec children was disclosed and many of the scientific theories of their origin were corroborated. As early as 1854 a letter in *The Scotsman* had argued that the Aztecs were actually two mixed-race and mentally deficient children, taken (or perhaps purchased) from their parents in San Salvador for the purposes of exhibition.[175] Quoting Karl Scherzers's 1857 *Travels in the Free States of Central America,* a correspondent to *Notes and Queries* in 1858 attempted to substantiate this version of their history. They were, he insisted, merely "mulatto children" of "mixed descent," specifically of "mixed Indian and Negro blood," which was apparently a "very common mixture" in San Salvador, their homeland.[176] In the 1860s the Aztecs' racial identity was further clarified: according to another contributor to *Notes and Queries,* Maximo and Bartola were members of a "hybrid race called 'Sambo' that is a cross between the American Indian and the Negro." Their Indian blood was not even Aztec, he maintained, as the "aborigines of San Salvador belong to the Quiche family."[177] A correspondent to the *Anthropological Review,* calling himself "A Traveller in the New World," similarly maintained that the Aztecs were a "Zambo-Mulatto breed," their mother being "a vigorous Mulatto" and their father merely an ordinary "Mulatto."[178] While "Zambo" or "Sambo" had earlier in the century referred to the child of a "Negro" and a "mulatto," and later in the century became a common racial slur for an African-American, in the 1850s it was largely applied to the offspring of a South or Central American "Indian" and a "Negro."[179] That a particular hybrid combination found a name that was used in both professional and common parlance suggested that even people who appeared at first to resist classification could nevertheless eventually be categorized as a distinct, if not pure, racial type. Although at the height of their popularity their racial classification was puzzling, a fact that allowed them to be imagined as members of a nearly extinct race, they were soon exposed as a fraud and subsumed within a definable, and thus knowable, racial schema.

This unraveling of the true nature of the Aztecs' ancestry changed the specific meaning of the act. Their inevitable decline was interpreted in this context not as a consequence of inbreeding, as the publicity materials insisted, but rather as the opposite—the result of miscegenation in general, and, more specifically, the intermingling of races believed to be particularly degenerate. This did not, however, diminish their appeal. The Aztecs, even if they were not authentic, confirmed popular and professional theories about the dangerous effects of racial mixing and played to anxieties prevalent in Britain about the physical consequences of miscegenation. Indeed, even long after they had been exposed as fakes, the Aztecs kept performing for curious audiences who eagerly consumed the narrative of degeneration that continued to frame the act. The moral of the Aztecs' exhibition—that some civilizations are fated to decline because of indolence, vice, cultural stagnation, innate racial inferiority, and, paradoxically, both inbreeding and miscegenation—was in fact perpetuated into the 1890s.

A MONSTROUS MARRIAGE

In 1867, when the Aztecs returned to the United Kingdom, their manager attempted to revive interest in the act by staging a wedding between Maximo and Bartola. Freak weddings were a common publicity stunt, a way to draw attention to the difference between the couple and thus enhance their respective acts (such as the marriage of a "fat lady" and a "skeleton dude") or, as in this case, to revive interest in performers who were no longer a novelty by exhibiting them in a new manner.[180] By 1867 the Aztecs had done the European and American circuits and had just returned to England from Russia, which necessitated that they be repackaged for audiences already familiar with the exhibition. Maximo and Bartola's promoters staged a wedding complete with a breakfast at Willis's Rooms, a fashionable St. James's venue, a dress reputed to have cost £2000,

Figure 14. Souvenir painted *carte de visite* of the Aztecs in their wedding clothes, ca. 1867. The Bodleian Library, University of Oxford, John Johnson Collection, Human Freaks Box 4.

and, of course, a *carte de visite* of the Aztecs in their wedding clothes, which was available for purchase.[181]

The press eyed the event with suspicion. The *Penny Illustrated Paper* reported that "having now attained to adult age," Maximo and Bartola were "'married' by the Registrar of the district of St. George's, Hanover-square."[182] The quotation marks around the word *married* suggest that the author believed the wedding to be an entirely staged event. When Edward Wood chronicled the event in his 1868 compendium of giants and dwarfs, he suggested that the marriage was merely another outlandish yarn. The "first story of these children being brother and sister," he pointed out, "has recently been ignored," replaced by this new, more exciting tale of a freak wedding. However, as he had himself reproduced the narrative of their "degenerative and diminutive forms" being the result of their injunction "to marry only among themselves," the staged marriage actually fit brilliantly into the original account and was, in fact, legally binding.[183]

The idea that the two would eventually marry each other had been part of the original presentation of the act in 1853, but when they returned to London in 1855 their new manager no longer stressed their impending nuptials.[184] When they did, in fact, legally marry in 1867, the earlier narrative of them being siblings was either debunked or entirely ignored. Although the *Daily News* argued that the original story that had asserted that they were brother and sister was "entirely without foundation," the *Daily Telegraph* alluded to their possible consanguinity. The *Morning Post,* however, was clearly much more concerned with their racial relationship than with their familial one. Twice in one column it stated that Maximo was "of a pure race" while Bartola was "of more mixed extraction." Similarly, the *British Medical Journal* was "disgust[ed]," not by the idea that their marriage would inevitably lead to incest, but rather that they might now "perpetuate a race" of "diminutive idiots."[185] Marrying the last two remaining members of the sacerdotal caste to each other, however, ultimately reinscribed their impending disappearance through inbreeding, which could only lead to degeneration and eventually annihilation, which remained the central theme of their exhibition.

After their 1867 marriage, the Aztecs were regularly displayed in their wedding clothes, which the press often described as a "costume proper to modern European civilization." Maximo's suit was so "intensely respectable," reported the *Times,* that it would "do credit to a missionary tea party."[186] The Aztecs' publicity materials nevertheless continued to advertise them as a "newly-discovered Tribe of Human Beings. The Only

Aztecs Yet Introduced to Civilized White People," suggesting that despite their fine clothes, they were neither white nor civilized.[187] A series of publicity photographs produced in Belgium around 1875 depicted them garbed in explicitly savage costumes trimmed with animal fur.[188] When they were exhibited at the Crystal Palace in Sydenham in 1870, the Aztecs were actually placed beside the monkey house. A reporter for the *Times* argued that this would be "suggestive to the disciples of Professor Huxley," the most vocal proponent of Darwinian evolution, and remarked that it was still difficult to determine whether or not the Aztecs were indeed human.[189]

When the Aztecs reappeared in England in 1889 with Barnum's Greatest Show on Earth as the "Last of the Mysterious Aztecs," their promotional material continued to frame them as "the Only Two" people left "from a Nation of over 19 millions, Hundreds of years ago," or alternatively as "the only Survivors of a Race of many Millions." By the end of the nineteenth century, then, after forty years of intermittently touring the United Kingdom, the Aztecs had become emblematic of the inevitable annihilation of civilizations unable to modernize and thus progress. The last trace of the Aztecs on the British show circuit was as a minor exhibit at the Royal Aquarium in the early 1890s. Their publicity materials, short on space, billed them as "once a most powerful and prosperous race in Central America," but now, "through War and degeneration, dwindled down to THE ONLY TWO PERSONS NOW ON VIEW HERE."[190] When they finally disappeared from view in 1893, then, no one could possibly have been surprised.

FIVE

"When the Cannibal King Began to Talk"

Performing Race, Class, and Ethnicity

WHEN THE AZTECS WERE EXHIBITED in London in 1853, the *Dublin Medical Press* proclaimed that the "owners of these small people might better perhaps have exhibited them in England as a variety of the wild Irish, for by so doing they might have tickled John Bull's pride as well as his curiosity."[1] Ireland's premier medical journal was here alluding to the widespread propensity in Britain for reading all ethnographic acts in relation to the archetypal Celtic "primitive." The Barnum and Bailey Circus, which generally featured ethnographic acts, responded to this tendency by including a ditty in their 1899 British songbook that made the connection between the "wild Irish" and their own "wild man" exhibit explicit. The song, "The Barnum and Bailey Show," contained the following verse: "When the cannibal king began to talk, / You could tell by his accent he'd been in Cork / With the Barnum and Bailey Show."[2] The song played on the widely held belief that the "cannibal king" not only had been to Cork but was just as likely to have been born there. Indeed, it was relatively common knowledge in the late nineteenth century that freak show entrepreneurs who could not afford to import troupes of exotic foreigners regularly employed locals, often working-class Irishmen, to play the role of African "savages." While scholars have examined the exhibition of non-Western peoples at freak shows and noted that many of the "cannibals" and "savages" on display were actually fakes, none have explored in earnest either the preconditions for, or the ramifications of, this particular artifice. This chapter interrogates the cultural attitudes that bound class, ethnic,[3] and racial otherness together, and the ways in which these relationships were embodied and performed, in order to explain what made these fake African shows not only possible, but appealing to a broad public.

EXHIBITING THE ETHNOGRAPHIC

Most scholars have been much more interested in the exhibition of "real" Africans than they have been in known fakes, that is, British or Irish performers costumed and painted to pass as Africans.[4] Historians and anthropologists have focused on ethnographic displays as a crucial component of imperial culture and have paid particular attention to the exhibition of non-Western peoples at international expositions. At these exhibitions Africans were generally displayed in the context of "native villages" where they lived in grass huts, cooked their own food, performed "tribal" dances, and wore "traditional" clothing, despite the often inclement European weather. These "native villages" thus offered the European public access to live examples of seemingly archaic peoples whose undeveloped societies appeared static and thus who reflected back to the audience the modernity and progressive nature of their own European cultures and societies. These exhibits thus rationalized the imperial project by constructing non-Western people as savage and primitive, and thus as "living proof" of the blessings of Western civilization. In this context, then, much emphasis was placed on the presumed authenticity of the "natives" on display.[5]

The exhibitions of savages, cannibals, and wild men in show shops and at fairgrounds, circuses, freak museums, and seaside resorts were perhaps more influential than those "native villages," as they were a permanent feature, or at least an annual seasonal one, of all major cities and most smaller towns. Audiences across England, Wales, Scotland, and Ireland were exposed to the same performers, who either moved with their troupes or contracted individually with venue managers. This meant that the population of the United Kingdom consumed a relatively consistent set of entertainers. Although the international exhibitions encouraged a cross-class audience, they were more expensive to attend than these cheaper shows, whose price—often a penny—made them a truly democratic form of entertainment. These shows are thus deserving of much closer attention as popular imperial spaces, particularly since the itinerant freak show was likely the first way that those living outside major metropolitan areas came into close contact with non-Western peoples.[6]

From the exhibition of "the Hottentot Venus" in 1810 until the First World War, a variety of different types of so-called savages were on display across the United Kingdom outside the auspices of the international exhibitions. Laplanders, Inuit, Ojibbeways, Australian Aborigines, New Zealand Maoris, Hurons, Tierra del Fuegans, Brazilian Botocudos, and a range of African peoples, including Zulus, "Bushmen," and, as we have seen, "Earthmen," all took the stage at fairs, music halls, show shops, and other entertainment venues. Demand for these shows increased over the nineteenth century as interest in African peoples intensified during the "Scramble for Africa." The British public was particularly interested in Zulus and other southern Africans in the period between the 1879 Zulu War and the Boer War, which drew to a close in 1902. In the late 1870s and early 1880s the inveterate showman G. A. Farini's star attraction was invariably a Zulu act: "Genuine Zulus," "Zulu Kaffir Boy," "Friendly Zulus," "Umgame, the Baby Zulu," and "Cetewayo's Daughters" all attracted curious crowds.[7] By displaying people of color alongside other "human oddities," these types of shows served to reinforce the Victorian construct of the white, healthy, middle-class Englishman as the norm of the perfectly evolved body.[8] As Rebecca Stern has argued, by "aligning display (the principal of exhibition) with racial color and cultural barbarism, these exhibitions tacitly erected the guidelines that regulated civilization and, hence, inclusion with the category of 'white.'"[9] The construction of the white civilized / black savage imperial binary was heightened by patently fraudulent freak shows in which colonial bodies were literally manufactured for display.

The significance of fake savage shows to the production of racial categories and the dissemination of ideas about them is evidenced by the fact that anthropologists, newly emerging as experts on race, became highly concerned about the impact of these shows on the general public. As early as 1855 John Conolly, president of the Ethnological Society, encouraged his colleagues to visit and report on freak shows in order to distinguish the authentic displays of "real" Africans from the increasingly common "frauds." Ethnologists, he argued, should instruct the public and prevent them from "imbibing erroneous information" about "the races of mankind." The "deceptive shows would, doubtless, still be followed," he argued, "but followed as mere shows, suitable as parts of the wonders of a fair, or a mere means of making money; but not ranking among objects of real instruction, and perverting knowledge."[10] Anthropologists were thus concerned to distinguish the real from the fake because they believed that these shows were instrumental in shaping popular understandings of race.

As Robert Bogdan has noted, showmen in the United States often employed locals to perform the role of savages, wild men, or cannibals because phony natives were easier to hire, cheaper to employ, and more cooperative than the authentic variety.[11] By the end of the nineteenth century, "painted Irishmen or indigenous British blacks were now displacing true Africans in British show business" as well.[12] Indeed, there were so many fake Africans on the fairgrounds circuit that by the turn of the century the term "Zulu" had become "synonymous with artifice and disguise."[13] Although historical evidence of this type of fakery is difficult to uncover, the nostalgic memoirs of showmen often reveal the secrets of the trade and testify to the frequency of the showman's reliance on "the arts of deception." British showmen followed in the tradition of P. T. Barnum, who famously aphorized that the "public appears disposed to be amused even when they are conscious of being deceived." Barnum and many other successful showmen combined the genuine and the fake, drawing on a mixture of illusion, assumption, and reality.[14] According to the English showman Tom Norman, it was not the show itself that entertained but rather "the tale that you told."[15]

While some audience members were clearly angered by being duped, in the case of fake savages the deception appears to have been successful more often than not—meaning people continued to pay to see what they may or may not have known was a fraud—primarily because they were entertained and reassured by the imperial ideologies at play. It was not the specific authenticity of the exhibition that was important, but rather the security of one's own relationship to the performance. As Vincent Cheng has argued, "the nature of what one formulates as 'other' and 'barbarian' tells us much more about the Self than about the Other."[16] Similarly, although the exhibition of fake savages tells us nothing about Africans, it reveals a great deal about imperial British identities in the age of an expanding empire. The fraudulent shows are, in fact, much more instructive than the authentic variety, for they expose the complex ways in which racial, class, and ethnic relationships were articulated and, crucially, staged.

In the second half of the nineteenth century the "wild man" character at the sideshow was generally portrayed as an African. African-American and other men of color were regularly employed to play these parts, regardless of their ethnicity or nationality, particularly in the late nineteenth century, when demand for these shows reached its peak. Thomas "Whimsical"

Walker, a professional clown, remembered that it was during the 1879 Zulu War that a showman first conceived of the idea of exhibiting Zulu warriors. Since none could be found he was forced to use "a party of ordinary niggers" instead. Similarly, Tom Norman declared that he got his "savages" from the Sailor's Home or "the wilds of Ratcliffe-highway" near the docks situated in the East London neighborhoods of Limehouse and Poplar. The poorest part of London, Limehouse and Poplar were also among the most ethnically diverse neighborhoods, as the docks were the entry point not only for foreign goods but also for foreign people (particularly Asians and Africans) who worked on the shipping vessels that daily arrived at Europe's largest port. Norman maintained that he chose "men of colour and mixed nationality . . . provided that they were black" to play "South Sea Islanders" or "Zulus."[17] By the early twentieth century, as the want ads in showmen's trade journals illustrate, it had become common practice to employ "Niggers, or any kind of Coloured People" to play the role of "Dahomey Warriors" or to perform in other novelty shows.[18]

It is not difficult to imagine how audiences made the imaginative leap from a "Negro" to a "Zulu Warrior" or "South Sea Islander." The showmen relied on the public's association of dark skin with primitive cultures and savage peoples, for there were relatively few communities of people of color in Britain between the early nineteenth century and the West Indian immigration of the post–World War II period.[19] These ruses, however, were sometimes surprisingly unsuccessful. Walker reported that when the troupe of "ordinary niggers" posing as Zulus played a seaside town it encountered an audience that consisted of sailors who had just returned from South Africa. The sailors knew "something of the Zulu lingo" and soon identified "Cetewayo's savage soldiery" as decidedly inauthentic. According to Walker, "they went for the Zulus, the proprietor and the show. There wasn't much of the latter left whole when they had finished."[20] A similar incident occurred at Norman's "Savage South Africa" show, for by the 1880s it was increasingly common to find audience members who were familiar with the newly important South African colonies.[21] Indeed, when English working-class men attacked these fake shows, they revealed their investment in their own imperial identities by evoking their proprietary and sophisticated knowledge of the geography, languages, and peoples of the empire. That the public itself maintained its ability to distinguish between an African-American, or ordinary "Negro," and a Zulu warrior also indicates that what they had paid to see was not merely a racial type but a particular kind of imperial Other whose racial difference could not merely be displayed but in fact had to be actively performed.[22]

Michael Ragussis has argued that in the eighteenth century the British theater served as the "central arena" for the construction and performance of ethnic difference and identity.[23] In the nineteenth century, the freak show joined the stage as a crucial space not merely for exhibiting but for enacting imperial ideologies of otherness. Indeed, although Victorians, and late Victorians in particular, believed that race was a fixed category by which humans could be hierarchically organized, the significance of racial difference needed to be exhibited and demonstrated, for it relied on understandings of primitiveness and savagery. Thus even authentic "natives" were dressed for the part and performed choreographed routines. When Farini exhibited a group of Khoisan in 1883 he garbed them in leopard-skin shorts—certainly not their traditional clothing—and advertised them as "Earthmen."[24] A newspaper report on the 1853 appearance of real Zulus in London remarked on the "almost perfect dramatic effect with which these wild men *play their parts.*" Another proclaimed that if "English actors could be found so completely to lose themselves in the *characters* they assumed, histrionic art would be in a state truly magnificent."[25] The press thus reviewed these ethnographic shows as a type of theater that involved a considerable degree of performance. So formulaic was this performance of savagery by authentic and fraudulent acts alike that John Conolly remarked in 1855 that the "genuine character" of ethnographic exhibitions was sometimes more evident "behind the scenes," after "the close of the public performances," than on stage.[26] The freak show thus relied on certain performative tropes of otherness that were continuously and necessarily reproduced even by "authentic natives" who were forced to conform to the conceits of sideshow spectacle and thus, ironically, to mimic their own impersonators.[27]

While Africans themselves were generally coached and costumed to conform to the audience's expectations, this was even more crucial in the case of entirely fraudulent acts. The showman James McKenzie maintained in his memoir that very little training was needed for actors who had previously performed in savage shows because the routine generally remained the same. "The Wild Man," he recalled, was exhibited behind prison bars, "wildly pacing up and down occasionally shaking the bars, almost naked with ornaments of teeth, and coins, he would glare at the people with grimaces, showing his teeth."[28] These performances relied on widespread assumptions about the primitive nature of non-Western peoples. The scantily clad performers decked out in animal skins suggested a proximity to nature that, paired with a gibberish language, indicated a primeval people.

But the freak show "native" was invariably not merely unevolved but explicitly savage, as the pacing, grimacing, and baring of teeth made crystal clear. Indeed, at fake shows much more so than at authentic exhibitions, the trope of savagery prevailed over that of primitiveness. This ensured a more exciting experience, but it also reveals an understanding of what audiences wanted to see, what images of Africanness they demanded to be shown, when they attended a "Zulu" show. At St. Giles's fair in 1878 the "imitation South African savage" startled the audience by "rushing forth and brandishing what the proprietor informed his hearers was the leg of his sister."[29] This claim was not merely threatening but suggested one of the fundamental taboos of Western culture: cannibalism. That this wild man was likely going to eat the leg—a leg that belonged not only to another human being but to his sister—illustrated the innate depravity that made the savage uncivilizable and thus fit only to be ruled and restrained. Indeed, the trope of cannibalism, so prevalent in "savage" shows, served an important ideological function, as it "displaced the violence of the colonisers onto the colonized" and thus justified the imperial project.[30]

These shows thus cast Africans as a brutal race that needed to be subdued because their passions were animalistic; unlike civilized Englishmen, they lacked self-control. Although, as Michael Pickering has argued, "'savagery' as spectacle was 'savagery' domesticated and tamed," a demonstration of the disciplining of the wild man was nevertheless central to the performance.[31] Ropes and cages were used as containment devices, but, more significantly, the wild man was also seen to be actively tamed: the circus showman "Lord" George Sanger used to parade his savages around the fairground buying them sweetmeats, thus showing that they could be restrained and controlled by a benevolent keeper.[32]

The showman's narrative and the promotional materials that surrounded these shows reinforced these themes of primitiveness, savagery, and thus the necessity of imperial rule. Freak shows were highly structured experiences that were invariably framed by a story about the anomalous body on display. The presenter's patter, important at most freak show performances, was particularly essential to the success of these shows, as it transformed otherwise unremarkable individuals into bloodthirsty savages. These "wonderful people," Sanger's father had proclaimed of two "mulatto" children whom he attempted to pass off as African "pigmies," "are fully grown, being, in fact, each over 30 years of age. They were captured by Portuguese traders in the African wilds, and are incapable of ordinary human speech. Their food consists of raw meat, and if they can capture a small animal they tear it to pieces alive with their teeth, eagerly devouring its flesh and drinking its blood."[33] As this spiel suggests, showmen advertised these acts as wild, dangerous, and depraved, thus strengthening the message of the props and costumes. But showmen also clearly preyed on humanitarian sentiments in order to make the wild man show respectable to middle- as well as working-class audiences. The "'story' of [the] slave trader of Africa and quoting 'Uncle Tom['s] Cabin' in all the tribulation of slavery, brought a good deal of sympathetic hearing," maintained McKenzie, "and it 'went down' [if] the 'tale' was told well."[34] Showmen thus manipulated both of the dominant nineteenth-century discourses of Africanness: that Africans were bloodthirsty savage cannibals, and, as the abolitionist movement had argued, that they were men and brothers who had been degraded by slavery. Although these were contradictory messages, they worked together to construct the African as a savage that must be—and, crucially, could be—subdued, if not entirely civilized.

Showmen thus guided audiences to see exactly what they had expected to observe, for these shows relied on imperial assumptions about the distance between the evolved British body and that of the colonial savage. Freak show entrepreneurs could thus easily employ locals to stand in for unattainable Africans by dressing them for the part, by exploiting popular assumptions about the nature and behavior of "primitive" and "savage" peoples, and by drawing on a variety of different racial narratives to frame the exhibition. But exactly which locals were chosen to enact Africanness was crucial to the success of the show, for imperial hierarchies were intimately bound up in class and ethnic, as well as racial, difference.

WHITENESS AND THE WORKING CLASS

An article in *Strand Magazine* in 1897 maintained that it is "more or less well known that vigilant agents are for ever scouring the universe, from Whitechapel to Central Africa, for freaks of Nature."[35] It was also widely understood that wild men could be found as easily in Whitechapel as in Central Africa, and thus a trip beyond "the dark continent" of the East End of London was rarely necessary to procure this type of exhibit. George Burchett, "the King of Tattooists," worked for a time at the Westminster

Aquarium, where he made friends with many of the "human oddities" on display. The "South Seas swimming ladies" and "one or two of the Zulus," he claimed, were all born "within the sound of Bow Bells," meaning in the center of the old City of London; even the "tattooed savages," he recalled, were true cockneys who spoke "in the accents of Bermondsey and Limehouse."[36]

Throughout the nineteenth and early twentieth centuries stories circulated widely about working men like Rupert Brown, who deserted from the army in order to become an actor and landed a job as a wild man. Brown, who dressed up in a leopard skin and performed a savage dance in a show shop, was apparently so convincing as an African warrior that a black widow took a fancy to him. To get out of this unwelcome predicament, "he 'ad to pretend 'e was a Zulu of an evening," claimed the night watchman, "and try and persuade Kumbo that he was an English gentleman of a daytime."[37] The insinuation was that both roles were equally challenging for a working-class man: while not exactly "black," neither was Brown an "English gentleman," and thus perhaps not exactly "white" either, as his name, likely invented for the purposes of this story, suggested.

That working-class performers like Rupert Brown and the Westminster Aquarium's East End oddities were employed to portray sideshow savages was not merely reflective of the low-paid nature of this type of semiskilled show work. In the nineteenth century, race and class were interrelated ways of categorizing difference. According to Douglas Lorimer, in the 1850s and '60s the English middle class imagined the working class to be a "distinct caste," placed by God in a subordinate social position. Social Darwinists similarly theorized that race and class were interconnected and often interchangeable typologies of inferiority, but focused on the biological rather than religious basis of social and racial inequality. This suggests that class was widely understood to be a fixed social category, dictated not by economics but rather by innate, immutable, God-given or hereditary differences by which people could be hierarchically organized. Class relationships at home, as historians have frequently argued, thus served as an important model for understanding race relations abroad.[38] European appeals to "superiority over other races," which manifested in both race prejudice and institutionalized racism, were thus always "projected over perceptions of social divisions at home."[39] Class ideologies were thus central to the production of Victorian racial categories.

The nineteenth-century sciences contributed to this elision between race and class. Physiognomy, still widely popular at midcentury, insisted that class differences could be distinguished through physical traits, that each person's social rank was labeled on them as "legibly as arms are painted on a carriage-panel."[40] Evolutionary anthropologists, who dominated the field of anthropology in the nineteenth century, furthered this essentialization of the working class by claiming that non-Western "primitives," children, women, and criminals were, like the poorer classes, examples of less developed peoples. This meant that class and racial differences could be read as analogous expressions of different stages of human evolution from savage to civilized.[41] Class and race thus became mutually reinforcing "scientific" classificatory schemes, such that by midcentury the London poor in particular had come to be seen not merely as a different class or even "nation," as Benjamin Disraeli had argued, but "as a 'race' apart."[42]

By the middle decades of the nineteenth century this racialization of class difference had become widespread in popular culture. As many scholars have noted, the literature of urban exploration so central to mid- and late Victorian journalism modeled itself on travelogues, guidebooks, and voyages of discovery, emphasizing the "exoticism of urban poverty." The slums of the metropolis became "darkest England," penetrated by urban explorers seeking to uncover the habits and dwellings of "savage tribes."[43] From Henry Mayhew to Jack London, journalists and writers cast themselves as anthropologists who chronicled their journeys "into a dark continent that is within easy walking distance of the General Post Office."[44]

The late Victorian dramatist and journalist George Sims explicitly linked this racial discourse to that of freakery. He declared that the London slums were in fact a "Chamber of Horrors," replete with "natural curiosities" who, he maintained, were "the strangest collection of human beings." In the poorer districts of the great cities, he reported in 1883, the same year that Krao debuted at the aquarium, there are "hidden away from general observation marvels as great as any of those which the enterprising Farini imports from the Cannibal Islands . . . for the amusement and edification of the shilling-paying public. Missing links abound, and monstrosities are plentiful."[45] The urban poor, Sims suggested, were freakish in exactly the same way as non-Western peoples. This racial reading of the poor was not, however, restricted to the residuum of Outcast London. The settlement movement that flourished in the East End in the final decades of the nineteenth century sought to establish cross-class bonds of brotherly love between an educated elite and respectable but disadvantaged men and boys. These social reformers also reiterated the race-class relationship by self-consciously constructing "colonies" in what was clearly imagined to be an outpost of empire.[46]

This racialization of the working class reached its peak in the 1880s, during heightened concern over urban degeneration, race deterioration, and national efficiency,[47] and at the same moment that the Third Reform Act expanded the franchise to a large majority of working men. The use of this language of racial otherness thus had a particular political valence, as it expressed imperial fears about who could claim to be not merely a subject of Great Britain, but a citizen who participated in governing the nation and the empire. Indeed, as Michael Pickering has argued, the "reciprocity between conceptions of race and class" was a crucial aspect of debates over representative democracy in Britain in the final decades of the nineteenth century.[48] When Lord Milner remarked, after seeing soldiers bathing during the First World War, that "he never knew the working classes had such white skins," he thus reinforced long-standing interdependent racial and class hierarchies that were central to the "demarcating imperative" of colonialism both abroad and at home.[49]

Fake savages were thus possible in part because of widespread assumptions about the relationship between racial and class difference. Michael Mark Chemers has argued that American freak shows sought to accentuate racial divides while obfuscating class gulfs.[50] British shows, however, clearly embedded class messages within racial ones, for, as I have argued, in the late Victorian period in particular the working class functioned in both popular and elite culture as the "internal counterpart" to the "external Other."[51] Because the possibility that the savage African on display was actually a working-class Englishman was ever present, class ideologies were always already present in the imperial and racial messages of sideshow savagery. This conflation of the working poor with the savage African likely appealed to middle-class freak show audiences because it established that the category of "whiteness," with its concomitant implication of fitness for imperial rule, was dependent not only upon racial distinctions, but also upon those of social class, something that real ethnographic exhibitions could not communicate.

The presence of working-class spectators in freak show audiences, however, complicated the meaning and reception of fake savage shows. Although there is considerable scholarly debate about when and how the British working class "became" white, it is clear that whiteness was and remains a highly contested category precisely because of its unstable and unbounded character.[52] Since at least the 1830s, as historians of both the abolitionist movement and the factory system have demonstrated, members of the English working class had lobbied for entitlements on the basis

of their perceived racial superiority.[53] That this racial status had to be rene-
gotiated throughout the nineteenth and twentieth centuries in both imperial and domestic settings reveals the extent to which whiteness was
dependent upon "a shifting set of subjective criteria rather than a fixed
group of innate characteristics" that included class, gender, and geography.[54] It also suggests that whiteness is always relational, for racial identi-
fication requires the presence, symbolic or actual, of an Other. For English
working-class freak show audiences, that other was an Irishman. For fake
savage shows to appeal to working-class spectators then, the "cannibal
king" needed to be constructed as a distinctly Irish African.

THE IRISH AFRICAN

By performing as Africans, individual working-class performers unwit-
tingly undermined claims to white identity and actually colluded with the
dominant middle-class ideology of whiteness that excluded the lower
orders. British working-class freak show audiences, however, were able to
recuperate their imperial identities through a discourse that cast Anglo-
Saxons—and indeed all other British (as opposed to Celtic) peoples,
regardless of their social status—as a ruling elite. This was a common
tactic of the Victorian theater, where every Briton, "however humble," was
encouraged to imagine himself "not as a member of his class but as an
empire-builder, and a natural superior of the other races and nations of the
world."[55] In this case, this shared positioning was made possible by a widespread belief—often borne out in fact—that many of the savages on display
were actually Irishmen in disguise.

   The class and racial messages of fake African exhibits were intensified by
the presence of Irish performers who throughout the nineteenth century
were regularly employed to play savages of one variety or another. "Lord"
George Sanger remembered that when his father ran a show of "living
curiosities" in the 1820s, his "savage cannibal pigmies," Tamee Ahmee and
Orio Rio, were in reality "two rather intelligent mulatto children, their
mother being a negress and their father an Irishman." These children were
chosen largely because of the color of their skin, but their half-Irish pedi-
gree is nevertheless significant, as it was typical—or, perhaps more significantly, believed to be typical—of these types of fraudulent acts. When
Sanger wanted to stage his own "Red Indian" show many years later, he
went to the slums of Liverpool, where in half an hour he engaged "eight
wild men and two savage women."[56] These savage slum dwellers were

likely members of the Irish migrant community. Indeed, it was common knowledge that most of the "Red Indians" on display in the early nineteenth century were in reality what were termed "Paddy Murphy" Indians, that is, only run-of-the-mill Irishmen. In 1835 a newspaper report on Greenwich Fair maintained that there were the "usual number of Indian warriors (thick lipped Irishmen from St. Giles [London's quintessential Irish slum] painted, with their ears and noses adorned with rings)."[57] In his semiautobiographical picaresque novel *The Confessions of Harry Lorrequer*, published serially in the *Dublin University Magazine* in 1837, the Anglo-Irish writer Charles Lever recounted a similar story. After an authentic troupe of "North American Indians" had abandoned their performance in Dublin, their "theatrical speculator" employed some "country fellows" to play their parts. With their "wild looks, their violent gestures, and, above all, their strange and guttural language," these Irish Indians proved to be "better savages than their prototypes."[58]

The exhibition of Irishmen as "Red Indians" signaled a long-held cultural understanding of savagery in which the Irish, as the first of Britain's colonized natives, were paradigmatic.[59] As early as the twelfth century Europeans had imagined the Irish to be not only culturally inferior but wild and bestial.[60] Although Joep Leerssen maintains that contact with the Americas shifted these understandings and allowed the Irish to be incorporated back into "England's inner sphere," no longer wild but merely "irksome,"[61] other scholars have challenged this interpretation. Luke Gibbons has suggested instead that the indigenous peoples of the New World did not replace the Irish as prototypical savages. Rather, the Irish peasant functioned in the Elizabethan period as a, if not the, model of the primitive and savage "native" through which the peoples of the Americas could be understood and interpreted.[62] That Charles Darwin compared New Zealand Maoris to Irish peasants[63] reveals the ways in which the "wild Irish" continued into the Victorian period to serve the English as the prime example of the primitive that newly encountered peoples could be measured against. This perceived relationship took on new political import in the age of Irish attempts to gain Home Rule. In a presentation to the Ethnological Society in 1868, Reverend William Houghton declared that hairy "wild men" had inhabited Ireland many years ago. "I hazard the conjecture," he declared, implicitly rejecting Irish claims to be self-governing, "that they were the primitive stock whence the Fenians have descended."[64]

In the second half of the nineteenth century the African replaced the Native American in the Victorian mind as the quintessential savage.

What seemed to remain constant, however, was the Irish reference point, for "Paddy Murphy" Indians were quickly superceded by "African Irishm[e]n," whom Charles Lever also described performing at a London freak show.[65] As the first colonized "natives," it was thus the Irish that provided the model for mid- and late Victorian attitudes toward newly colonized African subjects. For, as Kenan Malik has argued, nineteenth-century racial discourse arose out of perceived differences within European society and was only later applied to non-Europeans.[66] It was not, therefore, that Africanness was mapped onto Irish bodies, as historians have often suggested, but rather that the category of "Negro" was constructed in relationship to, and built upon, that of "Celt."

The publication of L. Perry Curtis's influential *Apes and Angels* in 1971 opened up debate within Anglo-Irish studies about the extent to which the Irish were racialized in the nineteenth and early twentieth centuries. Noel Ignatiev's influential history of "how the Irish became white" in the United States has fueled this debate in recent years, despite the fact that the cultural and political history of race relations in the United States differs greatly from that of the United Kingdom and thus cannot be used as a template for understanding British attitudes toward race and ethnicity.[67] Curtis has argued that British animosity toward and discrimination against the Irish was based not merely on anti-Catholic sentiment but on a specifically racial reading of Celtic peoples as distinctly nonwhite. Curtis's argument has been advanced and supported by scholars from a variety of disciplines who have insisted that, even though race was a highly flexible term in the nineteenth century, and could not be entirely separated from ethnicity, religion, and class,[68] it was nevertheless central to British perceptions of Irish difference. Indeed, the flourishing of postcolonial studies in recent years has allowed scholars to refine and expand on Curtis's theory, revealing the extent to which up until at least 1922 the British public understood the Irish as colonial subjects whose racial otherness was central to constructions of British national identity and to the maintenance of imperial hierarchies.[69] Indeed, several scholars have noted that, even in the post-independence period, the English in particular continued to conceive of Irish difference as racial and biological—and thus immutable—rather than as simply religious or cultural.[70]

The idea that the British understood the Irish as a separate race and treated them accordingly has been controversial, and a small but important and vocal group of historians have rejected it outright. Sheridan Gilley, Roy Foster, Alan O'Day, and G. K. Peatling have insisted that

Curtis's argument is historically inaccurate and politically expedient and that it trivializes the plight of other colonized groups.[71] Their critiques, while multifaceted, return to two major themes: that the Irish *are* white, appear to be white, and therefore could not have been understood as analogous to visibly nonwhite colonial subjects; and that although some racialized images of the Irish did circulate in popular culture, they were clearly comic, not malicious, had little to no impact on political decision making, and thus in no way influenced Britain's governance of Ireland.

The first of these critiques—that "unlike Anglo-Saxons and Celts, Caucasians and Negroes are in fact different races," and that while a "Negro is identifiable at once," "a 'Celt' does not have this separate racial character so visibly stamped upon him"—has largely been promoted by Gilley but rejected by Peatling.[72] By using quotations marks around the word *Celt* but not *Negro,* Gilley marked off the Celtic fringe as a socially constructed group while at the same time naturalizing the Negro as a visible and clearly demarcated racial category. Although in the 1970s, when Gilley launched this critique, race was still widely imagined to be a natural, if hierarchical, way of ordering humanity, scholars in recent decades have overwhelmingly rejected this idea, instead analyzing race as a culturally produced way of organizing difference and thus as deeply imbedded within specific political and social contexts.[73] Moving beyond the black/white binary to understand the multiple different ways—bodily and otherwise—in which a variety of groups have been excluded from whiteness has allowed for a more nuanced reading of the specific cultural and political meanings behind, and uses of, English demarcations of Irish otherness.[74]

The second critique, launched most clearly by Peatling, is that the "locations" of the discourses of anti-Irish racism did not give them "the requisite access to influence over the political process." Curtis's work, Peatling maintains, relies on sources that provide little insight into "the attitudes of 'the British ruling class'" and that therefore remain "distant from the political decision-making process."[75] Peatling, like many political and intellectual historians, explicitly attacks the work of "'cultural studies' scholarship" for refusing to privilege certain kinds of sources as inherently more important. He insists that documents produced by politicians and intellectuals are intrinsically more significant because he assumes that power operates only from the top down. Peatling thus discounts theories of anti-Irish racism largely because they rely on evidence drawn from popular culture, which he insists had no impact on the larger political landscape. He dismisses outright the contention of cultural historians that British racial ideologies were produced, reproduced, and in the process reworked by a much broader public than merely those with access to Whitehall and Westminster. In his haste to reject the practices of cultural history, however, Peatling has overlooked the crucial role that widespread popular attitudes have played in the production of knowledge. As Nancy Stepan has argued, in nineteenth-century Britain "science followed rather than led public opinion on race."[76]

John Belchem has demonstrated that popular performances were critical to the production and circulation of ethnic and racial representations and had political effects beyond the confines of the "'low' concert hall."[77] Although the music hall and the freak show were not the Houses of Parliament, they were, nevertheless, important spaces where racial and ethnic stereotypes were enacted and imperial hierarchies constructed and contested by a heterogeneous public whose support was essential to the maintenance of empire.[78] They were sites where race needed to be displayed and performed precisely because racial difference—and, crucially, the meanings attached to it—was not, as Gilley and others have imagined, transparent or self-evident, for according to Belchem, ethnic identities are always constructed in "complex, contingent, and contested contextual interaction."[79] Because freak shows relied on patently fake "cannibal kings," widely believed to be "blacked-up" Irishmen, these cheap entertainments were crucial to the articulation of the affinity between Irishmen and Africans, who were both classified as primitive, savage, colonial others best understood in relationship to each other.

The belief that the Africans on display in the halls and show shops were merely Irishmen in disguise emerged as early as the first widely popular African exhibit of the Victorian era. In 1847 a group of Khoisan, who were then called "Hottentots," "Bushmen," or "Bosjesmans," appeared at venues in London and Dublin, where they were hailed as authentic specimens.[80] When this same troupe was exhibited in Glasgow they were dismissed variously as "Paisley weavers," "Irishmen," "[chimney] sweeps," or "Highlandman." The accusation was that these savages were members of the Celtic fringe, whose primitiveness and wildness made them easy to pass off as Bushmen, who were seen as the most archaic of African peoples. According to David Prince Miller, one of the showmen who contracted to exhibit the Bushmen at Glasgow Fair, a street bookseller made much of these "aspersions" by flogging a "true account" of the interaction between one of the "Bosjesmans and an Irishman." On visiting the show, the pamphlet maintained, an unsuspecting "Paddy" found that one of the Bushmen on display was really a fellow "Patlander" who had robbed him months earlier:

> If others were astonished, what must Paddy have been when he beheld crouching at a fire, clothed in skins, and smoking a short dhudee, the treacherous blackguard who had robbed him. "Arrah, you devil," said he, making up to him, "do you think I don't know you? Is it bekase you got a cat's skin on, and them *fismygigs* (the arrows) sticking in your head, I don't know you? Where's me watch, and me money, and me clothes, ye spalpeen ye?" The Bosjesman, as he was called, (for it was really he who had robbed the Irishman) jabbered some unintelligible jargon. Paddy was not to be done, and swore that if he did not give them to him or their value, he would knock him into smithereens.[81]

Although Miller, who recounted this story in his memoirs, maintained that it was purely fictional, and that the Bushmen were authentic, his retelling of the popular pamphlet is significant, for it reveals the ways in which even an "authentic" African body was cast in Irish terms.

Indeed, whether the story is true or not is irrelevant, for the relationship between the Celts and the Bushmen was repeatedly drawn. John Pinkerton, Edinburgh geographer, antiquarian, and onetime editor of the *Critical Review,* had in the 1780s, according to the ethnologist J. C. Prichard, identified the Celts as distinct from the other races, having a mythology most closely resembling "the Hottentots, or others of the rudest savages."[82] By the mid-eighteenth century "Hottentot" had become a "common slur for someone of congenital stupidity" or a person who was "uncivilized, filthy, or ill-mannered," and was often applied to the Irish. The pipe, ubiquitous in representations of both the Irish and the "Hottentot," symbolized laziness and somnolence, which served to justify British colonial rule of both Ireland and South Africa.[83] The use of Gaelic words here for the oddities of Irish culture, such as *fismygigs* for arrows, *spalpeen* for scamp, and *dhudee* for the small clay pipe typical of the stage Irishman, was significant, for it cast the Irish as a quaint people of as much ethnological interest as the stone-age Bushmen. Indeed, during the famine—which had not yet abated when the Khoisan were exhibited in 1847—the Irish were often constructed in the same terms as the Bushmen: as a dying race that had only themselves to blame for their own extinction.[84]

The use of stereotypical Irish dialect in this narrative also linked the Celt to the Bushman, for in the 1840s racial categories were often constructed along linguistic lines. At this time ethnology, which focused in part on philology (as opposed to scientific anthropology, which focused on biology), dominated ethnographic discourse.[85] Language was thus a prime signifier of racial difference in the 1840s and '50s, a point that was well established in both popular and scientific circles. A surgeon who had spent much of his life in the West Indies declared, "How forcibly does language illustrate the characteristics of a people? We cannot for an instant compare the jabbering jargon of the Negro to the bold, forcible cosmopolitan tongue of the Anglo-Saxon. An Englishman can imitate the nigger dialect, but the Negro cannot speak English."[86] In the 1890s the American author W. L. Alden, whose work had been published widely in Britain, maintained in a fictional story of a freak show that the "Wild Man's" Irish "brogue" would surely give him away.[87] But at midcentury English showmen actually drew attention to the relationship between African and Celtic languages. When this Irish Bushman replied with "some unintelligible jargon," intending to mimic the distinctive, and to the European ear bestial, "Hottentot stammer," Miller implied that the Celtic language was itself equally opaque. Miller claimed, in fact, that the Bushmen's "words are very similar to the Gaelic."[88] Similarly, when Julia Pastrana was on display in the late 1850s, her souvenir pamphlet maintained that the language of the "Root-Digger" Indian tribe to which she belonged was similar to "Welsh and Celtic."[89] When the first group of Zulus was exhibited in London in 1853 Charles Dickens drew connections between the excited speeches of the staged Zulu war council and "an orator in an Irish House of Commons."[90] When another group of "Bosjesmen" were exhibited at the Egyptian Hall in London in 1847, their handbill advertised that their "shouts" were very "Irish in their explosiveness." Indeed, it billed them as "The White Negroes of Africa."[91]

This reference to "white Negroes" reveals the complicated understanding of race in the mid-nineteenth century. What made the Bushmen "Negroes" was clearly not the color of their skin, which throughout the eighteenth and nineteenth centuries was repeatedly described as "yellow," "tawny," or even, as in this case, white.[92] Indeed, in the nineteenth and early twentieth centuries there were many so-called "white Negroes" on public display; Africans and African-Americans who suffered from albinism, and whose skin thus appeared more white than black, were a popular sideshow attraction.[93] This implied that white skin did not actually make the Irish, who were also referred to as "white Negroes," truly "white," particularly as their language—which in the 1840s and early '50s was a key marker of racial affiliation—was here cast as much more similar to African than to European dialects. Indeed, Dickens accentuated the cultural relationship between the Zulus and the Irish: "several of the scenes of savage life," he commented, "bear a strong generic resemblance to an Irish election, and I think would be extremely well received and understood at Cork."[94] The seemingly comic accounts of the relationship between the Irish and the Bushmen and Zulus in the 1840s and '50s thus drew on contemporary anthropological theories that stressed language and cultural difference rather than skin color and other biological traits as prime signifiers of racial otherness.[95]

These scientific theories that connected Africans and Irishmen were echoed in a variety of popular entertainments that reinforced the relationship between "Negro" and Irish cultures and bodies. The music hall emerged in the nineteenth century as a significant space for the popularization of racist and imperialist discourses,[96] most clearly through the genre of blackface minstrelsy, which was an integral part of the music hall lineup in Britain from the 1840s until well into the twentieth century. Blackface minstrelsy—the practice of white entertainers painting their faces with burnt cork to perform as "Negro delineators" or "Ethiopian serenaders"—tied African-Americans and the Irish together in important ways. Henry Mayhew documented in the 1850s and '60s that some of London's blackface street minstrels and clowns were in fact Irish.[97] Indeed, blackface minstrelsy was popular in Ireland, where performers often included indigenous Irish songs and dances in their programs.[98] Since the Celtic peoples had such a rich tradition of popular music and dance, this was an obvious source to draw on. But this syncretism also reinforced the relationship between different primitive forms of bodily movement.[99] While, as Belchem has argued, "emerald minstrelsy" allowed the Irish "to confirm their whiteness" while articulating their "ethnic difference,"[100] by drawing African-American and Irish dance forms together, blackface performances also, perhaps inadvertently, reinscribed assumptions about primitive bodily expression and the relationship between these groups.

Parallels between the comic stage "Negro" and the stage Irishman, the so-called "funny man of the empire," were also frequently drawn. The characters in the minstrel show—Jim Crow, the plantation slave, and Dandy Jim or Zip Coon, the northern swell—drew on the conventions of the stage Irishman, who was similarly distinguished by his "endless flow of illogical talk." Indeed, it is not hard to discern in the disheveled and ragged appearance of the stage Irishman, with his "idiotic grin," naïveté, and stupidity, the roots of the blackface clown.[101] This relationship was cemented over the course of the second half of the nineteenth century such that in 1896 a "Stage Strucked Darkey," who claimed to be of African descent, sought to perform as an Irish comedian and advertised in a music hall journal for appropriate songs and scenarios.[102]

If "the Celt" and "the Negro" functioned in the 1840s and '50s as interchangeable comic characters, they were equally bound together by the melodramatic, and politically salient, trope of the suffering slave. Douglas Riach has argued that the Irish identified with slaves as a similarly oppressed people, stripped of liberty and dignity. Indeed, Daniel O'Connell and other Irish political leaders repeatedly drew connections between the Irish peasantry and Jamaican plantation slaves.[103] The former American slave Frederick Douglass also articulated this comparison. Touring Ireland in 1845 he was struck by the similarity between plantation slaves and the gaunt, deformed bodies of famine victims, who, he maintained, sang plaintive songs of grief and sorrow. All the Irish lacked was "a black skin and wooly hair," Douglass noted, "to complete their likeness to the plantation Negro."[104] An English review of *Uncle Tom's Cabin* in 1852 drew attention to this relationship, noting "how constantly we are reminded both of the good and evil traits in the *Irish* character by the language and deportment of these sable gentlemen and ladies."[105] Indeed, in many of the countless contemporary stage versions of the novel, and when the novel was read out loud in domestic settings, cockney, Irish, and Scottish accents often substituted for "Negro dialects."[106]

The relationship between the bodies, languages, and cultures of the Irish and the "Negro" was thus well established in Britain by midcentury. While Miller had insisted that his Bushmen were authentic specimens, the popular interpretation of them as Irishmen in disguise reveals the ways in which popular culture and the new science of anthropology colluded to construct widespread assumptions about the relationship between Africans and Celts that in turn made possible the fairgrounds' ruse of the "blacked-up" Irish cannibal king. This relationship intensified over the course of the second half of the nineteenth century as scientific anthropology became a tool for the racialization of not only class but also ethnic difference, and as both Africans and the Irish came to be understood as violent peoples in need of subjugation.

By midcentury middle-class Victorians firmly believed in a racial hierarchy in which Anglo-Saxons were at the pinnacle of physical and cultural evolution and all other peoples either ranked lower on the monogenetic tree or, according to polygenesists, had developed from entirely separate and inferior origins.[107] In 1850 Robert Knox, a Scottish surgeon, published *The Races of Men,* in which he argued that the Saxon and the Celt were racially distinct and that the survival of British civilization depended upon the outcome of this racial struggle. The "source of all evil," Knox proclaimed, lay in "the Celtic race of Ireland," which, he argued, must be forced from English soil.[108] These beliefs were reinforced by scientific racism, which gained momentum throughout the second half of the nineteenth century. Scientific racism deployed anthropometrics, comparative anatomy, and composite photography rather than ethnographic explorations of linguistic and cultural difference to demonstrate the inferiority of non-Western peoples. In 1885 the anthropologist John Beddoe developed an "index of nigrescence" to scientifically distinguish "Africanoid Celts," a category that he invented to account for dark-haired Irish peoples who were descended from a racial group in North Africa, he claimed.[109] The scientific anthropology of the later nineteenth century was thus deployed to construct the Irish as a savage people that, like their African counterparts, required colonization.

The Irish were not merely cast as racially inferior, but they were often depicted as among the least evolved, or most degenerate, of the human species, depending on which anthropological theory was at play. As Curtis has argued, starting in the 1860s popular political cartoons depicted the Irish as closer to the apes than to the angels. This was a response to both the rise of Irish nationalist violence and the availability of the new discourse of Darwinian theory. Marrying the older science of physiognomy to the new theory of evolution, political cartoonists drew Irish bodies as apelike prognathous monstrosities. This established the Irish in the popular mind as an inferior people unfit for self-rule. Indeed, from the 1860s, which was marked by the rise of Fenian violence, the popular press depicted the Irish as a savage race that had more in common with African peoples than with their British neighbors. This simianizing of the Irish was a racial discourse in that it allied Celts to Africans through the figure of the ape. Much more so than the Irish, African peoples were in the age of Darwin frequently depicted as unevolved apelike peoples. Casting the Irish as monkeys was a way of signaling their savage and primitive natures and thus allying them to Africans. A Belgian political economist noted in 1880 that English newspapers never failed to represent the Irish as "white negroes." During the Home Rule crisis and the African wars of the 1880s, these links between the Irish and Africans grew more explicit: an 1881

Punch cartoon depicted an Irish nationalist beside a Zulu warrior in a wax-work exhibition of imperial troublemakers. An 1882 cartoon titled "The King of A-Shantee" linked the Irish peasant to the Ashanti tribe.[110]

The idea that the black body was really "green" underneath was perpetuated in the 1880s and '90s through showmen's use of Irishmen to portray Zulus at freak shows and fairgrounds. This practice was apparently so widespread in both the United States and Britain that an American naturalist felt compelled to testify that not all "Dime Museum Zulus were manufactured to order." The Zulus he saw on display were not, he claimed, "as some of the journalists have wickedly insinuated, Irish immigrants cunningly painted and made up like savages."[111] These sideshow Zulus, whether from Belfast or from Bloemfontein, were always exhibited with assegais (spears), shields, and knobkerries (wooden clubs). This focus on weaponry was widespread in the late nineteenth century. At ethnographic and international exhibitions and at the new anthropological museums, weapons occupied a central place in displays of African goods and artifacts. Their primitive but demonstrably effective weapons were seen as an integral element of Zulu society and considered to epitomize their violent, warlike natures.[112] This was particularly true in the late 1870s and 1880s, when the British suffered embarrassing defeats at the hands of Zulu warriors. When showmen staged displays of Zulu culture, then, they drew on the assegai or knobkerrie as a synecdoche of the savage African and capitalized on public demand for staged re-creations of famous battle scenes from recent colonial wars.[113]

No exhibition of Zulus, authentic or fake, seems to have been without a knobkerrie fight. Even Farini's "Friendly Zulus," exhibited in 1880, were advertised as enacting this type of battle scene, despite the fact that this clearly undermined the narrative of their friendly natures. Similarly, "Cetewayo's Daughters," also known as the "Zulu Princesses," although feminized and maternalized, were also pictured on their poster with a raised knobkerrie.[114] The similarity between the knobkerrie—a wooden baton—and the shillelagh—a billy club that the stage or cartoon Irishman was never without—would not have been lost on a British audience. The violent nature of the Zulus and their weapons of choice, then, invoked the trope of the "fighting Irish," who were never happier, the English consistently maintained, than with a raised shillelagh, midbattle.[115]

Rather than merely casting the Irish as an archaic people such as the Bushmen, this late Victorian staging of the relationship between the Irish and the Zulus emphasized the violence of Irish nationalism that had

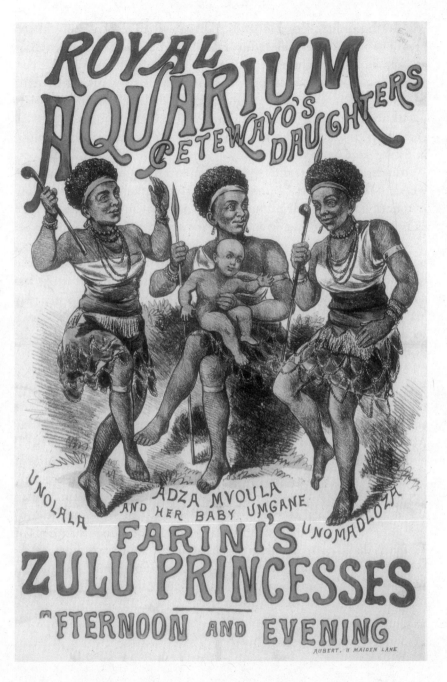

Figure 15. Poster for Cetewayo's Daughters, Royal Aquarium, Westminster, ca. 1882. ©British Library, Evanion Collection 341.

erupted in the late 1860s and 1880s and had evoked fears of vengeful savages. The knobkerrie/shillelagh parallel linked colonial savages at home and abroad by highlighting their threatening and violent natures. The performance of the knobkerrie fight was thus the freak show equivalent of the requisite, and gratuitous, shillelagh fight in the plethora of popular plays on Irish themes. Both served to justify Britain's use of force in colonial encounters, for they established that the "natives" were not only primitive but savage and dangerous.

Irish performers were thus regularly employed to play sideshow savages, whether "Red Indians," Bushmen, or Zulus, because of long-standing assumptions about their primitive, wild, and violent natures. Showmen cast them in these roles, and audiences allowed themselves to be deceived, because the ruse reinforced widespread beliefs about the racial inferiority of Irish people and, conversely, the whiteness of other Britons. The racial representations evident in these shows made it possible for working-class audiences to enjoy themselves alongside middle-class spectators precisely because these performances enabled "Anglo-Saxons" to distinguish themselves from the savage but subjugated "Africanoid Celt" and imagine instead that they were members of an imperial ruling race.

A successful savage show thus relied much less on an "authentic" body than it did on a choreographed performance that was framed by a familiar narrative and conformed to stereotypes of savage behavior and appearance. The use of the working class, and the Irish in particular, to portray Africans at sideshows was both dependent upon and contributed to already widespread beliefs about the relationship between the categories of class, ethnicity, and race. While most audience members were probably not fooled by the fraudulent acts, they could nevertheless be entertained and reassured by their messages, perhaps more so than by authentic exhibitions. For this particular artifice was predicated on understandings of otherness that allowed members of even a mixed-class British audience, far from the sinews of parliamentary power, to participate in the production and reinforcement of imperial ideologies and identities.

CONCLUSION

The Decline of the Freak Show

THE FREAK SHOW NO LONGER exists in Britain as a cultural institution. There is no equivalent to the Sideshows by the Seashore at Coney Island, which has kept the tradition alive in the United States. In fact, by the late twentieth century the British public had deemed the exhibition of human anomalies inappropriate, indecent, and indefensible. When referred to at all in late twentieth- and early twenty-first century discourse, the freak show has been widely condemned as a product of "the worst traditions of Victorian ghoulishness," an institution that inhabited "the backwaters of civilisation in the nineteenth century."[1] The freak show's seemingly inevitable demise has become part of a new national narrative of moral progress, multiculturalism, and civil rights. Britons in the new millennium have begun explicitly to construct their identities by distancing themselves from what is now seen as the more reprehensible "excesses and ignorances of [their] Victorian ancestors."[2] But the disappearance of freakery from British culture was a gradual process caused not only by the rise of "political correctness" but also by a variety of other factors. These included changes in attitudes toward deformity triggered by the First World War; the introduction of legislation that restricted the employment of foreign laborers; the emergence of the beauty industry; advances in medicine; and the rise of the disability rights movement, all of which significantly affected the British public's willingness to ogle Others.

The freak show's decline began in the second decade of the twentieth century. Although many show shops, seaside resorts, and freak museums continued to flourish until well after the Second World War, the end of the Edwardian period was also the end of an era for human oddities. In 1910 *World's Fair* remarked mournfully that there had been a "steady slump in the human freak market for the last three or four years." Quoting an "old showman," it maintained that "you couldn't get sixpence a head now for the turtleboy, the bearded lady and the two-headed girl combined."[3] Indeed, its own classified advertisements reveal a gradual decline in the demand for freak exhibits.

In part this was because tastes were changing. As early as the late nineteenth century showmen themselves had begun to distinguish between exhibitions that they felt were merely prurient and those that could be deemed tasteful. In 1898 *The Era,* the most important journal of the late nineteenth-century entertainment industry, printed an advertisement for "High Class Freaks and Monstrosities," suggesting that some human oddities were considered more refined than others.[4] A few weeks later, however, *The Encore,* a music hall and theatrical review, published an article denouncing freak shows in general. "Barnum and Bailey's freaks are neither funny nor interesting, entertaining or elevating," it opined. "To make a public exhibition of these poor things is horrible," it continued, "and to go see them displays a low form of mind"; audiences should be spared "the horror of seeing Nature's misfits," the article insisted.[5] By the 1920s this type of critique appears to have been widespread. In a book celebrating the fairgrounds published in 1929, Kenneth Grahame—best known as the author of *The Wind in the Willows*—commented that perhaps "the greatest change that has taken place in show-life in our generation is the disappearance of freaks and monstrosities." "It will surely be agreed by all," he concluded, that this "is a change entirely for good."[6] Even the clown Whimsical Walker—who had spent the better part of his life dedicated to shows and circuses—declared in his 1922 memoir that "the taste for freaks and monstrosities once so marked a characteristic of the British sightseer has disappeared. If so, it is hardly to be regretted."[7]

The vague sense that freaks were somehow indecent was beginning to dominate at least middle-class morality in the early twentieth century and eventually translated into government action. In 1907 the London County Council (LCC), responsible for overseeing the licensing of entertainment venues in the capital, decided that freaks would no longer be allowed to be exhibited at the Earl's Court exhibition grounds due to their "objectionable" nature.[8] Mr. Hart, who managed the London Exhibition Buildings at Earl's Court, did not protest this ruling. Although he insisted that freaks were not "in any sense indecent," such attractions, he agreed, were "not up to the high class standard that obtains at Earl's Court."[9] The showman Tom Norman argued that the formation of the LCC in 1889 had, in fact, led directly to the decline of the freak show. He remembered an old show-man predicting the change about to take place when the LCC began to license venues. "When it does," he asserted, "your and my occupation is gone." As far as the show shops were concerned, Norman maintained, "he was right, those that do not believe me, just test it in one shop alone, why you would get closed up, before you got open."[10] Similarly, circus entre-preneurs complained that excessive national and local regulations pertain-ing to public safety, cruelty to animals, and labor in general were sounding the death knell of the British big top.[11]

If the active policing of popular recreations, which had begun in earnest in the early nineteenth century, contributed to the decay of these types of exhibitions, so too did natural market trends in the leisure industry.[12] *World's Fair* suggested that the waning of the freak show, while "partly owing to the change in public taste," was also a product of "the slow but sure extinction of the old showman by the increase in music halls and the-atres throughout the country."[13] Seasonal fairs and itinerant shows had gone into sharp decline by 1850, and over the course of the late nineteenth century they were replaced by more permanent venues for popular enter-tainments. In 1874 Thomas Frost, writing on the closing of the fairs, noted the parallel rise of music halls, theaters, aquariums, and zoological gardens in the major British cities, which had become easily accessible even to those in smaller towns because of the expansion of the railways. The fairs were becoming "extinct," he argued, for "with the progress of the nation, they have ceased to posses any value in the social economy, either as marts of trade or as means of popular amusement." The nation had outgrown the fairs, he argued, and the "last showman will soon be as great a curios-ity as the dodo."[14]

Although some fairs have survived to the present day, the rise of music halls, zoos, aquariums, and other urban entertainments did contribute to the collapse of many fairgrounds, which had been key sites for human oddities. But these new venues were not *always* detrimental to freak shows, as they provided new spaces for these types of performances. Although the circus also created new opportunities for freak performers, the arrival of the American big top did negatively impact smaller independent freak shows. By the turn of the century the Barnum and Bailey Circus had become an annual feature of the London Christmas season. Because Barnum and Bailey could offer steady, well-paid work not only in the United Kingdom but in Europe and North America as well, this circus show began to monopolize the freak market. According to A. St. John Adcock, writing in 1902, "good live freaks gravitate to Barnum's nowadays unless a minor showman is lucky enough to hear of them in time and intercept them." This meant, Adcock maintained, that living freaks (as opposed to waxworks and "pickled punks"—preserved still births and the like) were becoming scarce outside the major circuses, even in London.[15]

These shifts in the leisure market altered the nature and prevalence of displays of anomalous bodies, but it was the cinema—which became the most important form of popular culture in the years after the First World War—that permanently displaced the freak show in the public's affection.[16] Even before British soldiers crossed the Channel, the cinematograph machine had invaded not only the theaters but also fairground booths, replacing the human prodigies with moving pictures.[17] In 1898 the *Hull News,* reporting on the local fair, remarked that this new form of public entertainment was taking over the show booths.[18] Consumer demand for these astonishing new moving pictures spelled demise for the no-longer novel "novelties" that had been such a draw in the nineteenth century.

By the 1930s, not only had the cinema driven the freak show to the margins of popular culture, but in the process it had absorbed its monsters, thus rendering exhibitions of human oddities obsolete. Audiences were still demanding to be frightened by abnormal bodies, but these no longer appeared in the form of the "freak of nature." Rather, by the 1930s horror movies had emerged as a popular cinematic genre. These films featured fantasy monsters that, like freaks, tapped into a variety of cultural anxieties that were being played out at the site of the deformed body. But these monsters were clearly imaginative creations that audience members knew they would never actually encounter. They were thus in many ways less frightening and less socially disruptive than freaks, whose very real transgressive bodies could be seen in the flesh and actually touched; freaks were so real, in fact—in the barker's patter, so "alive!"—that they might in fact touch one back. When Tod Browning's film *Freaks*—which featured an all-star cast of sideshow novelties—crossed the Atlantic in 1932, the British Board of Film Censors banned it. Feeling no need to offer an elaborate explanation, they maintained simply that its depiction of "revolting monstrosities" was inappropriate for British audiences.[19] Although they were not without controversy, neither Browning's 1931 version of *Dracula* nor James Whale's *Frankenstein* (released in Britain in 1932) met the same fate. Indeed, they were wildly popular with both the public and film critics, suggesting that the desire for deformity that had been fed by the freak show had not entirely disappeared. Rather, it was displaced onto new types of monsters and a new mode of consuming corporeal abnormalities. Horror movies thus replaced freak shows as a mean through which the threat that anomalous bodies posed to the social body could be managed.[20]

While it is often difficult to track transformations in taste or morality or to account for the capriciousness of consumer desire, as these types of cultural shifts rarely have a single root cause, the cataclysmic events of the First World War immediately wrought changes to the ways in which British audiences engaged with freakery. This was both because the war triggered changes to the entertainment industry that had long-term effects and because it compelled British society to engage with physical deformity in new ways. During World War I the War Office took control over several major exhibition venues, including the resort and theme park of Kursaal at Southend-on-Sea and the Crystal Palace in Sydenham, which was transformed into a Royal Navy depot.[21] Horses, steam engines, and other staples of the fairground were also commissioned by the government, which led to a steady decline in itinerant shows during the war. The government encouraged the closing of fairs and shows that detracted from war work, seeking to prioritize the production of munitions and discourage leisure activities. While showmen fought hard to sustain the fairs, the war took its toll. Human and animal acts in particular went into sharp decline, surviving primarily within the context of the circus.[22]

Perhaps more significantly, the war also led to new understandings of deformity and the development of the category of "the disabled." The widespread use of the term *the disabled* in Britain can be dated to the First World War. It initially referred almost exclusively to those wounded in the war, as medical practitioners, charitable institutions, and government officials began to address the care and employment of injured veterans. "Disabled," the *Oxford English Dictionary* maintains, in this context designates a status conferred by the state that entitles an individual to certain rights and privileges. This special status was bestowed on the war-wounded, who could make claims on the state because they had sacrificed their bodily integrity in service to the country.[23] Unlike those who had had the misfortune to be born with nonstandard and sometimes less than fully functional bodies, or who had suffered an injury, "the disabled" could demand preferential treatment in employment, housing, medical care, and other social services. The category of "the disabled" thus did not replace either "the cripple" or "the freak" because it was coterminous with the war-wounded. In fact, however parsimonious the British government actually was with respect to maimed former servicemen, from the very early years of the war public opinion strongly supported their right to demand state compensation for bodily losses.[24] This suggests that the British public as well as the state itself acknowledged and established a social and legal distinction between "the disabled" and all others who inhabited nonstandard bodies.

Those who performed as freaks, therefore, were not subsumed under the new category of "the disabled." Indeed, the distinction between disabled veterans and others with bodily deformities not only remained, but in many ways it intensified during the interwar period in Britain. In Germany, Herr Unthan, "the Armless Wonder," gave lectures and presentations to soldiers who had lost limbs during the war and wrote a small book for "war cripples" on how to adjust to a new life without arms. He eventually received a Red Cross Medal and a Medal for Distinguished Service to the Country from the German government for his role in the war effort.[25] In Britain, however, sideshow performers' expertise at living with atypical bodies was never called upon to help rehabilitate amputees. In fact, rather than enjoying new services or opportunities in the aftermath of World War I, those born with anomalous bodies saw a marginalization of "the cripple," "the infirm," "the handicapped," and others whose bodies had been compromised or injured other than in military service. Although in the end the British government actually provided very few services and benefits to disabled ex-servicemen, leaving voluntary associations to fill this need,[26] the civilian population who were armless or legless, for example, fared even worse. This was in part because any governmental or charitable funds available were channeled primarily toward "war cripples." But it was also because their ability to earn money through their own exhibition was severely hampered by the decline of the freak show in the wake of the emergence of new attitudes toward bodily deformity that the war had itself provoked.

The visibility of injured soldiers within almost every British community, and the widespread desire on the part of both the public and Parliament to valorize these bodies as a way to manage the trauma engendered by the war, seems to have rendered displays of deformity unseemly and inappropriate in the 1920s.[27] But even these shifts were gradual. A careful examination of showmen's journals published during the war and its immediate aftermath suggests that despite the sudden and pervasive presence of war amputees, the British public did not immediately sour on armless and legless entertainers. These performers continued to advertise their acts and were sought after by venue managers throughout the war years.[28] Over the long run, however, these types of exhibitions clearly became less common, as the British public struggled to incorporate large numbers of the war-wounded back into families, communities, and society more generally. Indeed, by the end of the First World War, however marginal they were within British society, the physically deformed could no longer be comfortably "othered," for they were undeniably sons, fathers, husbands, brothers, fellow citizens, and even national heroes.

If the war forever altered the nation's relationship to the deformed body, it also brought about changes to the labor market that significantly affected the exhibition of freaks. In the interwar period government officials intent on policing the borders of the United Kingdom and controlling the slumping economy attempted to curtail the importation of foreign workers. The 1920 Aliens Order had specified that noncitizens could enter the United Kingdom only if they had a work permit issued by the Ministry of Labour, which supplied these permits only for jobs that no British workers could fill. Since the freak show had always been a cosmopolitan space, peopled by performers from around the world, these new government initiatives to clamp down on alien workers necessarily impacted British exhibitions of human oddities.

In 1927 Bertram Mills—whose circus shows at Olympia were extremely popular—won his case for the importation of twelve foreign freaks, but only after significant debate. The Home Office officials who examined the case clearly hoped to find some basis to deny their entrance but found this position difficult to sustain. Mills drew on both humanitarian and labor arguments when pleading his case, stressing that without this kind of work, "people of abnormal weight, height, and colour" might become "a serious handicap to their families." He also maintained that he had tried to staff his show entirely with domestic performers but had found that of "the suitable English abnormal people" who chose to make their living through exhibitions, only six were currently in the United Kingdom, as most found that they could make more money in the United States or on the Continent. He assured the government that he would be entirely responsible for his employees once they had entered the country, and that his own willingness to pay their high salaries was evidence that these were not "undesirable people" but rather unique and skilled performers.

This application placed the government in a difficult situation. On the one hand, it was compelled to defend the rights of British workers and to restrict the importation of foreign laborers; on the other, denying work permits to these performers meant acknowledging the presence of British freaks. By claiming that there were only half a dozen British freaks available, Mills was able to capitalize on the more comfortable location of the abnormal body outside the boundaries of the nation. That he needed to import human oddities—and was eventually allowed to do so—reassured a state still recovering from the trauma of World War I that the modern British body was healthy, whole, and normal.

Mills won his case in part by appealing to these nationalist understandings of the fitness and normality of the British body. Three years later, in 1930, however, the government revisited the issue when W. W. Lennard, secretary of the London section of the Showmen's Guild, applied to import nine foreign freaks, all of whom had been previously admitted for the Mills show. The Ministry of Labour—which sought to prevent the importation of alien workers—argued that the salaries the foreign freaks were paid were not high enough to suggest that their talents were of any "exceptional merit." They did not, however, claim that there were domestic freaks who could do the job. Instead, they merely raised the specter of foreign freaks settling in United Kingdom, the implication being that they could cause trouble, become a burden on the state, or—worse still—breed. Problems of repatriation frequently arose when foreign freaks were admitted, the Ministry of Labour argued, and thus it was undesirable to allow this to continue. Seeking support for this decision, the Ministry of Labour approached the Home Office. The Aliens Branch strongly supported the Ministry of Labour's attempt to curtail the presence of foreign (particularly German and Austrian) performers, maintaining that it was time to put a stop to the issuing of permits for "alien freaks," as their itinerant nature made them difficult to control and to trace. There was no reason, one official maintained, why "alien abnormalities" should be considered essential to British shows.

But underlying this concern to control the entry of foreigners and to ensure that they did not compete with British workers was a moral argument that freak performers were, if not obscene, at least improper. "It does not seem desireable [sic]," the Aliens Branch maintained, "to have aliens of this description drifting round the country—one is described as a boy with a bird's head, another as an elephant girl, another as a paradox girl, and yet another as a half lady." Exactly what was improper about these particular acts remained unspoken, and indeed the government officials who commented on both cases, though clearly desirous of limiting the admittance of foreign freaks, were unclear on what basis they could be denied entry. Several people who reviewed the Mills case had declared that "these poor brutes do no good to our people," that they had a "demoralizing effect," or were in some way not "wholesome." But despite the fact that freaks were not "to everyone's taste," the government had ruled in favor of Mills's application, declaring that those who were not "indecent, repulsive, or likely to bring in some disease" could not legally be restricted entry. That Lennard lost his appeal a mere three years later suggests that moral discomfort with the freak show was intensifying in the interwar period, and was in fact helping to shape the laws pertaining to foreign workers. Despite the fact that no one in the government wanted "the invidious duty of discriminating between degrees of 'freakishness' e.g. midgets, giants and half ladies"—and thus, by implication, degrees of propriety—the Home Office decided henceforth to deal with each case on its merits, thus overturning their previous decision.[29]

If issues of propriety and morality emerged in discussions over what was essentially a legal issue around rights to labor, so too did the issue of beauty. The discourses of bodily beauty were newly important in the 1920s, as the early twentieth century saw the rise of a consumer culture focused on the perfection of the body. In the 1840s the British public had been under the thrall of what *Punch* had termed the "deformito-mania": flocks of people thronged to see the human exhibits at what it had sarcastically termed "the Hall of Ugliness." Indeed, the journal continued, if *"Beauty and the Beast* should be brought into competition in London, at the present day, *Beauty* would stand no chance against the *Beast* in the race for popularity."[30] But the same could not be said in 1920s. It was during this period that the beauty and cosmetic industries became fully commercialized and began to cater to a mass consumer public.[31] Indeed, by the 1920s and '30s the demand for more physically attractive bodies had led not only to the proliferation of temporary remedies for gray hair or thin lips but also to an explosion in the market for aesthetic surgery.[32]

In his 1927 request for work permits for his foreign freaks, Mills had attempted to distinguish between bodies that were unattractive and those that were merely unusual. "I have always refused applications from physically abnormal people who were really freaks of nature of a repulsive type," he asserted, claiming he tried only to "engage those that are attractive as well as being abnormal." Providing photographs of the individuals in question, Mills carefully detailed the physical appearance of each performer, arguing that "there is nothing repulsive" about them, and that "they will not exhibit themselves in any way that would be repulsive." When not actually performing, he claimed, many of these people would attract little attention on the street. The bearded woman's beard was "imperceptible" while she wore a fur coat; similarly, the elastic-skinned man, he proclaimed, looked "absolutely normal" when not stretching his skin. Mills felt obliged to assuage fears about the attractiveness of his performers because, while this was technically a legal matter, it was the respectability of the freak show itself that troubled the government officials reviewing the case. This seemed to hinge at least in part on the beauty of the performers rather than on the precise nature of their physical anomalies. One government official wrote (presumably sarcastically) on Mills's file that the freaks were "good looking" and had "nice hair," comments that underscore the centrality of beauty to debates over the propriety of looking at difference.[33] These concerns suggest that by the end of the 1920s the government's sensibilities were in line with "the public taste," which, according to Kenneth Grahame writing in 1929, "no longer demand[ed] to be disgusted."[34]

In a climate in which the distinction that Mills had attempted to uphold between anomalousness on the one hand and ugliness on the other had ultimately collapsed, disfigurement necessarily became recategorized. No longer associated primarily with rare congenital anomalies, even a longer-than-average nose could be classified as a "deformity" that required medical attention, which was now made more widely available.[35] The idea that even the slightest imperfection could, and therefore should, be corrected by cosmetic surgery epitomizes not only the emergence of a consumer culture focused on the beautiful body, but also the twentieth century's pathologization of many forms of physical difference. Writing in 1971 the showman Duncan Dallas maintained that the only freaks remaining "have been narrowed down to dwarfs, giants and very fat or very thin people. It is doubtful whether any showman today would exhibit the unfortunate medical specimens of the previous two centuries, like the elephant man."[36] That this late twentieth-century showman himself interpreted "the Elephant Man" as essentially a "medical specimen" reveals the extent to which the medical model of difference had taken root in the twentieth century even among show folk. This recasting of corporeal deviations as pathologies made the propriety of the freak show highly questionable, as it suggested that those on exhibit were in fact afflicted with a medical condition. This interpretation had consistently been resisted by performers and showmen in the nineteenth and early twentieth centuries, precisely because it appears to have been generally established that it was inappropriate and impolite to stare at those who were sick and thus presumed to be suffering.

This gradual medicalization of freakish bodies was, as I have argued, well under way in the Victorian period. Medical practitioners such as Frederick Treves and John Bland Sutton used the freak show to access medical research subjects and began to construct anomalous bodies as diseased rather than as merely deviating from the norm. Indeed, in the early twentieth century freak performers suffering from the slow decline of the market for human anomalies began to sell their bodies to medical professionals for the purposes of research in order to make ends meet. A showman interviewed in *World's Fair* in 1910 maintained that since the public demand for freaks had waned in recent years, the only way for a freak to make a living was "with the doctors." In an article titled "Doctors Buy Freaks," he maintained that "nowadays people don't seem to care about looking at monstrosities, and unless you are a giant and can get a job outside a public-house as a chucker-out, or a dwarf, whom some kind lady will adopt as a page-boy, it seems to me that the only way for a freak to earn a living now is with the doctors . . . by selling yourself to the medical profession, in order that they may study your deformity."[37]

The long process of acquiring both the technological know-how and the cultural authority to define what made one body normal and another abnormal—and thus, in the age of medicalization, by definition diseased—was thus intimately bound up in the institution of the freak show. The freak show's decline, as the author of "Doctors Buy Freaks" suggested, may in fact have benefited the medical profession, since it provided the doctors with more willing "medical specimens." Indeed, in the period after the Second World War, medical knowledge about and the ability to treat both the symptoms and the root causes of many congenital deformities expanded. With the legalization of therapeutic abortion in Britain after 1967, and with the parallel emergence of the new technologies of ultrasound and other forms of fetal imaging and monitoring in the 1960s, bodily anomalies could now not only be cured or treated but even entirely eliminated. The freak show was all but dead by the 1970s, then, in large part because the medical profession could both correct what they had relabeled "birth defects" and terminate anomalous fetuses before they were even born. Ironically, then, freaks contributed to their own demise by furnishing doctors with the knowledge necessary to engineer them out of existence.

Those individuals whose anomalous bodies either survived prenatal detection or could not effectively be treated have often been socially marginalized, despite the state's best efforts to provide them with care. Duncan Dallas argued that the healthcare policies of the welfare state introduced in the 1940s ultimately undermined British society's ability to engage with corporeal difference and incorporate people with serious abnormalities into the social body. There used to be "plenty of fat ladies, tattooed ladies, armless men, midgets, dwarfs, etc.," commented Dallas. "But today, in a welfare state," he continued, "you never hear anything about these people." Those who in another age would have been exhibited as freaks, and thus publicly visible, now "seem to be smothered," he maintained. "They seem to be kept out of the way in the background."[38] Instead of seeing the welfare state as leading only to improvements in the health and well-being of the general public, Dallas feared that it had merely led to a rise in the institutionalization, and thus the further marginalization, of those born with unusual bodies.

In reaction to these "advances" in both medicine and social policy, an emerging disability rights movement in the 1970s began to campaign against the practices of "enforced normalization" (such as the use of cochlear implants for the hearing impaired), the institutionalization of the physically and mentally impaired, and selective abortion, which they condemned as a type of eugenics or even genocide, which would exterminate those with nonstandard bodies.[39] Building on the claims of other civil rights movements, which aimed to eliminate discrimination based on sex or race, disability rights activists argued that, rather than eliminating the disabled from the community, accommodations needed to be made to allow those with differently abled bodies equal access to all the rights and privileges of citizenship. Crucially, these activists redefined "the disabled" to include not only those injured in service to the state but all members of society born with or who acquired bodily anomalies that compromised their ability to function within the dominant social context and built environment. Their use of the term *TABs*—temporarily able-bodied—to refer to those individuals who considered themselves "normal" highlighted the fact that the categories of "disabled" and "able-bodied" were always unstable. Unlike sex or race, disability is "an identity category that anyone can enter at any time," either as the result of an accident or through the process of aging.[40] Conversely, technology might make the seemingly disabled not only able-bodied but perhaps even stronger, faster, or more agile than TABs themselves. By 1995, with the passage of the Disability Discrimination Act, disability rights advocates had successfully lobbied Britain's welfare state to provide all of its citizens, temporarily able-bodied or not, with equal employment and educational opportunities, as well as access to housing, goods, services, public and private space, and transport.

This understanding of disability that resists the "othering" of those with bodies that deviate from the norm and at least attempts to accommodate them within the dominant culture has reshaped British society and in turn encouraged a widespread condemnation of the exhibition of human oddities—both physical and cultural—as fundamentally exploitative. By the last decades of the twentieth century, at the very latest, British public opinion had therefore pronounced the freak show a sordid institution, a product of the seedy and sensational side of the nineteenth century that gave birth to Jack the Ripper, the trade in pornography, and "the shilling shocker." This interpretation cast the Victorians as regressive rather than modern, barbaric rather than civilized, and vulgar rather than refined, intimating that there exists a wide gulf between this uncomfortable but distant chapter in the nation's past and current and seemingly more progressive attitudes toward both the physically disabled and people of color.

This pervasive and reproving discourse that separates Us from Them, however, is really just an extension of the cultural work of the Victorian and Edwardian freak show. These shows were, above all else, about exploring and making meaning out of exactly these types of binaries that had structured nineteenth- and early twentieth-century society and which have had complicated legacies in contemporary Britain. But if one moves beyond these simplistic narratives that presuppose that freaks could only ever be victims of exploitation or objects of derision to a more nuanced analysis of the social function of spectacles of deformity, the freak show emerges as much more than a skeleton best left undisturbed in the closet of Britain's past. Rather, it was a significant cultural institution that was both explicitly and implicitly engaged in producing and reproducing ideas about the nation and the self at a key moment in the making of modernity.

The freak show illuminates one of the ways in which British citizens and subjects came to understand themselves in relation to a wide range of Others and thus how they negotiated their roles within the hierarchical structure of imperial British society. As the case studies in this book have demonstrated, freak performances forced into the public sphere a discussion of where the boundaries between sexes, races, classes, species, nations, and civilizations could be drawn and how and why these distinctions should be upheld. Freak shows, however prurient they might seem in retrospect, thus served an important social purpose: they provided a forum for reinforcing, but also for interrogating and sometimes challenging, the classificatory schemata that became central to the making of modern and imperial culture.

NOTES

INTRODUCTION

1. "A Collection of Handbills, Newspaper Cuttings, and Other Items, 1820–96," G.R.2.5.7, opposite 24, Guildhall Library.

2. "Freak, n.1," *Oxford English Dictionary*, 2d ed., 1989, *OED Online*, Oxford University Press, 25 July 2008, http://dictionary.oed.com.tproxy01.lib.utah.edu/cgi/entry/50089602; Robert Aguirre, *Informal Empire* (Minneapolis: University of Minnesota, 2005), 107; Marlene Tromp and Karyn Valerius, "Introduction" to *Victorian Freaks: The Social Context of Freakery in Britain*, ed. Marlene Tromp (Columbus: Ohio State University Press, 2008), 1.

3. Laura Lunger Knoppers and Joan B. Landes, eds., *Monstrous Bodies/Political Monstrosities in Early Modern Europe* (Ithaca, NY: Cornell University Press, 2004); Kathryn M. Brammall, "Monstrous Metamorphosis: Nature, Morality, and the Rhetoric of Monstrosity in Tudor England," *Sixteenth Century Journal* 27(1) (1996): 3–21; Jorge Flores, "Distant Wonders: The Strange and the Marvelous Between Mughal India and Habsburg Iberia in the Early Seventeenth Century," *Comparative Studies in Society and History* 49(3) (2007): 553–81; Kevin Stagg, "Representing Physical Difference: The Materiality of the Monstrous," in *Social Histories of Disability and Deformity*, ed. David M. Turner and Kevin Stagg (London: Routledge, 2006), 19–38; Julie Crawford, *Marvelous Protestantism: Monstrous Births in Post-Reformation England* (Baltimore, MD: Johns Hopkins University Press, 2005).

4. A. W. Bates, *Emblematic Monsters: Unnatural Conceptions and Deformed Births in Early Modern Europe* (Amsterdam: Rodopi, 2005), 15, 147.

5. Kathryn A. Hoffman, "Sutured Bodies: Counterfeit Marvels in Early-Modern Europe," *Seventeenth-Century French Studies* 24 (2002): 57–70.

6. Paul Semonin, "Monsters in the Marketplace: The Exhibition of Human Anomalies in Early Modern England," in *Freakery: Cultural Spectacles of the Extraordinary Body,* ed. Rosemarie Garland Thomson (New York: New York University Press, 1996), 69–81; Robert M. Isherwood, "Entertainment in the Parisian Fairs in the Eighteenth Century," *Journal of Modern History* 53(1) (1981): 24–48.

7. Anthony Anemone, "The Monsters of Peter the Great: The Culture of the St. Petersburg Kunstkamera in the Eighteenth Century," *Slavic and East European Journal* 44(4) (2000): 583–602.

8. Tromp and Valerius, "Introduction," 1.

9. Leslie Fiedler, *Freaks: Myths and Images of the Secret Self* (New York: Simon and Schuster, 1978).

10. Jami Moss, " 'A Body of Organized Truth': Freaks in Britain, 1830–1900," PhD diss., University of Wisconsin–Madison, 1999, 22.

11. James Twitchell, *Dreadful Pleasures: An Anatomy of Modern Horror* (Oxford: Oxford University Press, 1985); Marlene Tromp, "Empire and the Indian Freak: The 'Miniature Man' from Cawnpore and the 'Marvellous Indian Boy' on Tour in England," in Tromp, *Victorian Freaks,* 176; Rosemarie Garland Thomson, "Freakery Unfurled," in Tromp, *Victorian Freaks,* xi; Crawford, *Marvelous Protestantism,* 1–26.

12. Judith Halberstam, *Skin Shows: Gothic Horror and the Technology of Monsters* (Durham, NC: Duke University Press, 1995), 21.

13. Roger Lund, "Laughing at Cripples: Ridicule, Deformity and the Argument from Design," *Eighteenth-Century Studies* 39(1) (2005): 91–114.

14. Matt Houlbrook, " 'The Man with the Powder Puff' in Interwar London," *The Historical Journal* 50(1) (2007): 165.

15. Semonin, "Monsters in the Marketplace," 78.

16. Henry Morley, *Memoirs of Bartholomew Fair* (London: Frederick Warne and Co., 1874 [1859]), 246.

17. Thomas Frost, *The Old Showmen and the Old London Fairs* (London: Tinsley Brothers, 1874), 60.

18. Diana Snigurowicz, "The Phenomène's Dilemma: Teratology and the Policing of Human Anomalies in Nineteenth- and Early Twentieth-Century Paris," in *Foucault and the Government of Disability,* ed. Shelley Tremain (Ann Arbor: University of Michigan Press, 2005), 172–88.

19. Neil McKendrick, John Brewer, and J. H. Plumb, eds., *The Birth of a Consumer Society* (Bloomington: Indiana University Press, 1982); John Brewer and Roy Porter, *Consumption and the World of Goods* (London: Routledge, 1994); Richard D. Altick, *The Shows of London* (Cambridge: Belknap Press, 1978);

Hugh Cunningham, *Leisure in the Industrial Revolution c. 1780–1880* (London: Croom Helm, 1980); James Walvin, *Leisure and Society, 1830–1950* (London: Longman, 1978); Peter Bailey, *Leisure and Class in Victorian England: Rational Recreation and the Contest for Control, 1830–1885* (London: Routledge and Kegan Paul, 1987).

20. Julia V. Douthwaite, *The Wild Girl, Natural Man, and the Monster: Dangerous Experiments in the Age of Enlightenment* (Chicago: University of Chicago Press, 2002), 48.

21. Vanessa Toulmin, "'Curios Things in Curios Places': Temporary Exhibition Venues in the Victorian and Edwardian Entertainment Environment," *Early Popular Visual Culture* 4(2) (2006): 113–37.

22. Montagu Williams, *Round London: Down East and Up West* (London: Macmillan and Co., 1894), 6–11. A similar freak museum on the Whitechapel Road makes an appearance in Margaret Harkness's 1889 novel, *Captain Lobe: A Story of the Salvation Army*. This book was originally published as *In Darkest London* under the pseudonym John Law.

23. Barbara Benedict actually dates the concept of curiosity to the period between 1660 and 1820. See her *Curiosity: A Cultural History of Early Modern Inquiry* (Chicago: University of Chicago Press, 2001). For Victorian curiosity see Brenda Assael, *The Circus and Victorian Society* (Charlottesville: University of Virginia Press, 2005); Thomas Richards, *The Commodity Culture of Victorian England* (Stanford, CA: Stanford University Press, 1990).

24. Robert W. Malcolmson, *Popular Recreations in English Society, 1700–1850* (Cambridge: Cambridge University Press, 1973), 15–33; Douglas A. Reid, "Interpreting the Festival Calendar: Wakes and Fairs as Carnivals," in *Popular Culture and Custom in Nineteenth-Century England,* ed. Robert D. Storch (London: Croom Helm, 1982).

25. P. T. Barnum, *Struggles and Triumphs* (Buffalo, NY: The Courier Company, 1875), 508. Fish's daughter became Barnum's second wife several years later.

26. "Miss C. Heenan," Broadsides BF 24b/65, Wellcome Library; Playbills Folder (Miscellaneous): American Museum, Guildhall Library; Playbills Folder (Miscellaneous): Ferguson's, Guildhall Library; Playbills Folder (Miscellaneous): Linwood Gallery, Guildhall Library; "A Collection of Handbills," 92; Evanion 827 and 1398, British Library.

27. Erika Rappaport, *Shopping for Pleasure* (Princeton, NJ: Princeton University Press, 2000); Judith Walkowitz, *City of Dreadful Delight* (Chicago: University of Chicago Press, 1992).

28. "P. T. Barnum's Greatest Show on Earth Programme," Olympia, November, ca. 1889, 2, Barnum Folder, Circus Box, Guildhall Library.

29. Judith Walkowitz, "The 'Vision of Salome': Cosmopolitanism and Erotic Dancing in Central London, 1908–1918," *American Historical Review* 108(2) (2003): 336–76.

30. "P. T. Barnum's Greatest Show on Earth Programme," 2.

31. Playbills Folder (Miscellaneous): Linwood Gallery, Guildhall Library.

32. "Patronized by the Faculty," 50274/D, Wellcome Library.

33. Evanion 1505, British Library. For a discussion of marketing respectability, see Heather McHold, "Even as You and I: Freak Shows and Lay Discourse on Spectacular Deformity" in Tromp, *Victorian Freaks,* 26.

34. [Thomas] Whimsical Walker, *From Sawdust to Windsor Castle* (London: Stanley Paul and Co., 1922), 60–61.

35. Timothy Neil has noted that human freaks often appeared alongside both normal and freakish animal exhibits, thus further troubling the presumed divide between human and animal. See his "White Wings and Six-Legged Muttons: The Freakish Animal," in Tromp, *Victorian Freaks,* 60–75.

36. Elizabeth Stephens, "Twenty-First Century Freak Show: Recent Transformations in the Exhibition of Non-Normative Bodies," *Disability Studies Quarterly* 25(3) 2005, www.dsq-sds.org/_articles_html/2005/summer/stephens.asp, 7.

37. Rosemarie Garland Thomson, "Preface" and "Introduction" to Thomson, *Freakery,* xviii, 7; see also Robert Bogdan, *Freak Show* (Chicago: University of Chicago Press, 1988), 3.

38. Elizabeth Stephens, "Cultural Fixions of the Freak Body: Coney Island and the Postmodern Sideshow," *Continuum: Journal of Media & Cultural Studies* 20(4) (2006): 487.

39. Arthur Goddard, "'EVEN AS YOU AND I' At Home with the Barnum Freaks," Human Freaks Box 4, John Johnson Collection, Oxford University.

40. "Miss Julia Pastrana, The Nondescript," Human Freaks Box 2, John Johnson Collection, Oxford University.

41. Playbills Folder (Miscellaneous): Linwood Gallery, Guildhall Library.

42. Rachel Adams, *Sideshow U.S.A.* (Chicago: University of Chicago Press, 2001), 13. A similar point has been made by Eric Ames regarding the ethnographic exhibition in Germany. See his "From the Exotic to the Everyday: The Ethnographic Exhibition in Germany," in *The Nineteenth-Century Visual Culture Reader,* ed. Vanessa Schwarz and Jeannene Przyblyski (London: Routledge, 2004), 313–27.

43. Sarah Mitchell, "Exhibiting Monstrosity: Chang and Eng, the 'Original' Siamese Twins," *Endeavour* 27(4) (2003): 151; Irving Wallace and Amy Wallace, *The Two* (New York: Simon and Schuster, 1978), 91.

44. *Lancet,* 9 July 1853, 44.

45. On the politics of staring see Rosemarie Garland Thomson, "Staring at the Other," *Disability Studies Quarterly* 25(4) (2005), www.dsq-sds.org/_articles_html/2005/fall/garland-thomson.asp.

46. Francis Buckland, *Curiosities of Natural History,* 4th series (London: Macmillan, 1905), 52.

47. *The Era,* 27 May 1899, 26.

48. For a discussion of the production of freak publicity photographs, see Christopher R. Smit, "A Collaborative Aesthetic: Levinas's Idea of Responsibility and the Photographs of Charles Eisenmann and the Late Nineteenth-Century Freak-Performer," in Tromp, *Victorian Freaks,* 283–311.

49. This is based on my sustained reading of *World's Fair* from its origin in 1904 to 1918. For an excellent analysis of nineteenth-century freak advertisements in *The Era,* see Ann Featherstone, "Shopping and Looking: Trade Advertisements in the *Era* and Performance History Research," *Nineteenth Century Theatre* 28(1) (2000): 26–61.

50. Tom Norman, "Memoirs of Tom Norman," unpublished typescript, 1928, Q/Norm/575, 61, National Fairgrounds Archive, Sheffield.

51. Smit, "Collaborative Aesthetic," 291.

52. A. St. John Adcock, "Sideshow London," in *Living London,* ed. George Sims (London: Cassell, 1902), 285.

53. Roslyn Poignant, *Professional Savages* (New Haven, CT: Yale University Press, 2004).

54. *The Era,* 6 May 1899, 19.

55. "Wild Men Zulu Kaffirs," Broadsides, BF 24b, Wellcome Library.

56. Pamela Scully and Clifton Crais, "Race and Erasure: Sara Baartman and Hendrik Cesars in Cape Town and London," *Journal of British Studies* 47(2) (2008): 301–23.

57. "Exhibitions at Westminster Aquarium," HO 45/9710/A51137, National Archives.

58. "Fraud," MEPO 3/1482, National Archives. She continued, however, to perform, particularly at Australian freak shows, and allegedly saved nine thousand pounds by the end of her career. See Richard Broome, "Windows on Other Worlds: The Rise and Fall of Sideshow Alley," *Australian Historical Studies* 112 (1999): 1–22.

59. Matthew Sweet, *Inventing the Victorians* (New York: St. Martin's Press, 2001), 153.

60. E. P. Thompson, *The Making of the English Working Class* (London: Victor Gollancz, 1963), 12.

61. This point has also recently been made in relationship to the U.S. freak show. See Michael M. Chemers, "Introduction: Staging Stigma: A Freak Studies Manifesto," *Disability Studies Quarterly* 25(3) (2005), www.dsq-sds.org/_articles_html/2005/summer/intro_chemers.asp.

62. *Strand Magazine,* April 1897, 410.

63. Norman, "Memoirs," 108.

64. McHold, "Even as You and I," 27–28.

65. David Gerber, "The 'Careers' of People Exhibited in Freak Shows," in Thomson, *Freakery,* 38–54; David Gerber, "Pornography or Entertainment? The Rise and Fall of the Freak Show," *Reviews in American History* 18(1) (1990):

15–21; David Mitchell and Sharon Snyder, "Exploitations of Embodiment: *Born Freak* and the Academic Bally Plank," *Disability Studies Quarterly* 25(3) (2005), www.dsq-sds.org/_articles_html/2005/summer/mitchell_snyder.asp.

66. Tom Norman and George Barnum Norman, *The Penny Showman: Memoirs of Tom Norman "Silver King"* (London: Privately published, 1985), ii.

67. Scully and Crais, "Race and Erasure," 303. For similar arguments see Smit, "Collaborative Aesthetic," and Rebecca Stern, "Our Bear Women, Ourselves: Affiliating With Julia Pastrana" in Tromp, *Victorian Freaks,* 200–233.

68. See, for example, Gerber, "The 'Careers' of People Exhibited"; Mitchell and Snyder, "Exploitations of Embodiment."

69. Sarah F. Rose, "'Crippled' Hands: Disability in Labor and Working-Class History," *Labor* 2(1) (2005): 30. For an excellent summation of disability studies see Lennard J. Davis, "Crips Strike Back: The Rise of Disability Studies," *American Literary History* 11(3) (1999): 500–512.

70. Rosemarie Garland Thomson, "Redrawing the Boundaries of Feminist Disability Studies," *Feminist Studies* 20(3) (1994): 584.

71. Catherine J. Kudlick, "Disability History: Why We Need Another 'Other,'" *American Historical Review* 108(3) (2003): 763–93. See also Douglas Baynton, "Disability: A Useful Category of Historical Analysis," *Disability Studies Quarterly* 17 (1997): 81–87.

72. David T. Mitchell and Sharon L. Snyder, "Introduction: Disability Studies and the Double Bind of Representation," in *The Body and Physical Difference,* ed. David T. Mitchell and Sharon L. Snyder (Ann Arbor: University of Michigan Press, 1997), 5–6.

73. Douglas Baynton, "Disability History: No Longer Hidden," *Reviews in American History* 32(2) (2004): 286.

74. Quoted in Shelley Tremain, "On the Subject of Impairment," in *Disability/Postmodernity: Embodying Disability Theory,* ed. Mairian Corker and Tom Shakespeare (London: Continuum, 2002), 33.

75. Thomas Laqueur, *Making Sex* (Cambridge, MA: Harvard University Press, 1992); Londa Schiebinger, "Skeletons in the Closet: The First Illustrations of the Female Skeleton in Eighteenth-Century Anatomy," *Representations* 14 (1986): 42–82.

76. Mairian Corker and Tom Shakespeare, "Mapping the Terrain," in Corker and Shakespeare, *Disability/Postmodernity,* 3 (emphasis in the original).

77. Tremain, "On the Subject of Impairment," 34.

78. Mitchell and Snyder, "Introduction," 2–3.

79. Rosemarie Garland Thomson, *Extraordinary Bodies: Figuring Physical Disability in American Culture and Literature* (New York: Columbia University Press, 1997), 58.

80. A sustained search of the catalogues of the Wellcome Library and the British Library as the well as the *Times* reveals that the term first appears in this context around 1900 and is used widely only during and after World War I.

81. Seth Koven, "Remembering and Dismemberment: Crippled Children, Wounded Soldiers and the Great War in Great Britain," *American Historical Review* 99 (1994): 1167–1202. See also Anne Borsay, "Disciplining Disabled Bodies: The Development of Orthopaedic Medicine in Britain, c. 1800–1939," in Turner and Stagg, *Social Histories of Disability and Deformity,* 97–116.

82. For a similar argument about France, see Henri-Jacques Stiker, *A History of Disability* (Ann Arbor: University of Michigan Press, 2000), 121–89. For British policies on dealing with disabled soldiers, see Deborah Cohen, *The War Come Home* (Berkeley: University of California Press, 2001), and Jeffrey S. Reznick, *Healing the Nation* (Manchester: Manchester University Press, 2004).

83. Georges Canguilhem, *The Normal and the Pathological* (New York: Zone, 1991), 132.

84. Simi Linton, *Claiming Disability: Knowledge and Identity* (New York: New York University Press, 1998); Patrick Devlieger, "'Handicap' and Education in the United States of the 1930s: Discursive Formations in the *New York Times*," *Paedagogica Historica* 37(2) (2001): 279–89; Paul K. Longmore and David Goldberger, "The League of the Physically Handicapped and the Great Depression: A Case Study in the New Disability History," *Journal of American History* 87(3) (2000): 888–922; Brad Byrom, "Joseph F. Sullivan and the Discourse of 'Crippledom' in Progressive America," in *Disability Discourse,* ed. Mairian Corker and Sally French (Philadelphia: Open University Press, 1999), 156–63.

85. On the discourse of pity and the freak show, see Stern, "Our Bear Women, Ourselves," 203.

86. Sidney Webb and Beatrice Webb, *English Poor Law Policy* (London: Archon Books, 1963), 51.

87. Deborah A. Stone, *The Disabled State* (Philadelphia: Temple University Press, 1985), 55.

88. Clarence Dean, *The Official Guide. Book of Marvels in the Barnum and Bailey Greatest Show on Earth with Full Descriptions of the Human Prodigies and Rare Animals* (London: Barnum and Bailey, 1899), 10–11.

89. Evanion 923, British Library.

90. "The Real Lobster-Clawed Lady," Human Freaks Box 2, John Johnson Collection, Oxford University.

91. Mitchell and Snyder, "Exploitations of Embodiment."

92. "P. T. Barnum's Greatest Show on Earth Programme," 11.

93. Mitchell, "Exhibiting Monstrosity," 151.

94. Evanion 827, British Library.

95. "Field Marshall Tom Thumb," Broadsides BF 24b/5, Wellcome Library.

96. *The Era,* 14 January 1899, 19.

97. George Buckley Bolton, "Statement of the Principal Circumstances Respecting the United Siamese Twins Now Exhibiting in London," *Philosophical Transactions of the Royal Society of London* 120 (1830): 185.

98. *Account of the Siamese Twin Brothers from Actual Observations* (London: W. Turner, ca. 1830), 8.

99. Mitchell and Snyder, "Exploitations of Embodiment."

100. Lennard J. Davis, "Constructing Normalcy: The Bell Curve, the Novel and the Invention of the Disabled Body in the Nineteenth Century," in *The Disability Studies Reader*, ed. Lennard J. Davis (New York: Routledge, 1997), 10. As Georges Canguilhem has argued, this term emerged much earlier in France, where it had a different trajectory that cannot necessarily be mapped onto the British context. See his *The Normal and the Pathological.*

101. Joyce L. Huff, "Freaklore: The Dissemination, Fragmentation, and Reinvention of the Legend of Daniel Lambert, King of Fat Men," in Tromp, *Victorian Freaks,* 37–38.

102. Dudley Wilson, *Signs and Portents* (London: Routledge, 1993), 1; Marie-Hélène Huet, *Monstrous Imagination* (Cambridge, MA: Harvard University Press, 1993), 101–23; Javier Moscoso, "Monsters as Evidence: The Uses of the Abnormal Body During the Early Eighteenth Century," *Journal of the History of Biology* 31 (1998): 355–82; Stephen Pender, "In the Bodyshop: Human Exhibition in Early Modern England," in *"Defects": Engendering the Modern Body,* ed. Helen Deutsch and Felicity Nussbaum (Ann Arbor: University of Michigan Press, 2000), 95–126; Katharine Park and Lorraine J. Daston, "Unnatural Conceptions: The Study of Monsters in Sixteenth-Century France and England," *Past and Present* 92 (1981): 20–54; Lorraine Daston and Katharine Park, *Wonders and the Order of Nature, 1150–1750* (New York: Zone Books, 1998); Michael Hagner, "Enlightened Monsters," in *The Sciences in Enlightened Europe,* ed. William Clark, Jan Golinski, and Simon Schaffer (Chicago: University of Chicago Press, 1999), 175–217; Andrew Curran and Patrick Graille, "The Faces of Eighteenth-Century Monstrosity," *Eighteenth-Century Life* 21(2) (1997): 1–15; Alan W. Bates, "Good, Common, Regular, and Orderly: Early Modern Classifications of Monstrous Births," *Social History of Medicine* 18(2) (2005): 141–58.

103. Harriet Ritvo, *The Platypus and the Mermaid* (Cambridge, MA: Harvard University Press, 1997), 137.

104. *Lancet,* 29 June 1833, 424–35.

105. Rosemarie Garland Thomson, "Introduction," in Thomson, *Freakery,* 4.

106. Benedict, *Curiosity,* 249.

107. Aileen Fyfe and Bernard Lightman, "Science in the Marketplace: An Introduction," in *Science in the Marketplace,* ed. Aileen Fyfe and Bernard Lightman (Chicago: University of Chicago Press, 2007), 1–22.

108. Ritvo, *Platypus and the Mermaid,* xii, 49, 50, 182, 187; Jonathan R. Topham, "Publishing 'Popular Science' in Early Nineteenth-Century Britain," in Fyfe and Lightman, *Science in the Marketplace,* 135–68; Iwan Rhys Morus, "'More the Aspects of Magic Than Anything Natural': The Philosophy of Demonstration," in Fyfe and Lightman, *Science in the Marketplace,* 336–70.

109. Wallace and Wallace, *The Two,* 97, 145.

110. H. Radcliffe Crocker, *Diseases of the Skin* (London: H. K. Lewis, 1893), 407, 410, 590.

111. *Guyoscope,* November 1898, 42–45. Thanks to Sam Alberti for this reference.

112. Buckland, *Curiosities,* 55.

113. See Francis T. Buckland, *Commonplace Books,* volume 1, Royal College of Surgeons Library, London; Bernard Lightman, "Lecturing in the Spatial Economy of Science," in Fyfe and Lightman, *Science in the Marketplace,* 109.

114. George M. Gould and Walter L. Pyle, *Anomalies and Curiosities of Medicine* (London: Rebman Publishing, 1897), 2.

115. *Lancet,* 27 December 1873, 903; 27 January 1900, 250–51.

116. E. J. Chance, *On the Nature, Causes, Variety and Treatment of Bodily Deformities* (London: T. T. Lemare, 1862), 82–83.

117. J. W. Ballantyne, *Manual of Antenatal Pathology and Hygiene: The Foetus* (Edinburgh: William Green and Sons, 1902), 3, 322–24.

118. See, for example, Barton Cooke Hirst and George Piersol, *Human Monstrosities* (Philadelphia: Lea Brothers and Co., 1891), 83; J. W. Ballantyne, *The Diseases and Deformities of the Foetus,* volume 2 (Edinburgh: Oliver and Boyd, 1892), 80–84.

119. Carrie Yang Costello, "Teratology: 'Monsters' and the Professionalization of Obstetrics," *Journal of Historical Sociology* 19(1) (2006): 1–33.

120. Sweet, *Inventing the Victorians,* 245; Heather McHold, "Diagnosing Difference: The Scientific, Medical, and Popular Engagement with Monstrosity in Victorian Britain," PhD diss., Northwestern University, 2002, 161.

121. *Lancet,* 2 February 1898, 451.

122. Ballantyne, *Manual of Antenatal Pathology,* 3.

123. "Miss Julia Pastrana, The Nondescript"; and "Wild Man of the Prairies," Entertainments Folder 8, John Johnson Collection, Oxford University. On the evolution of this term in natural history, see Ritvo, *The Platypus and the Mermaid,* 55.

124. Tromp, *Victorian Freaks,* 8.

125. "Mr. Tipney," Broadsides BF 24b/37, Wellcome Library.

126. *History of Miss Annie Jones, Barnum and Bailey's Esau Lady* (Glasgow: J. Lithgow, ca. 1891), unnumbered final page.

127. *Life of Miss Alice Bounds, The Bear Lady,* ca. 1911, 3–4, National Fairgrounds Archive, Sheffield.

128. "The Human Tripod," Human Freaks Box 2, John Johnson Collection, Oxford University.

129. *An Interesting Treatise on the Marvellous Indian Boy Laloo Brought to This Country by M. D. Fracis* (Leicester: n.p., n.d.), 4, Human Freaks Box 2, John Johnson Collection, Oxford University.

130. Erin O'Connor, *Raw Material: Producing Pathology in Victorian Culture* (Durham, NC: Duke University Press, 2000), 154.

131. McHold, "Diagnosing Difference," 67, 75, 159.

132. "Field Marshall Tom Thumb."

133. "Now Exhibiting at 66 Drury Lane," "Curious Exhibition Bills of Giants, Dwarfs, Monstrosities, &c., &c.," Hope Collection, Folder B29, Print Room, Ashmolean Museum, Oxford University.

134. "The Double Man," Broadsides BF 24b/16, Wellcome Library; "A Collection of Handbills," 105.

135. Playbills Folder (Miscellaneous): Adelaide Gallery, Guildhall Library; Playbills Folder (Miscellaneous): No. 1 Cross Street, Shoreditch, Guildhall Library; "Mr. Tipney"; "A Collection of Handbills," 105.

136. Edward J. Wood, *Giants and Dwarfs* (London: Richard Bentley, 1868), 432.

137. "The Giant Boy," Broadsides BF 24b/66, Wellcome Library.

138. *The Era,* 4 March 1899, 29.

139. Leslie Fiedler, *Tyranny of the Normal* (Boston: David R. Godine, 1996).

140. Rosemarie Garland Thomson, "Narratives of Deviance and Delight: Staring at Julia Pastrana, the 'Extraordinary Lady,'" in *Beyond the Binary: Reconstructing Cultural Identity in a Multicultural Context,* ed. Timothy B. Powell (New Brunswick, NJ: Rutgers University Press, 1999), 95.

141. Bernth Lindfors, ed., *Africans on Stage: Studies in Ethnological Show Business* (Bloomington: Indiana University Press, 1999), vii.

142. Playbills Folder (Miscellaneous): No. 31 Haymarket, Guildhall Library.

143. See, for example, Curtis M. Hinley, "The World as Marketplace: Commodification of the Exotic at the World's Columbian Exposition, Chicago, 1893," in *Exhibiting Cultures: The Poetics and Politics of Museum Display,* ed. Ivan Karp and Steven D. Lavine (Washington, D.C.: Smithsonian Institution Press, 1991), 346.

144. Sadiah Qureshi, "Displaying Sara Baartman, the 'Hottentot Venus,'" *History of Science* 42(2) (2004): 236–38.

145. Adcock, "Sideshow London," 281.

146. "The Leopard Boy," Royal Aquarium Folder 1876–84, London Theatre Museum.

147. John Conolly, *The Ethnological Exhibitions of London* (London: John Churchill, 1855), 5; Raymond Corbey, "Ethnographic Showcases, 1870–1930," *Cultural Anthropology* 8(3) (1993): 338–69. Poignant's *Professional Savages* is an extended discussion of this point.

148. *World's Fair,* 14 March 1908, 10.

149. "Krao, The Missing Link. A Living Proof of Darwin's Theory of the Descent of Man," ca. 1883, 8, Evanion 2474, British Library.

150. *Nature* 25 (1881): 3–4; R. H. W. Reece, "Introduction" to *The Head Hunters of Borneo,* by Carl Bock (Oxford: Oxford University Press, 1985.)

151. Conolly, *Ethnological Exhibitions of London*, 11. See also his *Address to the Ethnological Society of London Delivered at the Annual Meeting on the 25th of May 1855 and a Sketch of the Recent Progress of Ethnology by Richard Cull* (London: W. M. Watts, 1855).

152. Appendix to Z. S. Strother, "Display of the Body Hottentot," in Lindfors, *Africans on Stage*, 43.

153. Bernth Lindfors, "Hottentot, Bushman, Kaffir: Taxonomic Tendencies in Nineteenth-Century Racial Iconography," *Nordic Journal of African Studies* 5(2) (1996): 3. Baartman also had an elongated labia, but this was not available for either public or scientific consumption—at least not while she was alive.

154. Zine Magubane, "Which Bodies Matter? Feminism, Poststructuralism, Race, and the Curious Theoretical Odyssey of the 'Hottentot Venus,'" *Gender and Society* 15(6) (2001): 816–34.

CHAPTER ONE

A shorter version of this chapter was published as "Monstrosity, Masculinity and Medicine: Re-Examining 'the Elephant Man,'" *Cultural and Social History* 4(2) (2007): 193–213.

1. *World's Fair*, 17 February 1923, 9.

2. *World's Fair*, 24 February 1923, 5.

3. Frederick Treves, *The Elephant Man and Other Reminiscences* (London: Cassell and Co., 1923), 8.

4. Frederick Treves, *The Elephant Man: Amplified from an Account Published in the 'British Medical Journal'. December, 1888* (London: John Bale and Sons, 1888), 6; Treves, *Elephant Man and Other Reminiscences*, 13.

5. Tom Norman, "Memoirs of Tom Norman," unpublished typescript, 1928, Q/Norm/575 MSS, 56. National Fairgrounds Archive, Sheffield.

6. Tom Norman and George Barnum Norman, *The Penny Showman: Memoirs of Tom Norman "Silver King"* (London: Privately published, 1985), 103.

7. On recent debates in the field of masculinity studies, see John Tosh, "What Should Historians Do with Masculinity: Reflections on Nineteenth-Century Britain," *History Workshop Journal* 38 (1994): 184; Karen Harvey and Alexandra Shepard, "What Have Historians Done with Masculinity? Reflections on Five Centuries of British History, circa 1500–1950," *Journal of British Studies* 44(2) (2005): 274–80; Alexandra Shepard, "From Anxious Patriarchs to Refined Gentlemen? Manhood in Britain, circa 1500–1700," *Journal of British Studies* 44(2) (2005): 288–89; Karen Harvey, "The History of Masculinity, circa 1650–1800," *Journal of British Studies* 44(2) (2005): 305–11; Michael Roper, "Between Manliness and Masculinity: The 'War Generation' and the Psychology of Fear in Britain, 1914–1950," *Journal of British Studies* 44(2) (2005): 345.

8. Raphael Samuel, "The Elephant Man as a Fable of Class," *New Society*, 19 November 1981, 315.

9. Treves, *Elephant Man and Other Reminiscences*, 19.

10. Ibid., 4–8.

11. Ibid., 7–13.

12. Ibid., 24.

13. Peter W. Graham and Fritz H. Oehlschlaeger, *Articulating the Elephant Man: Joseph Merrick and His Interpreters* (Baltimore, MD: Johns Hopkins University Press, 1992), 60.

14. Michael Howell and Peter Ford, *The True History of the Elephant Man* (London: Allison and Busby, 1983), 72–92.

15. Stephen Trombley, *Sir Frederick Treves: The Extra-Ordinary Edwardian* (London: Routledge, 1989).

16. Norman, "Memoirs"; Vanessa Toulmin, "'It was not the show it was the tale that you told': The Life and Legend of Tom Norman, Silver King," www.shef.ac.uk/nfa/history/shows/norman.php.

17. What Merrick thought of his own exhibition is impossible to ascertain. His souvenir "autobiography" was produced to promote his act and is thus by its very nature unreliable. Although its modest tone and forthright narrative suggest that it is, in fact, an autobiography of sorts that was likely written by Merrick in collaboration with his first exhibitor, Sam Torr, it sheds little light on Merrick's true feelings. In it he asserts that he has "received the greatest kindness and attention" from his exhibitors and that "the public . . . have treated me well—in fact I may say I am as comfortable now as I was uncomfortable before." This declaration is echoed in a later statement that he added to the end of Treves's 1888 medical pamphlet on his case. Here Merrick proclaimed that he was thankful to his "kind doctor" and that he was "very comfortable, and I may say as happy as my condition will allow me to be." While both of these statements may have been true, their parallel structure and language also suggest that in both cases Merrick told his audience exactly what it expected and wanted to hear: that he was grateful for the kindness he had received, and that although his body was severely deformed, he was as well as could be expected. See *The Life and Adventures of Joseph Carey Merrick* (Leicester: H & A Cockshaw, ca. 1885), and Treves, *Elephant Man: Amplified from an Account*, 11.

18. Treves, *Elephant Man and Other Reminiscences*, 3–6.

19. Andrew Smith, *Victorian Demons: Medicine, Masculinity, and the Gothic at the Fin-de-Siècle* (Manchester: Manchester University Press, 2004), 45.

20. Sarah Mitchell, "From 'Monstrous' to 'Abnormal': The Case of Conjoined Twins in the Nineteenth Century," in *Histories of the Normal and the Abnormal*, ed. Waltraud Ernst (London: Routledge, 2006), 62.

21. John H. Appleby, "Human Curiosities and the Royal Society, 1699–1751," *Notes and Records of the Royal Society of London* 50(1) (1996): 13–27;

Erin O'Connor, *Raw Material: Producing Pathology in Victorian Culture* (Durham, NC: Duke University Press, 2000), 150.

22. John Bland Sutton, *The Story of a Surgeon* (London: Methuen, 1930), 8.

23. Ibid., 139.

24. Lisa Kochanek, "Reframing the Freak: From Sideshow to Science," *Victorian Periodicals Review* 30(3) (1997): 231; Trombley, *Sir Frederick Treves,* 22, 35. See also Heather McHold, "Diagnosing Difference: The Scientific, Medical, and Popular Engagement with Monstrosity in Victorian Britain," PhD diss., Northwestern University, 2002, 2, 30, 126.

25. *British Medical Journal* (hereafter *BMJ*), 6 December 1884, 1140.

26. *BMJ,* 25 February 1888, 416.

27. Bland Sutton, *Story of a Surgeon,* 40.

28. Bernard Lightman, "Lecturing in the Spatial Economy of Science," in *Science in the Marketplace,* ed. Aileen Fyfe and Bernard Lightman (Chicago: University of Chicago Press, 2007), 97–134. See also J. N. Hays, "The London Lecturing Empire, 1800–1850," in *Metropolis and Province: Science and British Culture, 1780–1850,* ed. Ian Inkster and Jack Morrell (London: Hutchinson, 1983), 91–119.

29. Iwan Rhys Morus, "'More the Aspect of Magic Than Anything Natural': The Philosophy of Demonstration," in Fyfe and Lightman, *Science in the Marketplace,* 337.

30. D. G. Halsted, *Doctor in the Nineties* (London: Christopher Johnson, 1959), 29.

31. Trombley, *Sir Frederick Treves,* 35.

32. On freak postcards see Ann Featherstone, "Showing the Freak: Photographic Images of the Extraordinary Body," in *Visual Delights,* ed. Simon Popple and Vanessa Toulmin (Trowbridge: Flicks Books, 2000); Christopher R. Smit, "A Collaborative Aesthetic: Levinas's Idea of Responsibility and the Photographs of Charles Eisenmann and the Late Nineteenth-Century Freak-Performer," in *Victorian Freaks: The Social Context of Freakery in Britain,* ed. Marlene Tromp (Columbus: Ohio State University Press, 2008), 283–311.

33. Register of Students, MC/S/1/8, London Hospital Museum and Archives (hereafter LHMA).

34. McHold, "Diagnosing Difference," 161–72.

35. Norman and Norman, *Penny Showman,* 103.

36. Lightman, "Lecturing in the Spatial Economy," 97–134.

37. Howell and Ford, *True History of the Elephant Man,* 104.

38. Norman and Norman, *Penny Showman,* 103.

39. Jan Bondeson, *A Cabinet of Medical Curiosities* (London: I. B. Tauris, 1997), 144–69; Marie-Hélène Huet, *Monstrous Imagination* (Cambridge, MA: Harvard University Press, 1993); Dennis Todd, *Imagining Monsters: Miscreations*

of the Self in Eighteenth-Century England (Chicago: University of Chicago Press, 1995), 44–63.

40. Norman and Norman, *Penny Showman,* 103–4; *Lancet,* 10 April 1852, 356; William C. Dabney, "Maternal Impressions," in *Cyclopaedia of the Diseases of Children,* ed. John M. Keating (Edinburgh: Young J. Petland, 1889), 196–202.

41. Huet, *Monstrous Imagination,* 1.

42. George M. Gould and Walter L. Pyle, *Anomalies and Curiosities of Medicine* (London: Rebman Publishing, 1897), 81.

43. *BMJ,* 3 October 1885, 672–73; *BMJ,* 9 June 1883, 1116; *Lancet,* 14 July 1888, 63; *Lancet,* 15 October 1887, 755–56.

44. Dabney, "Maternal Impressions," 191–216.

45. London Hospital In-Patients Register LH/M/1/14, 23–25 June 1886, LHMA; *East London Advertiser,* 19 April 1890, 6; *World's Fair,* 17 February 1923, 9; *World's Fair,* 24 February 1923, 5; Halsted, *Doctor in the Nineties,* 40.

46. *Life and Adventures of Joseph Carey Merrick.*

47. Norman and Norman, *Penny Showman,* 103.

48. Treves, *Elephant Man and Other Reminiscences,* 1.

49. Erwin Ackerknecht, *Medicine at the Paris Hospital* (Baltimore, MD: Johns Hopkins University Press, 1967); W. F. Bynum, *Science and the Practice of Medicine in the Nineteenth Century* (Cambridge: Cambridge University Press, 1994); N. D. Jewson, "The Disappearance of the Sick Man from Medical Cosmology, 1770–1870," *Sociology* 10 (1976): 225–44; N. D. Jewson, "Medical Knowledge and the Patronage System in Eighteenth-Century England," *Sociology* 12 (1974): 369–85.

50. Rosemarie Garland Thomson, *Extraordinary Bodies: Figuring Physical Disability in American Culture and Literature* (New York: Columbia University Press, 1997), 59.

51. Norman and Norman, *Penny Showman,* 103–4.

52. Treves, *Elephant Man: Amplified from an Account,* 6.

53. Norman, "Memoirs," 13.

54. Norman and Norman, *Penny Showman,* 102–4.

55. Treves, *Elephant Man and Other Reminiscences,* 10; Norman and Norman, *Penny Showman,* 109.

56. Heather McHold, "Even as You and I: Freak Shows and Lay Discourse on Spectacular Deformity," in Tromp, *Victorian Freaks* 274.

57. Norman and Norman, *Penny Showman,* 104.

58. John Tosh, "Masculinities in Industrializing Society: Britain 1800–1914," *Journal of British Studies* 44(2) (2005): 335.

59. Stefan Collini, *Public Moralists: Political Thought and Intellectual Life in Britain, 1850–1930* (Oxford: Oxford University Press, 1991), 106; Keith McClelland, "England's Greatness, the Working Man," in *Defining the Victorian Nation,* ed. Catherine Hall, Keith McClelland, and Jane Rendall (Cambridge:

Cambridge University Press, 2000); Anna Clark, "Manhood, Womanhood and the Politics of Class in Britain, 1790–1845," in *Gender and Class in Modern Europe,* ed. Laura L. Frader and Sonya O. Rose (Ithaca, NY: Cornell University Press, 1996), 278; John Tosh, "Gentlemanly Politeness and Manly Simplicity in Victorian England," *Transactions of the Royal Historical Society* 12 (2002): 466, 468.

60. Norman and Norman, *Penny Showman,* 108–9.

61. Ibid., 97, 104.

62. *Times,* 4 December 1886, 6; Treves, *Elephant Man: Amplified from an Account,* 5.

63. London Hospital In-Patients Register, LH/M/1/14, 23–25 June 1886, LHMA.

64. *Times,* 4 December 1886, 6.

65. On prostitution and Victorian morality, see Judith Walkowitz, *Prostitution and Victorian Society* (Cambridge: Cambridge University Press, 1980).

66. Norman and Norman, *Penny Showman,* 110.

67. *Times,* 5 January 1887, 10.

68. Norman and Norman, *Penny Showman,* 109.

69. Seth Koven, *Slumming: Sexual and Social Politics in Victorian London* (Princeton, NJ: Princeton University Press, 2004), 124–29.

70. Treves, *Elephant Man and Other Reminiscences,* 15, 31.

71. Jami Moss, "'A Body of Organized Truth': Freaks in Britain, 1830–1900," PhD diss., University of Wisconsin–Madison, 1999, 224, 227.

72. Treves, *Elephant Man and Other Reminiscences,* 2.

73. Ibid., 11, 14. On speech and language in relationship to Merrick, see Christine C. Ferguson, "Elephant Talk: Language and Enfranchisement in the Merrick Case," in Tromp, *Victorian Freaks,* 114–33.

74. Treves, *Elephant Man and Other Reminiscences,* 21.

75. Howell and Ford, *True History of the Elephant Man,* 150.

76. William E. Holladay and Stephen Watt, "Viewing the Elephant Man," *PMLA* 104(5) (1989): 871–73.

77. Treves, *Elephant Man and Other Reminiscences,* 17.

78. Ibid., 26.

79. Ibid., 36–37.

80. James Eli Adams, *Dandies and Desert Saints* (Ithaca, NY: Cornell University Press, 1995); O'Connor, "Raw Material," 104; J. A. Mangan, ed., *Making European Masculinities: Sport, Europe, Gender* (London: Frank Cass, 2000); J. A. Mangan and James Walvin, eds., *Manliness and Morality: Middle-Class Masculinity in Britain and America 1800–1940* (Manchester: Manchester University Press, 1991); Bruce Haley, *The Healthy Body and Victorian Culture* (Cambridge, MA: Harvard University Press, 1978); Seth Koven, "Remembering and Dismemberment: Crippled Children, Wounded Soldiers, and the Great War in Great Britain," *American Historical Review* 99 (1994): 1167–1202; Patrick

McDevitt, *May the Best Man Win: Sport, Masculinity, and Nationalism in Great Britain and the Empire, 1880–1935* (Houndmills: Palgrave, 2004).

81. Martin Francis, "The Domestication of the Male? Recent Research on Nineteenth- and Twentieth-Century British Masculinity," *The Historical Journal* 45(3) (2002): 639.

82. Koven, *Slumming*, 124–29; Trombley, *Sir Frederick Treves*, 30–31.

83. Frederick Treves, *Physical Education* (London: J & A Churchill, 1892), 2, 18.

84. Sir Wilfred Thomason Grenfell, *A Labrador Doctor* (London: Hodder and Staughton, 1929), 60.

85. Treves, *Elephant Man and Other Reminiscences*, 5.

86. On clothing and manhood, see David Kuchta, *The Three-Piece Suit and Modern Masculinity: England, 1550–1850* (Berkeley: University of California Press, 2002); Christopher Brewer, *The Hidden Consumer: Masculinities, Fashion, and City Life, 1860–1914* (Manchester: Manchester University Press, 1999); Brent Shannon, "ReFashioning Men: Fashion, Masculinity, and the Cultivation of the Male Consumer in Britain, 1860–1914," *Victorian Studies* 46(4) (2004): 597–630.

87. Treves, *Elephant Man and Other Reminiscences*, 27–28.

88. McHold, "Even as You and I," 30.

89. Norman and Norman, *Penny Showman*, 108.

90. Ibid., 105.

91. Ibid., 108.

92. Treves, *Elephant Man and Other Reminiscences*, 9.

93. *Times*, 5 January 1887, 10.

94. Norman and Norman, *Penny Showman*, 110.

95. F. Parkes Weber, "Cutaneous Pigmentation as an Incomplete Form of Recklinghausen's Disease, with Remarks on the Classification of Incomplete and Anomalous Forms of Recklinghausen's Disease," *British Journal of Dermatology* 21(2) (1909): 53.

96. Norman and Norman, *Penny Showman*, 110.

97. Grenfell, *A Labrador Doctor*, 60.

98. *Times*, 5 January 1887, 10.

99. London Hospital House Committee Minutes LH/A/5/43, 7 December 1886, LHMA.

100. Grenfell, *A Labrador Doctor*, 60.

101. Treves, *Elephant Man and Other Reminiscences*, 19.

102. Ibid., 22.

103. *BMJ*, 19 April 1890, 917; Bland Sutton, *Story of a Surgeon*, 140; *Illustrated Leicester Chronicle*, 27 December 1930, 3. Thanks to Jim Epstein for chasing down this last citation for me.

104. London Hospital House Committee Minutes LH/A/5/43, 7 December 1886, 81–82; 14 December 1886, 87–88; 15 February 1887, 133; 19 April 1887, 164; 29 April 1890, 243, LHMA; *Times*, 5 January 1887, 10.

105. Ann Featherstone, "Shopping and Looking: Trade Advertisements in the *Era* and Performance History Research," *Nineteenth Century Theatre* 28(1) (2000): 48.

106. Trombley, *Sir Frederick Treves,* 49.

107. Norman and Norman, *Penny Showman,* 109–10.

108. Ibid., 114.

109. *Times,* 16 April 1890, 6.

110. Treves, *Elephant Man and Other Reminiscences,* 36.

111. Treves, *Elephant Man and Other Reminiscences,* 24; Halsted, *Doctor in the Nineties,* 40.

112. *BMJ,* 19 April 1890, 917.

113. Norman and Norman, *Penny Showman,* 110.

114. Grenfell, *A Labrador Doctor,* 60.

115. London Hospital House Committee Minutes LH/A/5/44, 15 April 1890, 236; 29 April 1890, 243; 13 May 1890, 261; Register of Bodies Used for Anatomical Examination MC/A/31/9, 16 April 1890; London Hospital Medical College Minute Book MC/A/2/3, 23 May 1890, 300; 3 June 1890, 304, LHMA.

116. Since the original research for this chapter was undertaken the Pathological Museum has undergone a renovation. The Merrick relics, his model church, and the replica of his hood and visor have been transferred to the London Hospital Museum, which is open to the public. The skeleton will remain in the Pathological Museum, but at the time of this writing it is unclear what form the exhibition of the bones will take.

117. J. A. Tibbles and M. M. Cohen, "The Proteus Syndrome: The Elephant Man Diagnosed," *BMJ* (Clinical Research Edition), 13 September 1986, 683–85.

118. Norman and Norman, *Penny Showman,* 111.

CHAPTER TWO

1. Marlene Tromp, "Empire and the Indian Freak: The 'Miniature Man' from Cawnpore and the 'Marvellous Indian Boy' on Tour in England," in *Victorian Freaks: The Social Context of Freakery in Britain,* ed. Marlene Tromp (Columbus: Ohio State University Press, 2008), 167–75.

2. *Daily News,* 27 April 1886, 4; 7 May 1886, 4; 8 May 1886, 4; *New York Times,* 24 April 1886, 3. On these types of exhibitions, see Paul Greenhalgh, *Ephemeral Vistas* (Manchester: Manchester University Press, 1991). For ethnological exhibits at the 1886 exhibition, see Saloni Mathur, "Living Ethnological Exhibits: The Case of 1886," *Cultural Anthropology* 15(4) (2000): 492–524.

3. For a longer discussion of this point and of the racialization of Chang and Eng, who were ethnically Chinese though born in Siam, see Sarah Mitchell, "From 'Monstrous' to 'Abnormal': The Case of Conjoined Twins in the

Nineteenth Century," in *Histories of the Normal and the Abnormal,* ed. Waltraud Ernst (London: Routledge, 2006), 53–72.

4. George Buckley Bolton, "Statement of the Principal Circumstances Respecting the United Siamese Twins Now Exhibiting in London," *Philosophical Transactions of the Royal Society of London* 120 (1830): 177–86; *BMJ,* 13 February 1869, 139; *BMJ,* 13 March 1869, 232.

5. *An Interesting Treatise on the Marvellous Indian Boy Laloo Brought to This Country by M. D. Fracis* (Leicester: n.p., ca. 1886), Human Freaks Box 2, John Johnson Collection, Oxford University.

6. Evanion 2526 and 461, British Library.

7. Clarence Dean, *The Official Guide Book of Marvels in the Barnum and Bailey Greatest Show on Earth with Full Descriptions of the Human Prodigies and Rare Animals* (London: Barnum and Bailey, 1899), 10; *The Wonder Book of Freaks and Animals* (London: Walter Hill and Co., 1898), 6.

8. *Lancet,* 19 March 1898, 835.

9. David L. Clark and Catherine Myser, "Being Humaned: Medical Documentaries and the Hyperrealization of Conjoined Twins," in *Freakery: Cultural Spectacles of the Extraordinary Body,* ed. Rosemarie Garland Thomson (New York: New York University Press, 1996), 350.

10. Allison Pingree, "The 'Exceptions That Prove the Rule': Daisy and Violet Hilton, the 'New Woman,' and the Bonds of Marriage," in Thomson, *Freakery.* 173.

11. *Times,* 16 January 1911, 6; *World's Fair,* 21 January 1911, 5; R. Birnbaum, *A Clinical Manual of the Malformations and Congenital Diseases of the Foetus,* trans. G. Blacker (London: J & A Churchill, 1912), 321; *The Siamese Twins: Chang and Eng. A Biographical Sketch* (London: J. W. Last, ca. 1869), 15–16.

12. *The Siamese Twins,* 1.

13. Irving Wallace and Amy Wallace, *The Two* (New York: Simon and Schuster, 1978), 72, 81.

14. "A Collection of Handbills, Newspaper Cuttings, and Other Items, 1820–96," G.R.2.5.7, opposite 31, Guildhall Library; Evanion 2656, British Library.

15. "The Pygopagi Twins," EPH++42, Wellcome Library.

16. "A Collection of Handbills," opposite 66.

17. *Pearson's Weekly,* 23 July 1898, 23.

18. For an example of these types of experiments, see *Lancet,* 11 February 1888, 276.

19. *Times,* 25 November 1829, 2; *Lancet,* 13 February 1869, 230; *Times,* 11 February 1869, 12; *BMJ,* 13 February 1869, 141; *BMJ,* 13 March 1869, 229–33.

20. Clippings from *Illustrated Times,* 3 October 1868; *Illustrated Weekly News,* 20 March 1869, Human Freaks Box 2, John Johnson Collection, Oxford University.

21. *The Siamese Twins,* 2.

22. Clipping from unknown source, 24 January 1874, in Francis T. Buckland, *Commonplace Books,* vol. 1, Royal College of Surgeons. Wallace and Wallace, however, seem to give the story credence. See their account in Wallace and Wallace, *The Two,* 256–57, 266.

23. *The Showman,* 14 February 1902, 355; *World's Fair,* 20 March 1909, 10.

24. http://www.victorian-cinema.net/doyen.htm; Kelly Loughlin, "Spectacle and Secrecy: Press Coverage of Conjoined Twins in 1950s Britain," *Medical History* 49 (2005): 197–212; Alice Dreger, *One of Us: Conjoined Twins and the Future of the Normal* (Cambridge, MA: Harvard University Press, 2004); Clark and Myser, "Being Humaned."

25. Dreger, *One of Us.*

26. *Transactions of the Pathological Society of London* (hereafter *TPSL*), 25 February 1888, 437.

27. *Lancet,* 7 January 1928, 24.

28. Dreger, *One of Us,* 7.

29. This was not the first time this gimmick had been deployed. In 1855 "the Edmonton Twins" had tried this same marketing device, advertising that they had "Two perfect Heads with beautiful black hair, (Male & Female) united to one Body, with Two Spinal Columns,—Three Arms, Four Hands & Two Legs." See "The Edmonton Twins," Human Freaks Box 2, John Johnson Collection, Oxford University; Playbills Folder (Miscellaneous): Adelaide Gallery, Lowther Arcade, Guildhall Library.

30. Ironically, in India "Lala" would not necessarily have been considered a female name.

31. Alice Dreger, *Hermaphrodites and the Medical Invention of Sex* (Cambridge, MA: Harvard University Press, 1998), 30.

32. Dreger, *Hermaphrodites.*

33. Ruth Gilbert, "Seeing and Knowing: Science, Pornography, and Early Modern Hermaphrodites," in *At the Borders of the Human,* ed. Erica Fudge, Ruth Gilbert, and Susan Wiseman (Houndmills: Macmillan, 1999); Dreger, *Hermaphrodites,* 53.

34. Laurence Senelick, "Enlightened By Morphodites: Narratives of the Fairground Half-and-Half," *Amerikastudien* 44(3) (1999): 357–78; Elizabeth Grosz, "Intolerable Ambiguity: Freaks as/at the Limit," in Thomson, *Freakery,* 61. This conceit had in fact been manipulated fifty years earlier by at least one British sideshow performer. In 1871 James Taylor exhibited himself as "Half Man and Half Woman," though not necessarily as a hermaphrodite. Taylor had a skeletonlike right torso and arm and a similarly emaciated left leg. His left side was advertised as being "that of a woman, with a woman's breast, and one rib less than any other man." However, he deliberately sported a full beard and mustache on both sides of his face. While using a convention of representation

that prefigured the morphodite, Taylor exhibited himself largely as an anatomical anomaly, a "Double Man" with two hearts and a peculiar anatomy, rather than as a truly double-sexed body. "The Double Man," Broadsides BF 24b/16, Wellcome Library.

35. Harriet Ritvo, *The Platypus and the Mermaid* (Cambridge, MA: Harvard University Press, 1997), 168.

36. Anne Fausto-Sterling, *Sexing the Body: Gender Politics and the Construction of Sexuality* (New York: Basic Books, 2000), 3.

37. John Bland Sutton, *Tumours: Innocent and Malignant,* 7th ed. (London: Cassell, 1922), 507.

38. *Indian Medical Gazette,* July 1886, 220–21.

39. *BMJ,* 25 February 1888, 416.

40. *Lancet,* 7 January 1928, 24.

41. Bland Sutton, *Tumours,* 507.

42. The parasitic fetus covered in the *BMJ* and the *Indian Medical Gazette* may not be Lalloo, as the subject is unnamed. The reports are so similar, however, and this condition so rare that it would be surprising if this were not, in fact, the same case. Although Lalloo was already in England by July 1886, there is no indication when he was actually being exhibited in Hyderabad as opposed to when the report was published. In both the medical and promotional materials a wide span of ages is given for Lalloo (his birth year ranges from 1870 to 1875). The confusion likely stemmed from the fact that Lalloo was often said to look much younger than his years.

43. *BMJ,* 29 August 1885, 404–5.

44. *Lancet,* 18 August 1888, 318; *BMJ,* 25 February 1888, 416.

45. *BMJ,* 12 December 1885, 1104.

46. *Indian Medical Gazette,* July 1886, 219–21.

47. Fracis, *An Interesting Treatise,* 6.

48. Thomas Laqueur, *Making Sex* (Cambridge, MA: Harvard University Press, 1992), 149.

49. For a summary of these arguments, see Tim Hitchcock, *English Sexualities, 1700–1800* (New York: St. Martin's Press, 1997), 42–57.

50. Londa Schiebinger, "Skeletons in the Closet: The First Illustrations of the Female Skeleton in Eighteenth-Century Anatomy," *Representations* 14 (1986): 42–82.

51. *Lancet,* 11 February 1888, 276; *BMJ,* 11 February 1888, 312.

52. *Lancet,* 25 February 1888, 371.

53. George Gould and Walter Pyle, *Anomalies and Curiosities of Medicine* (London: Rebman Publishing, 1897), 192; *BMJ,* 11 February 1888, 312; *BMJ,* 25 February 1888, 436; *TPSL,* 21 February 1888, 429; Barton Cooke Hirst and George A. Piersol, *Human Monstrosities,* part 4 (Philadelphia: Lea Brothers and Co., 1893), 190.

54. Dreger, *Hermaphrodites*, 11, 29, 139–66.

55. *TPSL*, 21 February 1888, 432.

56. *BMJ*, 25 February 1888, 436.

57. Gould and Pyle, *Anomalies and Curiosities*, 192; *BMJ*, 25 February 1888, 416; *TPSL*, 21 February 1888, 430; Hirst and Piersol, *Human Monstrosities*, 190; *Lancet*, 25 February 1888, 371.

58. Suzanne Kessler, *Lessons from the Intersexed* (New Brunswick, NJ: Rutgers University Press, 1998); Kathleen Perry Long, "Sexual Dissonance: Early Modern Scientific Accounts of Hermaphrodites," in *Wonders, Marvels, and Monsters in Early Modern Culture,* ed. Peter G. Platt (Newark: University of Delaware, 1999), 157; Ambroise Paré, *On Monsters and Marvels,* trans. Janis L. Pallister (Chicago: University of Chicago Press, 1982 [1573]), 26–29.

59. Gould and Pyle, *Anomalies and Curiosities,* 192; Hirst and Piersol, *Human Monstrosities,* 190.

60. *BMJ*, 25 February 1888, 437; *BMJ*, 3 March 1888, 498.

61. Ritvo, *Platypus and the Mermaid,* 156.

62. Dreger, *One of Us,* 62–63.

63. Clark and Myser, "Being Humaned," 348.

64. George Buckley Bolton, *On the United Siamese Twins* (London: Richard Taylor, 1830), 179, 185.

65. *Times*, 23 November 1829, 2.

66. "Chang and Eng in an Oriental Setting," Iconographic Collection 2615i, Wellcome Library.

67. Dreger, *One of Us,* 24.

68. *BMJ*, 13 February 1869, 141.

69. *Times*, 17 May 1843, 6.

70. Evanion 482, British Library.

71. *The Siamese Twins,* 5.

72. Clipping from unknown source, 24 January 1874, in Francis T. Buckland, *Commonplace Books*, vol. 1.

73. Bland Sutton, *Tumours,* 502.

74. Wallace and Wallace, *The Two,* 183.

75. Quoted in Heather McHold, "Diagnosing Difference: The Scientific, Medical, and Popular Engagement with Monstrosity in Victorian Britain," PhD diss., Northwestern University, 2002, 101.

76. "Biographical Sketch of Millie-Christine," ca. 1885, 18, Human Freaks Box 2, John Johnson Collection, Oxford University.

77. "Biographical Sketch," 29.

78. Bland Sutton, *Tumours,* 503. Dreger reports that these details appeared on the American version of their publicity materials, but they did not appear on the British versions. See Dreger, *One of Us,* 121.

79. *BMJ*, 23 September 1911, 654.

80. For similar debates among American acts, see Dreger, *One of Us,* 49; Pingree, "The 'Exceptions That Prove the Rule,'" 181–82.

81. "Female Conjoined Twins from Berlin," Image V0029574, Wellcome Images.

82. *World's Fair,* 21 January 1911, 5.

83. Bland Sutton, *Tumours,* 502.

84. "Lalloo," ca. 1902, Image 406, Ronald G. Becker Collection of Charles Eisenmann Photographs, Syracuse University, http://library.syr.edu/information/spcollections/digital/eisenmann/.

85. *Wonder Book of Freaks and Animals,* 6.

86. Dean, *Official Guide Book of Marvels,* 10.

87. Allison Pingree, "America's 'United Siamese Brothers,'" in *Monster Theory,* ed. Jeffrey Jerome Cohen (Minneapolis: University of Minnesota Press, 1996), 106; Andrea Stulman Dennett, *Weird and Wonderful: The Dime Museum in America* (New York: New York University Press, 1997), 82.

88. *TPSL,* 21 February 1888, 430.

89. On the history of autoeroticism, see Thomas Laqueur, *Solitary Sex* (New York: Zone, 2004).

90. Quoted in Nancy F. Anderson, "The 'Marriage with a Deceased Wife's Sister Bill' Controversy: Incest, Anxiety, and the Defense of Family Purity in Victorian England," *Journal of British Studies* 21(2) (1982): 69.

91. James B. Twitchell, *Forbidden Partners: The Incest Taboo in Modern Culture* (New York: Columbia University Press, 1987), 41.

92. Anthony S. Wohl, "Sex and the Single Room: Incest Among the Victorian Working Classes," in *The Victorian Family: Structure and Stresses,* ed. Anthony S. Wohl (New York: St. Martin's Press, 1978), 197–216.

93. Louise A. Jackson, *Child Sexual Abuse in Victorian England* (London: Routledge, 2000), 29.

94. James R. Kincaid, *Child-Loving: The Erotic Child and Victorian Culture* (New York: Routledge, 1992), 198–99.

95. On the NSPCC see George Behlmer, *Child Abuse and Moral Reform in England, 1870–1908* (Stanford, CA: Stanford University Press, 1982); George Behlmer, *Friends of the Family: The English Home and Its Guardians, 1850–1940* (Stanford, CA: Stanford University Press, 1998). On the "Maiden Tribute," see Judith Walkowitz, *City of Dreadful Delight* (Chicago: University of Chicago Press, 1992).

96. Adam Kuper, "Incest, Cousin Marriage, and the Origin of the Human Sciences in Nineteenth-Century England," *Past and Present* 174(1) (2002): 180–81. On the "Deceased Wife's Sister" debate, see Anderson, "The 'Marriage with a Deceased Wife's Sister Bill,'" and Elisabeth Rose Gruner, "Born and Made: Sisters, Brothers, and the Deceased Wife's Sister Bill," *Signs* 24(2) (1999): 423–47.

97. Frank Mort, *Dangerous Sexualities: Medico-Moral Politics in England Since 1830* (London: Routledge and Kegan Paul, 1987), 135.

98. *Daily News,* 27 April 1886, 4; *Daily News,* 7 May 1886, 4; *Daily News,* 8 May 1886, 4. On nautch girls see Kenneth Ballhatchet, *Race, Sex and Class Under the Raj: Imperial Attitudes and Policies and Their Critics, 1793–1905* (London: Weidenfeld and Nicolson, 1980), 157–59.

99. "Lalloo the Double-Bodied Hindu," COPY 1/439/540, National Archives. This same backdrop, however, was also used for other Barnum and Bailey freaks, and thus should not entirely structure the reading of Lalloo.

100. Antoinette Burton, "From Child Bride to 'Hindoo Lady': Rukhmabai and the Debate on Sexual Respectability in Imperial Britain," *American Historical Review* 103(4) (1998): 1119–46.

101. Dagmar Engels, "The Age of Consent Act of 1891: Colonial Ideology in Bengal," *South Asia Research* 3(2) (1983): 107–34; Padma Anagol-McGinn, "The Age of Consent Act (1891) Reconsidered: Women's Perspectives and Participation in the Child Marriage Controversy in India," *South Asia Research* 12(2) (1992): 100–118; Mrinalini Sinha, "Nationalism and Respectable Sexuality in India," *Genders* 21 (1995): 30–57.

102. *BMJ,* 25 February 1888, 436.

CHAPTER THREE

A shorter version of this chapter was previously published as "The Missing Link and the Hairy Belle: Krao and the Victorian Discourses of Evolution, Imperialism and Primitive Sexuality," in *Victorian Freaks: The Social Context of Freakery in Britain,* ed. Marlene Tromp (Columbus: Ohio State University Press, 2008), 134–53.

1. Throughout this chapter I will be employing the nineteenth-century terms for the countries that make up the region we know today as Southeast Asia. I am using Victorian terminology because I am interested in British fantasies about the countries known today as Laos, Thailand, and Myanmar.

2. "Krao, the Missing Link. A Living Proof of Darwin's Theory of the Descent of Man," ca. 1883, Evanion 2474, British Library.

3. Shane Peacock, "Africa Meets the Great Farini," in *Africans on Stage: Studies in Ethnological Show Business,* ed. Bernth Lindfors (Bloomington: Indiana University Press, 1999), 84.

4. Erroll Sherson, *London's Lost Theatres of the Nineteenth Century* (London: John Lane, 1925), 296.

5. Sherson, *London's Lost Theatres,* 297; Edwin Adeler and Con West, *Remember Fred Karno? The Life of a Great Showman* (London: John Long, 1939), 56.

6. Administrative County of London, Sessions of the Licensing Committee, 9 October 1889, LCC/MIN/10, 891, London Metropolitan Archives.

7. Tracy C. Davis, "Sex in Public Places: The Zaeo Aquarium Scandal and the Victorian Moral Majority," *Theatre History Studies* 10 (1990): 1–13.

8. "Krao, the Missing Link," 1.

9. Kathryn A. Hoffmann, "Of Monkey Girls and a Hog-Faced Gentlewoman: Marvel in Fairytales, Fairgrounds, and Cabinets of Curiosities," *Marvels & Tales* 19(1) (2005): 67–85.

10. Michael Mitchell, *Monsters: Human Freaks in America's Gilded Age* (Toronto: ECW Press, 2002), 46.

11. Nigel Rothfels, "Aztecs, Aborigines, and Ape-People: Science and Freaks in Germany, 1850–1900," in *Freakery: Cultural Spectacles of the Extraordinary Body,* ed. Rosemarie Garland Thomson (New York: New York University Press, 1996), 162.

12. See the articles in Lindfors, *Africans on Stage,* on the display of ethnological types.

13. *Morning Post,* 1 January 1883, 2.

14. "Krao, the Missing Link," 13.

15. Ibid., 12.

16. Ibid., 14.

17. Shane Peacock, *The Great Farini: The High-Wire Life of William Hunt* (Toronto: Viking, 1995), 290.

18. *Sporting and Dramatic News,* 6 January 1883, 425.

19. *Penny Illustrated Paper,* 6 January 1883, 14.

20. This *carte de visite* is in the private collection of Shane Peacock, who kindly shared a reproduction of it with me.

21. Edward Caudill, "Victorian Satire of Evolution," *Journalism History* 20(3/4) (1994): 107–15.

22. Janet Browne, "Darwin in Caricature: A Study in the Popularisation and Dissemination of Evolution," *Proceedings of the American Philosophical Society* 145(4) (2001): 496–509.

23. Leo Henkin, *Darwinism in the English Novel, 1860–1910* (New York: Corporate Press, 1940); Jane R. Goodall, *Performance and Evolution in the Age of Darwin* (London: Routledge, 2002), 52.

24. James W. Cook Jr., "Of Men, Missing Links, and Nondescripts: The Strange Career of P. T. Barnum's 'What-is-It?' Exhibition," in Thomson, *Freakery,* 139–57.

25. Diana Snigurowicz, "Sex, Simians, and Spectacle in Nineteenth-Century France; or, How to Tell a 'Man' From a Monkey," *Canadian Journal of History* 34(1) (1999): 60.

26. *Billboard,* 21 February 1914, 32.

27. "Krao, the Missing Link," 1.

28. Ibid., ii.

29. Ibid., ii–iii.

30. *Morning Post,* 1 January 1883, 2.

31. *Sporting and Dramatic News,* 6 January 1883, 425.

32. Z. S. Strother, "Display of the Body Hottentot," in Lindfors, *Africans on Stage,* 31.

33. Francis T. Buckland, *Curiosities of Natural History* (London: Macmillan, 1900); G. H. O. Burgess, *The Curious World of Frank Buckland* (London: John Baker, 1967); Bernard Lightman, "Lecturing in the Spatial Economy of Science," in *Science in the Marketplace,* ed. Aileen Fyfe and Bernard Lightman (Chicago: University of Chicago Press, 2007), 103–11.

34. Peacock, *The Great Farini,* 298.

35. "Krao, the Missing Link," ii.

36. *Bell's Life in London,* 6 January 1883, 7.

37. "Krao, the Missing Link," 11.

38. *Nature,* 11 January 1883, 245. On Keane, see Douglas A. Lorimer, "Science and the Secularization of Victorian Images of Race," in *Victorian Science in Context,* ed. Bernard Lightman (Chicago: University of Chicago Press, 1997), 224–28. On Keane and Dubois's missing link, see Sumathi Ramaswamy, *The Lost Land of Lemuria* (Berkeley: University of California Press, 2004), 42–45.

39. *Nature,* 19 April 1883, 579. According to the thai2english.com dictionary, *krao* is a transliteration of the Thai word for *whiskers.*

40. *The Medical Press and Circular,* 3 January 1883, 6–7; *British Medical Journal,* 6 January 1883, 28–29; *Journal of the Anthropological Institute of Great Britain and Ireland* 13 (1884): 6–7.

41. *British Medical Journal,* 6 January 1883, 28–29.

42. *Daily News,* 1 January 1883, 2.

43. *London Figaro,* 6 January 1883, 4; *Morning Advertiser,* 2 January 1883, 2.

44. *Penny Illustrated Paper,* 6 January 1883, 14.

45. *Land and Water,* 6 January 1883, 14.

46. *Illustrated London News,* 27 January 1883, 105.

47. *The Medical Press and Circular,* 3 January 1883, 7.

48. Fred Bradna, *The Big Top: My Forty Years with the Greatest Show on Earth* (London: Hamish Hamilton, 1953), 197.

49. James McKenzie, "Strange Truth. The Autobiography of a Circus Showman, Stage and Exhibition Man," unpublished manuscript, ca. 1944–50, 218, Brunel University Library.

50. For a similar argument about the role of nondescripts and missing links at American freak shows, see Linda Frost, *Never One Nation: Freaks, Savages, and Whiteness in U.S. Popular Culture, 1850–1877* (Minneapolis: University of Minnesota Press, 2005), 6–9.

51. Anne McClintock, *Imperial Leather* (New York: Routledge, 1995), 30.

52. Patrick Brantlinger, *Rule of Darkness: British Literature and Imperialism, 1830–1914* (Ithaca, NY: Cornell University Press, 1988).

53. John Crawfurd, *Journal of an Embassy from the Governor-General of India to the Court of Ava in the Year 1827* (London: Henry Colburn, 1829), 184–87.

54. Charles Darwin, *The Variation of Animals and Plants Under Domestication,* vol. 2 (London: John Murray, 1868), 327; W. Houghton, "On a Hairy Family in Burmah," *Transactions of the Ethnological Society of London* 7 (1869): 53–59.

55. *Strand Magazine,* May 1897, 521–28; *British Medical Journal,* 12 June 1886, 1118.

56. "Krao, the Missing Link," 3.

57. For British imperialism in this region see V. G. Kiernan, "Britain, Siam, and Malaya: 1875–1885," *Journal of Modern History* 28(1) (1956): 1–20; Eric Tagliacozzo, "Ambiguous Commodities, Unstable Frontiers: The Case of Burma, Siam, and Imperial Britain, 1800–1900," *Comparative Studies in Society and History* 46(2) (2004): 354–77.

58. In 1883 the *British Medical Journal* suggested that Laos was part of Burma; in 1894, once Laos had been absorbed into French Indochina, the *English Mechanic* nonetheless maintained that it was part of Siam. See *English Mechanic and World of Science,* 28 December 1894, 429.

59. Deborah Deacon Boyer, "Picturing the Other: Images of Burmans in Imperial Britain," *Victorian Periodicals Review* 35(3) (2002): 216; D. M. Gray, ed., *Mandalay Massacres. Upper Burma During the Reign of King Theebaw* (Rangoon: Rangoon Gazette Press, 1884).

60. "Krao, the Missing Link," 5–6.

61. *Strand Magazine,* April 1897, 408–9.

62. "What we know of Waino and Plutano, Wild Men of Borneo. And some of the latest Popular Songs," ca. 1878, National Fairgrounds Archive, Sheffield. See also Robert Bogdan, *Freak Show* (Chicago: University of Chicago Press, 1988), 121–27.

63. "Krao, the Missing Link," 6–11. Neither book mentions the quest for the missing link. See Carl Bock, *The Head Hunters of Borneo* (London: Sampson Low, Marston, Searle & Rivington, 1881), and *Temples and Elephants: The Narrative of a Journey of Exploration through Upper Siam and Lao* (London: Sampson Low, Marston, Searle & Rivington, 1884).

64. "The Burmese Imperial State Carriage and Throne," London Play Places Box 10, John Johnson Collection, Oxford University. For a similar argument about the Kohinoor diamond at the Crystal Palace, see Lara Kriegel, "Narrating the Subcontinent: India at the Crystal Palace in 1851," in *The Great Exhibition of 1851,* ed. Louise Purbrick (Manchester: Manchester University Press, 2001).

65. *Strand Magazine,* May 1897, 521–28; *British Medical Journal,* 12 June 1886, 1118.

66. Newspaper clippings on and handbills for the exhibition of the Sacred Hairy Family can be found in "A Collection of Handbills, Newspaper Cuttings, and Other Items 1820–96," G.R.2.5.7, 87, Guildhall Library; Piccadilly Hall

Folder, London Theatre Museum. Ironically, as Frank Dikotter has argued, when Europeans arrived in China in the seventeenth century, it was their excessive hairiness that marked them as Other and thus barbarian. See his "Hairy Barbarians, Furry Primates, and Wild Men: Medical Science and Cultural Representations of Hair in China," in *Hair: Its Power and Meaning in Asian Cultures,* ed. Alf Hiltebeitel and Barbara D. Miller (Albany: State University of New York Press, 1998), 51–74.

67. "Krao, the Missing Link," 7.

68. Ibid., 12.

69. Ibid., 14.

70. *The Broad Arrow,* 6 January 1883, 22.

71. *Nature,* 11 January 1883, 245.

72. "Krao, the Missing Link," 11.

73. Rosemarie Garland Thomson, "Narratives of Deviance and Delight: Staring at Julia Pastrana, the 'Extraordinary Lady,'" in *Beyond the Binary: Reconstructing Cultural Identity in a Multicultural Context,* ed. Timothy B. Powell (New Brunswick, NJ: Rutgers University Press, 1999), 94.

74. *Daily News,* 1 January 1883, 2.

75. *Bell's Life in London,* 6 January 1883, 7; *Land and Water,* 6 January 1883, 14.

76. *Land and Water,* 6 January 1883, 14.

77. *Daily News,* 1 January 1883, 2; *London Figaro,* 6 January 1883, 4.

78. *London Figaro,* 6 January 1883, 4.

79. Peacock, *The Great Farini,* 289.

80. *Peru Republican,* 24 April 1885, in Newspaper Advertisements, 1884–91, Circus World Museum, Baraboo, Wisconsin.

81. Peter Stallybrass and Allon White, *The Politics and Poetics of Transgression* (Ithaca, NY: Cornell University Press, 1986), 41.

82. Tracy C. Davis, "The Actress in Victorian Pornography," *Theatre Journal* 41(3) (1989): 298; Snigurowicz, "Sex, Simians, and Spectacle," 76–77.

83. Wendy Cooper, *Hair: Sex, Society, Symbolism* (New York: Stein and Day, 1971), 7, 66.

84. Mary E. Fissell, "Hairy Women and Naked Truths: Gender and the Politics of Knowledge in *Aristotle's Masterpiece,*" *William and Mary Quarterly* 60(1) (2003): 43–74.

85. Cooper, *Hair,* 78.

86. Karen Harvey, *Reading Sex in the Eighteenth Century* (Cambridge: Cambridge University Press, 2004), 96–97.

87. "Krao, the Missing Link," 13.

88. Jami Moss, "'A Body of Organized Truth': Freaks in Britain, 1830–1900," PhD diss., University of Wisconsin–Madison, 1999, 185.

89. Arthur Goddard, "Even as You and I," 1898, Human Freaks Box 4, John Johnson Collection, Oxford University; *The Era,* 1 January 1898, 22.

90. *World's Fair,* 20 March 1909, 10.

91. Clarence Dean, *The Official Guide. Book of Marvels in the Barnum and Bailey Greatest Show on Earth With Full Descriptions of the Human Prodigies and Rare Animals* (London: Barnum and Bailey, 1899), 12–13; "Photograph of Annie Jones, the Bearded Lady," COPY 1/439/549, National Archives.

92. Playbills Folder (Miscellaneous): Linwood Gallery, Guildhall Library; "The Last Great Wonder of the World," Entertainments Folder 8, John Johnson Collection, Oxford University.

93. *Penny Illustrated Paper,* 6 January 1883, 14.

94. "Miss Julia Pastrana, The Nondescript," Human Freaks Box 2, John Johnson Collection, Oxford University; *Account of Miss Pastrana, the Nondescript; and the Double-Bodied Boy* (London: E. Hancock, 1860); Janet Browne and Sharon Messenger, "Victorian Spectacle: Julia Pastrana, the Bearded and Hairy Female," *Endeavour* 27(4) (2003): 155–59; Thomson, "Narratives of Deviance and Delight," 81–104; Rebecca Stern, "Our Bear Women, Ourselves: Affiliating with Julia Pastrana," in *Victorian Freaks: The Social Context of Freakery in Britain,* ed. Marlene Tromp (Columbus: Ohio State University Press, 2008), 200–233.

95. "Miss Julia Pastrana, The Nondescript."

96. *Account of Miss Pastrana,* 3.

97. *Lancet,* 3 May 1862, 468.

98. *Lancet,* 11 July 1857, 48; 15 March 1862, 294.

99. Darwin, *Variation of Animals and Plants,* 328.

100. "Miss Julia Pastrana," Iconographic Collection 38980i, Wellcome Library; *Lancet,* 11 July 1857, 48.

101. "New and Unparalleled Discovery in the Art of Embalming," Human Freaks Box 2, John Johnson Collection, Oxford University.

102. Evanion 2537, British Library.

103. "A Collection of Handbills," 94; Evanion 1635 and 375, British Library; "Madame Howard," Human Freaks Box 2, John Johnson Collection, Oxford University.

104. *World's Fair,* 16 October 1909, 12. The acts may in fact be the same person.

105. Sander Gilman, "Black Bodies, White Bodies: Toward an Iconography of Female Sexuality in Late Nineteenth-Century Art, Medicine and Literature," in *"Race," Writing and Difference,* ed. Henry Louis Gates Jr. (Chicago: University of Chicago Press, 1986); George W. Stocking Jr., *Victorian Anthropology* (New York: Free Press, 1987); Raymond Corbey, "Ethnographic Showcases, 1870–1930," *Cultural Anthropology* 8(3) (1993): 346–47.

106. Thomson, "Narratives of Deviance and Delight," 92.

107. These images are reproduced in Diana Snigurowicz, "Spectacles of Monstrosity and the Embodiment of Identity in France, 1829–1914," PhD diss., University of Chicago, 2000, 455–56.

108. Snigurowicz, "Sex, Simians, and Spectacle," 78.

109. "Krao, the Missing Link," 12.

110. *News of the World,* 31 December 1882, 5.

111. *Times,* 2 January 1883, 9; *Daily News,* 1 January 1883, 2.

112. *Land and Water,* 6 January 1883, 14.

113. *Morning Post,* 1 January 1883, 2.

114. "Krao, the Missing Link," ii.

115. Peacock, *The Great Farini,* 297–98.

116. Royal Aquarium Programme, 30 April 1887, Playbills Collection, British Library.

117. *English Mechanic and World of Science,* 28 December 1894, 429.

118. Griselda Pollock, *Vision and Difference* (London: Routledge, 1988), 133.

119. Elisabeth G. Gitter, "The Power of Women's Hair in the Victorian Imagination," *PMLA* 99(5) (1984): 938.

120. Unsigned letter to Clerk of London County Council, 22 December 1899, LCC/MIN/10, 891, London Metropolitan Archives.

121. *News of the World,* 14 January 1900, 6. See also a poster from the 1890s that used both phrases in Barbara Kirshenblatt-Gimblett, *Destination Culture* (Berkeley: University of California Press, 1998), 219.

122. "Inspection of Places of Public Entertainment Report," Royal Aquarium, 2 January 1900, LCC/MIN/10, 891, London Metropolitan Archives.

123. Snigurowicz, "Sex, Simians, and Spectacle," 67; McClintock, *Imperial Leather,* 22; Londa Schiebinger, *Nature's Body* (Boston: Beacon Press, 1993), 95.

124. According to her contract Krao was paid $50 for the 1916 season, as much as Frank Lentini, the spectacular three-legged boy. Many thanks to Fred D. Pfening for sharing his collection of contracts with me.

125. "Circus Folk Mourn 'Best-Liked Freak,'" *New York Times,* 19 April 1926, 7.

126. *The Broad Arrow,* 6 January 1883, 22.

CHAPTER FOUR

1. *Illustrated Magazine of Art,* November 1853, 444.

2. *Illustrated Memoir of an Eventful Expedition into Central America Resulting in the Discovery of the Idolatrous City of Iximaya, in an Unexplored Region* (London: R. S. Francis, 1853). A variety of versions of this pamphlet exist. This particular copy is available at the University of California, Berkeley and will be referred to here as *Illustrated Memoir.*

3. *Illustrated Memoir,* 19.

4. *Liverpool Mercury,* 21 June 1853, 483; *Liverpool Chronicle,* 25 June 1853, 7.

5. "Aztec Lilliputians!!," St. Martin's Scrapbook, Leicester Square vol. 1(2), City of Westminster Archives Centre.

6. Richard D. Altick, *The Shows of London* (Cambridge: Belknap Press, 1978), 284–86; Evanion 466, British Library; "Extraordinary Cheap Exhibition," in Ricky Jay, *Jay's Journal of Anomalies* (New York: Farrar, Straus and Giroux, 2001), 90.

7. *Times,* 5 July 1853, 5; *Morning Advertiser,* 25 July 1853, 6.

8. In 1856 the *Manchester Guardian* reported that "Theodore, aged 14," who was one of the "little 'Aztecs' lately exhibited in England" (clearly not Maximo) had died in Berlin. Another imitation act went bankrupt in Paris that same year. See *Manchester Guardian,* 14 March 1856, 3; *News of the World,* 11 May 1856, 7. For their American imitators, see Robert Bogdan, *Freak Show* (Chicago: Chicago University Press, 1988), 132–34.

9. Newspaper clipping about "The Aztec Children," Adelaide Gallery Folder, London Theatre Museum; Iwan Rhys Morus, "'More the Aspects of Magic Than Anything Natural': The Philosophy of Demonstration," in *Science in the Marketplace,* eds. Aileen Fyfe and Bernard Lightman (Chicago: University of Chicago Press, 2007), 340–41. While there is some conflicting evidence as to when the Adelaide Gallery actually closed or was renamed, advertisements for the Aztecs, who did not appear in London before 1853, clearly mention their appearance at a space named the Adelaide Gallery.

10. Minutes of the Ethnological Society Council Meeting, 30 June 1853, 141; Minutes of the Annual Meeting of the Ethnological Society Council, 26 May 1854, 160–61, Royal Anthropological Institute, London; *Lancet,* 9 July 1853, 44; *Lancet,* 29 September 1855, 306; *Lancet,* 18 August 1855, 154.

11. These photographs were purchased by the Natural History Museum, London at a sale of Owen's effects. They were pasted into the museum's copy of Richard Cull, "A Brief Notice of the Aztec Race," *Journal of the Ethnological Society of London* 4 (1856): 120–28.

12. *Illustrated Memoir,* 28, 36.

13. Ibid., 4.

14. Ibid., 25.

15. *Times,* 7 July 1853, 8; *Illustrated London News,* 9 July 1853, 11.

16. *Notes and Queries,* 29 September 1866, 252.

17. Richard Owen, "A Description of the So-Called Aztec Children Exhibited on the Occasion, By Professor Owen, F.R.S," *Journal of the Ethnological Society of London* 4 (1856): 135.

18. "Aztec Lilliputians!!,"; "Favour Ticket for the Aztecs and the Earthmen," St. Martin's Scrapbook, Leicester Square vol. 1(2), City of Westminster Archives Centre. Copies of this ticket are also archived in the Savile House Folder, London Theatre Museum.

19. "The Aztec Lilliputians and the Earthmen," Broadsides BF 24b/50, Wellcome Library.

20. Robert D. Aguirre, *Informal Empire* (Minneapolis: University of Minnesota Press, 2005), 104.

21. "The Aztec Polka, Composed and Dedicated to J. H. Anderson Esq. by J. Robinson," Human Freaks Box 4, John Johnson Collection, Oxford University; John Conolly, *The Ethnological Exhibitions of London* (London: John Churchill, 1855), 24. Interestingly, in the Jain religion, the end of humanity is signaled by the decrease of humans to the size of pigmies.

22. *Athenaeum*, 23 December 1854, 1561; "The Aztecs!," Human Freaks Box 4, John Johnson Collection, Oxford University; quoted in Jay, *Jay's Journal of Anomalies*, 90; *Times*, 7 July 1853, 8; *Illustrated London News*, 9 July 1853, 11; *Illustrated London News*, 23 July 1853, 43–44; "Extraordinary Cheap Exhibition."

23. *Lancet*, 7 April 1855, 494.

24. Owen, "Description of the So-Called Aztec Children," 137.

25. *Athenaeum*, 1 October 1853, 1170.

26. *Illustrated London News*, 23 July 1853, 43; *Dublin Medical Press*, 27 July 1853, 58.

27. Owen, "Description of the So-Called Aztec Children," 134, 136; *Anthropological Review* 1(1) (1863): 187–91.

28. *Anthropological Review* 7(25) (1869): 128–36; Nigel Rothfels, "Aztecs, Aborigines, and Ape-People: Science and Freaks in Germany, 1850–1900," in *Freakery: Cultural Spectacles of the Extraordinary Body*, ed. Rosemarie Garland Thomson (New York: New York University Press, 1996), 166–68.

29. William W. Ireland, "On the Diagnosis and Prognosis of Idiocy and Imbecility," *Edinburgh Medical Journal*, June 1882: 1072–85; John Langdon Down, *On Some of the Mental Affections of Childhood and Youth* (Oxford: Blackwell, 1990 [1887]), 18–19; George M. Gould and Walter L. Pyle, *Anomalies and Curiosities of Medicine* (London: Rebman Publishing, 1897), 248.

30. "Favour Ticket."

31. *Athenaeum*, 9 July 1853, 825; *Freeman's Journal*, 4 October 1853, 3; *Standard*, 12 July 1853, 1.

32. *Illustrated London News*, 23 July 1853, 43–44.

33. *Times*, 25 July 1853, 5. On Waterton, see Victoria Carroll, "Natural History on Display: The Collection of Charles Waterton," in Fyfe and Lightman, *Science in the Marketplace*, 271–300.

34. *Illustrated London News*, 30 July 1853, 66.

35. For similar discussion about language, speech, civilization, and the freak show, see Christine C. Ferguson, "Elephant Talk: Language and Enfranchisement in the Merrick Case," in *Victorian Freaks: The Social Context of Freakery in Britain*, ed. Marlene Tromp (Columbus: Ohio State University Press, 2008), 114–33.

36. *Household Words*, 13 August 1853, 573; *Notes and Queries*, 8 May 1858, 382; *Blackwood's Edinburgh Magazine*, February 1855, 200.

37. *Illustrated London News*, 23 July 1853, 43–44.

38. *Freeman's Journal*, 4 October 1853, 3.

39. *Household Words*, 13 August 1853, 576.

40. [Thomas] Whimsical Walker, *From Sawdust to Windsor Castle* (London: Stanley Paul and Co., 1922), 60.

41. Lori Merish, "Cuteness and Commodity Aesthetics: Tom Thumb and Shirley Temple," in Thomson, *Freakery,* 185–203.

42. Aguirre, *Informal Empire,* 119–20.

43. "Aztec Lilliputians!!"

44. Jane R. Goodall, *Performance and Evolution in the Age of Darwin* (London: Routledge, 2002), 62.

45. "Aztec Lilliputians!!"

46. Aguirre, *Informal Empire.*

47. L. Sprague de Camp, *Lost Continents: The Atlantis Theme in History, Science, and Literature* (New York: Dover, 1970), 105; Robert D. Aguirre, "Exhibiting Degeneracy: The Aztec Children and the Ruins of Race," *Victorian Review* 29(2) (2003): 44–45.

48. *Illustrated Memoir,* 34.

49. Ibid., 11, 14.

50. *Dublin Evening Post,* 4 October 1853, 3; *Dublin Evening Mail,* 5 October 1853, 3. For the way in which these kinds of costumes featured in the Victorian depiction of martians, see Jennifer Tucker, *Nature Exposed: Photography as Eyewitness in Victorian Science* (Baltimore, MD: Johns Hopkins University Press, 2005), 69–70. For their later sun worshiper costumes, see photographs by Charles Eisenmann in Bogdan, *Freak Show,* and in Michael Mitchell, *Monsters: Human Freaks in America's Gilded Age* (Toronto: ECW Press, 2002).

51. *Athenaeum,* 13 August 1853, 966; *Times,* 19 July 1853, 8.

52. *The Scotsman,* 18 February 1854, 2.

53. Austen Henry Layard, *Nineveh and Its Remains* (London: John Murray, 1849).

54. *Illustrated Memoir,* vii.

55. Ibid., 3.

56. Ibid., 23, 25.

57. See, for example, *Liverpool Chronicle,* 25 June 1853, 7. On the old-world origins of New World civilizations, see Robert Wauchope, *Lost Tribes and Sunken Continents: Myth and Method in the Study of American Indians* (Chicago: University of Chicago Press, 1962), 3; de Camp, *Lost Continents,* 105.

58. Austen Henry Layard, *Discoveries in the Ruins of Nineveh and Babylon* (London: John Murray, 1853).

59. Program for "Sardanapalus, or, the 'Fast' King of Assyria," Theatre Royal, Adelphi, 20 July 1853, London Theatre Museum; *The Leader,* 30 July 1853, 741.

60. Frederick N. Bohrer, *Orientalism and Visual Culture: Imagining Mesopotamia in Nineteenth-Century Culture* (Cambridge: Cambridge University Press, 2003); Altick, *Shows of London,* 182; Steven W. Holloway, "Biblical Assyria

and Other Anxieties in the British Empire," *Journal of Religion and Society* 3 (2001): 5; Nancy Aycock Metz, "*Little Dorrit's* London: Babylon Revisited," *Victorian Studies* 33(3) (1990): 468.

61. *Illustrated Memoir of an Eventful Expedition into Central America Resulting in the Discovery of the Idolatrous City of Iximaya, in an Unexplored Region* (London: n.p., 1853), viii. This version of the pamphlet, found at the British Library, is different from the other 1853 edition, found at the University of California, Berkeley, that I quote throughout this chapter. The Berkeley pamphlet does not contain the Layard drawings. The version from the British Library will be referred to throughout as *Illustrated Memoir of an Eventful Expedition* to distinguish it from the Berkeley edition.

62. "The Aztecs, the Earthmen, and a Concert," Entertainments Folder 6, John Johnson Collection, Oxford University.

63. *Athenaeum,* 9 July 1853, 828.

64. *Athenaeum,* 13 August 1853, 966–67; *Liverpool Mercury,* 21 June 1853, 483; *Bell's Life in London,* 17 July 1853, 8.

65. *Illustrated Magazine of Art,* September 1853, 77.

66. *Lancet,* 7 April 1855, 494. Knox was so interested in the Assyrian excavation that he later published "Abstract of Observations on the Assyrian Marbles, and on Their Place in History and in Art," *Transactions of the Ethnological Society of London* 1 (1861): 146–54.

67. *Freeman's Journal,* 3 October 1853, 3.

68. *Illustrated London Magazine* 1 (1853): 149, 152.

69. Robert Reid, "Observations on the Dentition of the 'Lilliputian Aztecs,'" *Monthly Journal of Medical Science* 18 (1854): 121.

70. *Illustrated London News,* 9 July 1853, 11.

71. Benjamin Keen, *The Aztec Image in Western Thought* (New Brunswick, NJ: Rutgers University Press, 1990), 113.

72. *Illustrated Memoir,* 29.

73. Bohrer, *Orientalism and Visual Culture,* 49, 50, 59.

74. *Illustrated Memoir,* 2, 22.

75. *Times,* 11 July 1853, 8.

76. Ibid.; *Standard,* 12 July 1853, 1.

77. *Catalogue of J. W. Reimer's Gallery of All Nations and Anatomical Museum* (Leeds: Jackson and Asquith, 1853), 43–44.

78. Shawn Malley, "Austen Henry Layard and the Periodical Press: Middle Eastern Archaeology and the Excavation of Cultural Identity in Mid-Nineteenth Century Britain," *Victorian Review* 22(2) (1996): 158, 165; Andrew M. Stauffer, "Dante Gabriel Rossetti and the Burdens of Nineveh," *Victorian Literature and Culture* 33(2) (2005): 369–70; Metz, "*Little Dorrit's* London," 470.

79. *Household Words,* 8 February 1851, 468–69; Deborah Thomas, "Uncovering Nineveh," *Archaeology Odyssey* 7 (2004): 30–31.

80. Troy Bickham, *Savages Within the Empire* (Oxford: Oxford University Press, 2005), 198; H. M Hopfl, "From Savage to Scotsman: Conjectural History in the Scottish Enlightenment," *Journal of British Studies* 17(2) (1978): 37.

81. Arthur Herman, *The Idea of Decline in Western History* (New York: The Free Press, 1997), 13–45.

82. Sumathi Ramaswamy, *The Lost Land of Lemuria* (Berkeley: University of California Press, 2004); de Camp, *Lost Continents;* Wauchope, *Lost Tribes and Sunken Continents;* Stuart Kirsch, "Lost Tribes: Indigenous People and the Social Imaginary," *Anthropological Quarterly* 70(2) (1997): 58–67; Kelly Hurley, "The Victorian Mummy Fetish: H. Rider Haggard, Frank Aubrey, and the White Mummy" in Tromp, *Victorian Freaks,* 180–99. I am grateful to John Gillis for pointing me in this direction.

83. Quoted in Malley, "Austen Henry Layard," 161.

84. Christopher Woodward, *In Ruins* (New York: Vintage, 2003), 5.

85. Quoted in Alun C. Davies, "Ireland's Crystal Palace, 1853," in *Irish Population, Economy and Society,* ed. J. M. Goldstrom and L. A. Clarkson (Oxford: Oxford University Press, 1981), 250, n. 3. See also Paul Greenhalgh, *Ephemeral Vistas* (Manchester: Manchester University Press, 1991); John E. Findling, ed., *Historical Dictionary of World's Fairs and Expositions, 1851–1988* (New York: Greenwood Press, 1988); Peter H. Hoffenberg, *An Empire on Display* (Berkeley: University of California Press, 2001); Leon Litvack, "Exhibiting Ireland, 1851–3: Colonial Mimicry in London, Cork, and Dublin," and A. Jamie Saris, "Imagining Ireland in the Great Exhibition of 1853," in *Ireland in the Nineteenth Century: Regional Identity,* ed. Leon Litvack and Glenn Hooper (Dublin: Four Courts Press, 2000). For the 1851 Crystal Palace exhibition, see Jeffrey Auerbach, *The Great Exhibition of 1851* (New Haven, CT: Yale University Press, 1999).

86. *Dublin Evening Mail,* 5 October 1853, 3.

87. *Dublin Evening Post,* 8 October 1853, 3.

88. *Freeman's Journal,* 4 October 1853, 3; Evanion 466, British Library; *Illustrated Memoir of an Eventful Expedition;* Poster for "The Aztec Wonders" at the Royal Aquarium, reprinted in Jay, *Jay's Journal of Anomalies,* 88; Conolly, *Ethnological Exhibitions,* 24.

89. *Household Words,* 13 August 1853, 576. On the contributors to this journal, see Anne Lohrli, *Household Words: A Weekly Journal 1850–1859 Conducted by Charles Dickens* (Toronto: University of Toronto Press, 1973).

90. *Athenaeum,* 23 December 1854, 1561.

91. Conolly, *Ethnological Exhibitions,* 22–24.

92. *Times,* 19 February 1867, 10; *Morning Post,* 8 January 1867, 3.

93. Johannes Fabian, *Time and the Other: How Anthropology Makes Its Object* (New York: Columbia University Press, 1983); Patrick Brantlinger, *Dark Vanishings* (Ithaca, NY: Cornell University Press, 2003), 2, 18.

94. *Times,* 19 July 1853, 8.

95. Jay, *Jay's Journal of Anomalies,* 89.

96. "Aztec Lilliputians!!"

97. Aguirre, *Informal Empire,* 112.

98. "A Collection of Handbills, Newspaper Cuttings, and Other Items, 1820–96," G.R.2.5.7, 16, Guildhall Library; J. S. Tyler, *The Bosjesmans: A Lecture on the Mental, Moral, and Physical Attributes of the Bush Men* (Leeds: C. A. Wilson, 1847), 2.

99. Tyler, *The Bosjesmans,* 6.

100. "Now Exhibiting at the Egyptian Hall, Piccadilly. The Bosjesmans, or Bush People" ca. 1847, 1856.g.15(16), British Library.

101. *Household Words,* 11 June 1853, 337–39.

102. *Illustrated Magazine of Art,* November 1853, 444–45.

103. For more details on their performance before they joined the Aztecs, see Bernth Lindfors, "Hottentot, Bushman, Kaffir: Taxonomic Tendencies in Nineteenth-Century Racial Iconography," *Nordic Journal of African Studies* 5(2) (1996): 10–16.

104. *Times,* 7 May 1853, 5; *The Erdemanne; or, Earthmen from the Orange River in South Africa* (London: John K. Chapman, 1853), 3.

105. *Journal of the Ethnological Society of London* 4 (1856): 149; *Lancet,* 7 April 1855, 495.

106. *Athenaeum,* 23 December 1854, 1561; Goodall, *Performance and Evolution,* 72; Handbill for "The Aztec Lilliputians, The Reputed Gods of Iximaya, and the Earthmen," in "A Collection of Handbills, Programmes, and Admission Tickets Relating to Exhibitions in Leicester Square, 1800–1870," British Library; P. T. Barnum, *Struggles and Triumphs* (Buffalo: The Courier Company, 1875), 544.

107. Conolly, *Ethnological Exhibitions,* 27; Minutes of the Ethnological Society Council Meeting, 2 June 1853, 141, Royal Anthropological Institute, London.

108. "The Earthmen," Human Freaks Box 4, John Johnson Collection, Oxford University; *Times,* 7 May 1853, 5; Lindfors, "Hottentot, Bushman, Kaffir," 16.

109. "Favour Ticket."

110. Ibid.

111. *Blackwood's Edinburgh Magazine,* September 1853, 360.

112. Goodall, *Performance and Evolution,* 66.

113. *Times,* 19 July 1853, 8.

114. *Illustrated Memoir,* vi.

115. "Aztec Lilliputians!!"; *Notes and Queries,* 8 May 1858, 382; *Times,* 19 July 1853, 8; *Illustrated London Magazine* 1 (1853): 150; *Bell's Life in London,* 17 July 1853, 8. On the relationship between the discourses of race and dwarfism, see

Marlene Tromp, "Empire and the Indian Freak: The 'Miniature Man' from Cawnpore and the 'Marvellous Indian Boy' on Tour in England" in Tromp, *Victorian Freaks*, 160–62.

116. J. Mason Warren, "An Account of Two Remarkable Indian Dwarfs Exhibited in Boston Under the Name of Aztec Children," *American Journal of the Medical Sciences*, April 1851, 288.

117. *Blackwood's Edinburgh Magazine*, February 1855, 200.

118. *Household Words*, 13 August 1853, 576; Conolly, *Ethnological Exhibitions*, 23.

119. *Illustrated London News*, 23 July 1853, 44.

120. Owen, "Description of the So-Called Aztec Children," 135; Evelleen Richards, "A Political Anatomy of Monsters, Hopeful and Otherwise: Teratogeny, Transcendentalism, and Evolutionary Theorizing," *Isis* 85(3) (1994): 377–411.

121. Carl Vogt, *Lectures on Man: His Place in Creation and in the History of the Earth* (London: Longman, Green, Longman and Roberts, 1864), 200.

122. *Illustrated London News*, 9 July 1853, 11; *Illustrated London Magazine* 1 (1853): 150.

123. As late as 1870 Luke Burke was declaring that skin and hair differences were of trivial value and "should not be taken as a basis in defining the primary divisions of the human race." See *Journal of the Ethnological Society of London* 2(4) (1870): 412.

124. *Athenaeum*, 23 December 1854, 1561; *Athenaeum*, 9 July 1853, 828; "Exhibitions for the Million," Broadsides BF 24b/50, Wellcome Library.

125. Cull, "Brief Notice of the Aztec Race," 123, 128.

126. *Illustrated Memoir*, v.

127. Gould and Pyle, *Anomalies and Curiosities of Medicine*, 248, provided this figure for their facial angle. See L. Perry Curtis, *Apes and Angels* (Washington, D.C.: Smithsonian Press, 1996), 8–9, for Camper's diagrams.

128. Aguirre, *Informal Empire*, 116–17.

129. William Henry West, "The Aztec Polka" (London: J. Duncombe, ca. 1853).

130. Reid, "Observations on the Dentition," 121–22; Edward J. Wood, *Giants and Dwarfs* (London: Richard Bentley, 1868), 437; *Illustrated London News*, 9 July 1853, 11–12.

131. Owen, "Description of the So-Called Aztec Children," 136–37.

132. Aguirre, *Informal Empire*, 122.

133. "Aztec Lilliputians!!"

134. *Times*, 7 July 1853, 8; "Exhibitions for the Million"; *Illustrated London News*, 9 July 1853, 11.

135. *Illustrated London News*, 23 July 1853, 44; "Extraordinary Cheap Exhibition."

136. *Times*, 19 February 1867, 10.

137. Reid, "Observations on the Dentition," 122.

138. *Journal of the Ethnological Society of London* 4 (1856): 149; H. F. Augstein, "Aspects of Philology and Racial Theory in Nineteenth-Century Celticism—the Case of James Cowles Prichard," *Journal of European Studies* 28(4) (1998): 367.

139. Owen, "Description of the So-Called Aztec Children," 132.

140. *Illustrated London Magazine* 1 (1853): 150.

141. *The Leader,* 27 August 1853, 836. For Burke, see his obituary in *Journal of the Anthropological Institute of Great Britain and Ireland* 15 (1886): 504.

142. *Anthropological Review* 1(1) (1863): 191.

143. *Journal of the Ethnological Society of London* 4 (1856): 297; Wood, *Giants and Dwarfs,* 436.

144. Altick, *Shows of London,* 342; R. J. Jordan, *Catalogue of the London Anatomical Museum* (London: n.p., ca. 1861), 37; *Handbook of Dr. Kahn's Museum* (London: W. Snell, 1863), catalogue nos. 158 and 159; *Catalogue of J. W. Reimer's Gallery of All Nations.* On the history of anatomical museums, see Samuel J. M. M. Alberti, "The Museum Affect: Visiting Collections of Anatomy and Natural History," in Fyfe and Lightman, *Science in the Marketplace,* 371–403.

145. Reid, "Observations on the Dentition," 122.

146. *Lancet,* 7 April 1855, 495.

147. Richards, "Political Anatomy of Monsters," 400–404.

148. *Times,* 14 July 1853, 8.

149. *Illustrated Magazine of Art,* September 1853, 77; Aguirre, *Informal Empire,* 127.

150. *Lancet,* 23 July 1853, 89.

151. "Caste," *Oxford English Dictionary,* 2nd ed., 1989, *OED Online,* Oxford University Press, 29 July 2008, http://dictionary.oed.com.tproxy01.lib.utah.edu/cgi/entry/50034207.

152. Owen, "Description of the So-Called Aztec Children," 136.

153. *Athenaeum,* 9 July 1853, 825.

154. *Anthropological Review* 1(1) (1863): 187.

155. *Journal of the Ethnological Society of London* 4 (1856): 149; *Athenaeum,* 9 July 1853, 825.

156. Reid, "Observations on the Dentition," 122.

157. *Household Words,* 13 August 1853, 576.

158. *The Leader,* 27 August 1853, 836.

159. *Dublin Evening Post,* 4 October 1853, 3.

160. Wauchope, *Lost Tribes and Sunken Continents,* 50–59; Gordon Goodwin, "King, Edward, Viscount Kingsborough (1795–1837)," rev. Alan Bell, in *Oxford Dictionary of National Biography* (Oxford: Oxford University Press, 2004). See also E. B. Tylor, *Anahuac* (London: Longman, Green, Longman, and Roberts, 1861), 17–18.

161. *Times,* 7 July 1853, 8; *Illustrated London News,* 9 July 1853, 11. See also *Morning Post,* 9 July 1853, 4.

162. *Notes and Queries,* 8 May 1858, 382.

163. *Daily News,* 12 July 1853, 5.

164. Quoted in Jay, *Jay's Journal of Anomalies,* 90.

165. Tylor, *Anahuac,* 62.

166. *Freeman's Journal,* 4 October 1853, 3.

167. Sander Gilman, *The Jew's Body* (New York: Routledge, 1991), 169–93.

168. Owen, "Description of the So-Called Aztec Children," 133.

169. *Bell's Life in London,* 17 July 1853, 8.

170. *Standard,* 12 July 1853, 1.

171. Walker, *From Sawdust to Windsor Castle,* 60.

172. *The Leader,* 27 August 1853, 836.

173. *Lancet,* 7 April 1855, 495.

174. Daniel Pick, *Svengali's Web* (New Haven, CT: Yale University Press, 2000); Jules Zanger, "A Sympathetic Vibration: Dracula and the Jews," *English Literature in Transition* 34(1) (1991): 33–44; Stephen D. Arata, "The Occidental Tourist: *Dracula* and the Anxiety of Reverse Colonization," *Victorian Studies* 33(4) (1990): 621–45.

175. *The Scotsman,* 18 February 1854, 2.

176. *Notes and Queries,* 10 July 1858, 39.

177. *Notes and Queries,* 27 October 1866, 343.

178. *Anthropological Review* 5(17) (1867): 252–53.

179. "Sambo," *Oxford English Dictionary,* 2nd ed., 1989, *OED Online,* Oxford University Press, 29 July 2008, http://dictionary.oed.com.tproxy01.lib.utah.edu/cgi/entry/50212589.

180. Andrea Stulman Dennett, "The Dime Museum Freak Show Reconfigured as Talk Show," in Thomson, *Freakery,* 322; Heather McHold, "Even as You and I: Freak Shows and Lay Discourse of Spectacular Deformity," in Tromp, *Victorian Freaks,* 26–27.

181. For coverage of the wedding, see *Daily Telegraph,* 8 January 1867, 3; *Morning Post,* 8 January 1867, 3; *News of the World,* 13 January 1867, 4; *Morning Advertiser,* 8 January 1867, 4; *British Medical Journal,* 12 January 1867, 45. This wedding stunt was copied two years later by another showman who also married his "Lilliputians," two children masquerading as a dwarf couple. The wedding took place at St. George's, Hanover Square, with a dinner following at Willis's Rooms. See John Pollocke, ed., *The Life of David Charles Donaldson Better Known as "Showman Charlie"* (London: Houlston and Son, 1875), 87–89.

182. *Penny Illustrated Paper,* 12 January 1867, 3.

183. Wood, *Giants and Dwarfs,* 434–38. The marriage between Maximo Nuñez and Bartola Velasquez is recorded in the index to the "Register of Marriages for the March Quarter of 1867 in the district of St. George's, Hanover Square," vol. 1a, p. 503.

184. Connolly, *Ethnological Exhibitions,* 22.

185. *The Daily News*, 8 January 1867, 3; *The Daily Telegraph*, 8 January 1867, 3; *Morning Post*, 8 January 1867, 3; *British Medical Journal*, 19 January 1867, 62.

186. Evanion 2530, British Library; *Times*, 16 April 1870, 9; *Times*, 19 February 1867, 10.

187. Evanion 2530, British Library.

188. This photograph and others are pasted into the copy of Richard Cull's "A Brief Notice of the Aztec Race," owned by the Natural History Museum's Zoological Library in London. Another from the same series is pasted into the *Illustrated Memoir of an Eventful Expedition into Central America* owned by the University of California at Berkeley.

189. *Times*, 16 April 1870, 9. When the Aztecs were on display in Germany in the last decades of the nineteenth century, Nigel Rothfels has argued, the discourses of evolution and recapitulation became even more central to their interpretation. See Rothfels, "Aztecs, Aborigines, and Ape-People," 166–68.

190. Evanion 1505 and 998, British Library; Programmes: Royal Aquarium, December 1893, City of Westminster Archives Centre; *Times*, 25 December 1891, 4. The Aztecs appeared at the aquarium from December of 1891 through March of 1892. They reappeared there in November and December of 1893, but after this they disappear from the historical record. For these appearances, see *Times*, 8 December 1891, 1; *Times*, 19 March 1892, 10; *Times*, 7 November 1893, 1. Although they were exhibited at least through 1901, there is no trace of them in the United Kingdom after 1893.

CHAPTER FIVE

1. *Dublin Medical Press*, 10 August 1853, 92.

2. *The Barnum and Bailey Songster. Railway Tour, Great Britain, 1899* (London: Barnum and Bailey, 1899), 3.

3. Although Victorians did not employ the term *ethnicity*, I use it here to refer to a social identity constructed in relation to national and cultural markers, which might overlap with, but nevertheless exist independently from, racial groupings. I do not intend to engage with debates over the definition of ethnicity here. Instead, I seek to use it as a useful term to differentiate understandings of Irishness and Englishness from concepts of racial types that were understood to be fixed and immutable.

4. Bernth Lindfors, ed., *Africans on Stage* (Bloomington: Indiana University Press, 1999); Nicolas Bancel et al., ed., *Zoos Humains* (Paris: La Découverte, 2002). On fakery and early modern marvels, see Kathryn A. Hoffmann, "Sutured Bodies: Counterfeit Marvels in Early-Modern Europe," *Seventeenth-Century French Studies* 24 (2002): 57–70.

5. Paul Greenhalgh, *Ephemeral Vistas* (Manchester: Manchester University Press, 1991), 82–111; John MacKenzie, *Propaganda and Empire* (Manchester:

Manchester University Press, 1984), 114–18; Michael Pickering, *Stereotyping: The Politics of Representation* (Houndmills: Palgrave, 2001), 51–60; Nicolas Bancel and Olivier Sirost, "Le corps de l'Autre: une nouvelle economie du regard," in Bancel et al., *Zoos Humains;* Annie Coombes, *Reinventing Africa* (New Haven, CT: Yale University Press, 1994), 85–108; Brian Street, "British Popular Anthropology: Exhibiting and Photographing the Other," in *Anthropology and Photography,* ed. Elizabeth Edwards (New Haven, CT: Yale University Press, 1992), 122–31; Raymond Corbey, "Ethnographic Showcases, 1870–1930," *Cultural Anthropology* 8(3) (1993): 338–69; J. S. Bratton, "Introduction," in *Acts of Supremacy,* ed. J. S. Bratton et al. (Manchester: Manchester University Press, 1991), 4; Eric Ames, "From the Exotic to the Everyday: The Ethnographic Exhibition in Germany," in *The Nineteenth-Century Visual Culture Reader,* ed. Vanessa Schwartz and Jeannene Przyblyski (London: Routledge, 2004), 317–18.

6. Bernth Lindfors, "Charles Dickens and the Zulus," in Lindfors, *Africans on Stage,* 63; Coombes, *Reinventing Africa,* 6; William Schneider, "Race and Empire: The Rise of Popular Ethnography in the Late Nineteenth Century," *Journal of Popular Culture* 11(1) (1977): 98.

7. "A Collection of Handbills, Newspaper Cuttings, and Other Items 1820–96," G.R.2.5.7, opposite 102, Guildhall Library; Royal Aquarium Folder, 1876–84, London Theatre Museum; Evanion 341, British Library; Shane Peacock, "Africa Meets the Great Farini," in Lindfors, *Africans on Stage.* For Cetewayo's visit to London, see Neil Parsons, "No Longer Rare Birds in London: Zulu, Ndebele, Gaza, and Swazi Envoys to England, 1882–1894," in *Black Victorians, Black Victoriana,* ed. Gretchen Holbrook Gerzina (New Brunswick, NJ: Rutgers University Press, 2003).

8. Bruce Haley, *The Healthy Body and Victorian Culture* (Cambridge, MA: Harvard University Press, 1978). Similar arguments for the American freak show are traced in Robert Bogdan, *Freak Show* (Chicago: University of Chicago Press, 1988), 176–99; and Thomas Fahy, "Exotic Fantasies, Shameful Realities: Race in the Modern American Freak Show," in *A Modern Mosaic,* ed. Townsend Ludington (Chapel Hill: University of North Carolina Press, 2000), 67–92.

9. Rebecca Stern, "Our Bear Women, Ourselves: Affiliating with Julia Pastrana," in *Victorian Freaks: The Social Context of Freakery in Britain,* ed. Marlene Tromp (Columbus: Ohio State University Press, 2008), 208.

10. John Conolly, *The Ethnological Exhibitions of London* (London: John Churchill, 1855), 11.

11. Bogdan, *Freak Show,* 176.

12. Bernth Lindfors, "Hottentot, Bushman, Kaffir: Taxonomic Tendencies in Nineteenth-Century Racial Iconography," *Nordic Journal of African Studies* 5(2) (1996): 21.

13. Bernth Lindfors, "Ethnological Show Business," in *Freakery: Cultural Spectacles of the Extraordinary Body,* ed. Rosemarie Garland Thomson (New York: New York University Press, 1996), 217.

14. James W. Cook, *The Arts of Deception: Playing with Fraud in the Age of Barnum* (Cambridge, MA: Harvard University Press, 2001), 16–18.

15. Tom Norman, "Memoirs of Tom Norman," unpublished typescript, 1928, Q/Norm/575 MSS, 13, National Fairgrounds Archive, Sheffield.

16. Vincent Cheng, *Joyce, Race, and Empire* (Cambridge: Cambridge University Press, 1995), 20.

17. Norman, "Memoirs of Tom Norman," 25–26; *The Era,* 26 October 1901, 22; On the port of London as a "nexus of empire," see Jonathan Schneer, *London 1900: The Imperial Metropolis* (New Haven, CT: Yale University Press, 1999), 37–63.

18. *World's Fair,* 25 January 1907, 14; *World's Fair,* 1 February 1908, 14.

19. James Walvin, *Black and White: The Negro and English Society, 1555–1945* (London: Allen Lane, 1973), 197.

20. [Thomas] Whimsical Walker, *From Sawdust to Windsor Castle* (London: Stanley Paul and Co., 1922), 130–31.

21. Norman, "Memoirs of Tom Norman," 17.

22. Bogdan has made a similar point for American shows. Bogdan, *Freak Show,* 187.

23. Michael Ragussis, "Jews and Other 'Outlandish Englishmen': Ethnic Performance and the Invention of British Identity under the Georges," *Critical Inquiry* 26 (2000): 773–97. On the performativity of race, see also Dorinne Kondo, *About Face: Performing Race in Fashion and Theater* (New York: Routledge, 1997).

24. London Theatres, Playbills and Programmes, Albert Palace, Guildhall Library; Peacock, "Africa Meets the Great Farini," 96–97.

25. "A Collection of Handbills," opposite 102; Lindfors, "Charles Dickens and the Zulus," 66–67 (emphasis mine). For an account of this visit told from the perspective of the Zulu performers, see Bernth Lindfors, "A Zulu View of Victorian London," *Munger Africana Library Notes* 48 (1979): 3–19.

26. Conolly, *Ethnological Exhibitions,* 7–8.

27. For an important discussion of ethnographic theatricality and the possibilities of resistance, see Jane R. Goodall, *Performance and Evolution in the Age of Darwin* (London: Routledge, 2002), 80–111. For the ways in which this manifested in the blackface arts, see Michael Pickering, "Mock Blacks and Racial Mockery: The 'Nigger' Minstrel and British Imperialism," in Bratton et al., *Acts of Supremacy,* 181.

28. James McKenzie, "Strange Truth. The Autobiography of a Circus, Showman, Stage and Exhibition Man," unpublished manuscript, Brunel University Library, London, 190.

29. Sally Alexander, "St. Giles's Fair, 1830–1914," *History Workshop Pamphlets* No. Two (Oxford: History Workshop, 1970), 57.

30. Roslyn Poignant, *Professional Savages: Captive Lives and Western Spectacle* (New Haven, CT: Yale University Press, 2004), 11.

31. Pickering, *Stereotyping,* 60.

32. Lord George Sanger, *Seventy Years a Showman* (London: C. Arthur Pearson, 1908), 99. Linda Frost has argued that P. T. Barnum deployed the same techniques in his exhibition of "a band of Indians from Iowa" at his American Museum in 1843. See Linda Frost, *Never One Nation* (Minneapolis: University of Minnesota, 2005), 23.

33. Sanger, *Seventy Years a Showman,* 14.

34. McKenzie, "Strange Truth," 190.

35. *Strand Magazine,* March 1897, 321–22.

36. George Burchett, *Memoirs of a Tattooist* (London: Oldbourne, 1958), 40–41.

37. Maurice Gorham, *Showmen and Suckers* (London: Percival Marshall, 1951), 115–16.

38. Douglas Lorimer, *Colour, Class, and the Victorians* (Leicester: Leicester University Press, 1978), 92–107; Greta Jones, *Social Darwinism and English Thought* (Atlantic Highlands: Humanities Press, 1980), 140–59; Susan Thorne, "'The Conversion of Englishmen and the Conversion of the World Inseparable': Missionary Imperialism and the Language of Class in Early Industrial Britain," in *Tensions of Empire,* ed. Frederick Cooper and Ann Laura Stoler (Berkeley: University of California Press, 1997), 238–62.

39. Daniel Pick, *Faces of Degeneration* (Cambridge: Cambridge University Press, 1989), 41; see also Kenan Malik, *The Meaning of Race* (New York: New York University Press, 1996), 91–100.

40. Mary Cowling, *The Artist as Anthropologist* (Cambridge: Cambridge University Press, 1989), 121–81.

41. Henrika Kuklick, *The Savage Within: The Social History of British Anthropology, 1885–1945* (Cambridge: Cambridge University Press, 1991), 84–86; George Stocking Jr., *Victorian Anthropology* (New York: Free Press, 1987), 219.

42. Gertrude Himmelfarb, *The Idea of Poverty* (New York: Vintage, 1983), 311.

43. Ellen Ross, *Love and Toil: Motherhood in Outcast London, 1870–1918* (Oxford: Oxford University Press, 1993), 11; Deborah Nord, "The Social Explorer as Anthropologist: Victorian Travellers Among the Urban Poor," in *Visions of the Modern City,* ed. William Sharpe and Leonard Wallock (Baltimore, MD: Johns Hopkins University Press, 1987), 123–24; Peter Keating, *Into Unknown England* (Manchester: Manchester University Press, 1976); Patrick Brantlinger, "Victorians and Africans: The Genealogy of the Myth of the Dark Continent," *Critical Inquiry* 12 (1985): 166–203.

44. George Sims, *How the Poor Live* (London: Chatto and Windus, 1889), 1.

45. Ibid., 3, 17, 69.

46. Seth Koven, *Slumming: Sexual and Social Politics in Victorian London* (Princeton, NJ: Princeton University Press, 2004).

47. Gareth Stedman Jones, *Outcast London* (Oxford: Clarendon Press, 1971); Anthony Wohl, *Endangered Lives* (Cambridge, MA: Harvard University Press, 1983); Pick, *Faces of Degeneration.*

48. Pickering, "Mock Blacks," 193.

49. Quoted in Philip Cohen, "The Perversions of Inheritance," in *Multi-Racist Britain,* ed. P. Cohen and H. S. Bains (Houndmills: Palgrave, 1988), 32; Peter Stallybrass and Allon White, *The Politics and Poetics of Transgression* (Ithaca, NY: Cornell University Press, 1986); Gail Ching-Liang Low, *White Skins/Black Masks: Representation and Colonialism* (New York: Routledge, 1996), 3; Ann Stoler, *Race and the Education of Desire* (Durham, NC: Duke University Press, 1996), 123–30; Peter Fryer, *Staying Power* (Atlantic Highlands, NJ: Humanities Press, 1984), 169–70; Brantlinger, "Victorians and Africans," 181–82.

50. Michael Mark Chemers, "Monsters, Myths, and Mechanics: Performance of Stigmatized Identity in the American Freak Show," PhD diss., University of Washington, 2001, 133.

51. Pickering, *Stereotyping,* 124.

52. Alastair Bonnett, "How the British Working Class Became White: The Symbolic (Re)formation of Racialized Capitalism," *Journal of Historical Sociology* 11(3) (1998): 316–40; Jonathan Hyslop, "The Imperial Working Class Makes Itself 'White': White Labourism in Britain, Australia, and South Africa Before the First World War," *Journal of Historical Sociology* 12(4) (1999): 398–421; Richard Dyer, *White* (London: Routledge, 1997), 57.

53. Robert Gray, *The Factory Question and Industrial England, 1830–1860* (Cambridge: Cambridge University Press, 1996); Patricia Hollis, "Anti-Slavery and British Working-Class Radicalism in the Years of Reform," in *Anti-Slavery, Religion, and Reform,* ed. Christine Bolt and Seymour Drescher (Folkestone: W. Dawson, 1980), 296.

54. Elizabeth Buettner, "Problematic Spaces, Problematic Races: Defining 'Europeans' in Late Colonial India," *Women's History Review* 9(2) (2000): 278.

55. J. S. Bratton, "Introduction," 5.

56. Sanger, *Seventy Years a Showman,* 99.

57. Douglas C. Riach, "Blacks and Blackface on the Irish Stage, 1830–60," *Journal of American Studies* 7(3) (1973): 237 n. 30; Newspaper clipping, Greenwich Fair, 1835, Noble Collection C 26.5, Guildhall Library. On the Irish character of St. Giles, see Pamela Gilbert, " 'Scarcely to Be Described': Urban Extremes as Real Spaces and Mythic Places in the London Cholera Epidemic of 1854," *Nineteenth Century Studies* 14 (2000): 149–72. For the use of Africans and African-Americans to portray Indians in the early nineteenth century, see "The Everyday Book, September 5, 1825," in "A Collection of Advertisements . . . Relating to

Bartholomew Fair," 1194, British Library; Sanger, *Seventy Years a Showman,* 99; David Prince Miller, *The Life of a Showman: To Which Is Added Managerial Struggles* (London: Lacy, 1849), 54.

58. Charles Lever, *The Confessions of Harry Lorrequer* (New York: The Century Co., 1904 [1837]), 224–26.

59. On Ireland as an internal colony, see Michael Hechter, *Internal Colonialism* (Berkeley: University of California Press, 1975).

60. Joep Leerssen, "Wildness, Wilderness, and Ireland: Medieval and Early-Modern Patterns in the Demarcation of Civility," *Journal of the History of Ideas* 56(1) (1995): 25–39; Michael de Nie, *The Eternal Paddy: Irish Identity and the British Press, 1798–1882* (Madison: University of Wisconsin Press, 2004), 5–6; James Muldoon, *Identity on the Medieval Irish Frontier* (Gainesville: University Press of Florida, 2003).

61. Leerssen, "Wildness, Wilderness, and Ireland," 33.

62. Luke Gibbons, "Race Against Time: Racial Discourse and Irish History," *Oxford Literary Review* 13(1–2) (1991): 97–99; Stocking, *Victorian Anthropology,* 234; Patrick Brantlinger, *Dark Vanishings: Discourse on the Extinction of Primitive Races, 1800–1930* (Ithaca, NY: Cornell University Press, 2003), 94; James Muldoon, "The Indian as Irishman," *Essex Institute Historical Collections* 111 (1975): 267–89.

63. Cheng, *Joyce, Race, and Empire,* 21.

64. W. Houghton, "On a Hairy Family in Burmah," *Transactions of the Ethnological Society of London* 7 (1869): 53–54.

65. Lever, *Confessions of Harry Lorrequer,* 376.

66. Malik, *Meaning of Race,* 82.

67. Noel Ignatiev, *How the Irish Became White* (New York: Routledge, 1995); Bonnett, "How the British Working Class," 317.

68. De Nie, *Eternal Paddy,* 5–6.

69. The literature on this subject is immense. For a representative sample, see Bill Roston, "Are the Irish Black?" *Race and Class* 41(1/2) (1999): 94–102; Michael de Nie, "The Famine, Irish Identity, and the British Press," *Irish Studies Review* 6(1) (1998): 27–35; Jim Mac Laughlin, "'Pestilence on Their Backs, Famine in Their Stomachs: The Racial Construction of Irishness and the Irish in Victorian Britain," in *Ireland and Cultural Theory,* ed. Colin Graham and Richard Kirkland (Houndmills: Macmillan, 1999); Gibbons, "Race Against Time"; Hazel Waters, "The Great Irish Famine and the Rise of Anti-Irish Racism," *Race and Class* 37(1) (1995): 95–108; Catherine Hall, "The Nation Within and Without," in *Defining the Victorian Nation,* ed. Catherine Hall, Keith McClelland, and Jane Rendall (Cambridge: Cambridge University Press, 2000), 207–13; Mary J. Hickman, *Religion, Class and Identity: The State, the Catholic Church and the Education of the Irish in Britain* (Aldershot: Averbury, 1995); Bronwen Walter, *Outsiders Inside: Whiteness, Place and Irish Women* (London: Routledge, 2001).

70. Mary J. Hickman, "Reconstructing Deconstructing 'Race': British Political Discourses About the Irish in Britain," *Ethnic and Racial Studies* 21(2) (1998): 288–307; R. M. Douglas, "Anglo-Saxons and Attacotti: The Racialization of Irishness in Britain Between the World Wars," *Ethnic and Racial Studies* 25(1) (2002): 40–63.

71. Sheridan Gilley, "English Attitudes to the Irish in England, 1780–1900," in *Immigrants and Minorities in British Society*, ed. Colin Holmes (London: Allen and Unwin, 1978); R. F. Foster, *Paddy and Mr. Punch* (Harmondsworth: Penguin, 1993); Alan O'Day, "Home Rule and the Historians," in *The Making of Modern Irish History: Revisionism and the Revisionist Controversy*, ed. David George Boyce and Alan O'Day (London: Routledge, 1996), 141–62; G. K. Peatling, "The Whiteness of Ireland," *Journal of British Studies* 44(1) (2005): 115–33. For further literature on this debate, see also Walter L. Arnstein, "Victorian Prejudice Re-Examined," *Victorian Studies* 12(4) (1969): 452–57; Paul B. Rich, "Social Darwinism, Anthropology and English Perspectives of the Irish, 1867–1900," *History of European Ideas* 19(4–6) (1994): 777–85; L. Perry Curtis, "Comment: The Return of Revisionism," *Journal of British Studies* 44(1) (2005): 134–45; John Belchem, "Comment: Whiteness and the Liverpool-Irish," *Journal of British Studies* 44(1) (2005): 146–52; David A. Wilson, "Comment: Whiteness and Irish Experience in North America," *Journal of British Studies* 44(1) (2005): 153–61; G. K. Peatling, "A Response to the Commentators," *Journal of British Studies* 44(1) (2005): 161–66.

72. Gilley, "English Attitudes to the Irish," 90–91.

73. Michael Banton, *Racial Theories*, 2nd ed. (Cambridge: Cambridge University Press, 1998).

74. Walter, *Outsiders Inside*; Cohen, "The Perversions of Inheritance"; Mary J. Hickman, "The Irish in Britain: Racism, Incorporation and Identity," *Irish Studies Review* 10 (1995): 16–19.

75. Peatling, "The Whiteness of Ireland," 125–26.

76. Nancy Stepan, *The Idea of Race in Science: Great Britain, 1800–1960* (London: Macmillan, 1982), 4.

77. Belchem, "Comment," 146–52.

78. MacKenzie, *Propaganda and Empire*.

79. Belchem, "Comment," 146.

80. For the history of the exhibition of Khoisan peoples, see Francois-Xavier Fauvelle-Aymar, "Les Khoisan: entre science et spectacle," in Bancel et al., *Zoos Humains*. For a discussion of the distinctions between the "Hottentot" and the "Bushmen," see Anne Fausto-Sterling, "Gender, Race, and Nation: The Comparative Anatomy of 'Hottentot' Women in Europe, 1815–17," in *The Gender and Science Reader*, ed. Muriel Lederman and Ingrid Bartsch (London: Routledge, 2001), 343–66.

81. Miller, *Life of a Showman,* 142–43.

82. H. F. Augstein, "Aspects of Philology and Racial Theory in Nineteenth-Century Celticism—the Case of James Cowles Prichard," *Journal of European Studies* 28(4) (1998): 357.

83. Z. S. Strother, "Display of the Body Hottentot," in Lindfors, *Africans on Stage,* 13, 29; Nicholas Hudson, "'Hottentots' and the Evolution of European Racism," *Journal of European Studies* 34(4) (2004): 309.

84. Brantlinger, *Dark Vanishings.*

85. See Augstein for how James Cowles Prichard used philology to elevate rather than denigrate the Irish race and culture.

86. Quoted in Christine Bolt, *Victorian Attitudes to Race* (London: Routledge and Kegan Paul, 1971), 150.

87. W. L. Alden, *Among the Freaks* (London: Longmans, 1896), 6.

88. Miller, *Life of a Showman,* 142. On British perceptions of the Bushmen's language, see Bernth Lindfors, "Clicks and Clucks: Victorian Reactions to San Speech," *Africana Journal* 14(1) (1983): 10–17.

89. *Account of Miss Pastrana, the Nondescript; and the Double-Bodied Boy* (London: E. Hancock, n.d.), 12.

90. Quoted in Lindfors, "Charles Dickens and the Zulus," 76.

91. "Now Exhibiting at the Egyptian Hall, Piccadilly, The Bosjesmans, or Bush People," n.p., ca. 1847, 1856.g.15(16), British Library.

92. On the racialization of the fair-skinned Khoisan who was not clearly "black," see Linda E. Merians, "What They Are, Who We Are: Representations of the 'Hottentot' in Eighteenth-Century Britain," *Eighteenth-Century Life* 17 (1993): 14–39; Hudson, "'Hottentots' and the Evolution of European Racism"; Zine Magubane, "Which Bodies Matter? Feminism, Poststructuralism, Race, and the Curious Theoretical Odyssey of the 'Hottentot Venus,'" *Gender and Society* 15(6) (2001): 816–34.

93. In his 1911 text on albinism Karl Pearson was quick to note that "albinism is very often associated with lowered physique and lessened mentality," thus dismissing the idea that "albinotic negroes," despite their white skin, could in any way be comparable to Europeans, and thus that race was much more complicated than mere skin color. See Karl Pearson, E. Nettleship, and C. H. Usher, *A Monograph on Albinism in Man,* part 1 (London: Dulau and Co., 1911), 28. On the exhibition of black albinos, see Charles Martin, *The White African American Body: A Cultural and Literary Exploration* (New Brunswick, NJ: Rutgers University Press, 2002).

94. Quoted in Lindfors, "Charles Dickens and the Zulus," 76.

95. Stocking, *Victorian Anthropology,* 50–51, 57–58, 68; Bolt, *Victorian Attitudes,* 17; Lorimer, *Colour, Class, and the Victorians;* Philip Curtin, *The Image of Africa* (Madison: University of Wisconsin Press, 1964), 233, 365.

96. Andrew Crowhurst, "Empire Theatres and the Empire: The Popular Geographical Imagination in the Age of Empire," *Environment and Planning D: Society and Space* 15 (1997): 155–73; Bratton, "Introduction," 3.

97. Walvin, *Black and White,* 189.

98. Michael Pickering, "White Skin, Black Masks: 'Nigger' Minstrelsy in Victorian England," in *Music Hall: Performance and Style,* ed. J. S. Bratton (Milton Keynes: Open University Press, 1986), 83.

99. For emotional music and sensual dancing as central to Victorian construction of African primitiveness, see Pickering, "Mock Blacks," 205.

100. Belchem, "Comment," 149.

101. Richard Allen Cave, "Staging the Irishman," in Bratton et al., *Acts of Supremacy,* 63; G. C. Duggan, *The Stage Irishman* (New York: B. Blom, 1969), 295; L. Perry Curtis, *Apes and Angels,* 2nd ed. (Washington, D.C.: Smithsonian Institution Press, 1997), xxi; Michael Pickering, "John Bull in Blackface," *Popular Music* 16(2) (1997): 181–201.

102. *The Era,* 10 October 1896, 19.

103. Brantlinger, *Dark Vanishings,* 98.

104. Riach, "Blacks and Blackface," 239–40; Patricia Ferreira, "All But 'A Black Skin and Wooly Hair': Frederick Douglass's Witness of the Irish Famine," *American Studies International* 37(2) (1999): 69–83.

105. Quoted in Lorimer, *Colour, Class, and the Victorians,* 84 (emphasis in the original).

106. Gretchen Holbrook Gerzina, ed., *Black Victorians/Black Victoriana* (New Brunswick, NJ: Rutgers University Press, 2003), 5–6.

107. L. Perry Curtis, *Anglo-Saxons and Celts* (New York: New York University Press, 1968); Curtis, *Apes and Angels.*

108. Quoted in Hickman, *Religion, Class and Identity,* 47; Banton, *Racial Theories,* 73.

109. John Beddoe, *The Races of Britain* (London: Hutchinson, 1971 [1885]); Stepan, *Idea of Race in Science,* 103.

110. Curtis, *Apes and Angels,* 1, 24; Cheng, *Joyce, Race, and Empire,* 40.

111. Quoted in Bernth Lindfors, "Circus Africans," *Journal of American Culture* 6(2) (1983): 11.

112. Coombes, *Reinventing Africa,* 63–83, 115.

113. For an example of Zulu theatricals, see J. S. Bratton, "British Heroism and the Structure of Melodrama," in Bratton et al., *Acts of Supremacy,* 25; Ben Shephard, "Showbiz Imperialism: The Case of Peter Lobengula," in *Imperialism and Popular Culture,* ed. John MacKenzie (Manchester: Manchester University Press, 1986), 94–112.

114. "A Collection of Handbills," opposite 102; Royal Aquarium Folder, 1876–84, London Theatre Museum; Evanion 341, British Library.

115. Richard Ned Lebow, *White Britain and Black Ireland* (Philadelphia: Institute for the Study of Human Issues, 1976), 45; James Malcolm Nelson, "From Rory and Paddy to Boucicault's Myles, Shaun and Conn: The Irishman on the London Stage, 1830–1860," *Eire-Ireland* 13(3) (1978): 86.

CONCLUSION

1. *Daily Mail,* 23 March 2002, 27; *Sunday Times,* 24 March 2002, 3G, 11.

2. Matthew Sweet, *Inventing the Victorians* (New York: St. Martin's Press, 2001), 140.

3. *World's Fair,* 23 April 1910, 9.

4. *The Era,* 1 January 1898, 34.

5. *The Encore,* 13 January 1898, 6.

6. Kenneth Grahame, *Fun O' The Fair* (London: J. M. Dent and Sons, 1929), 27.

7. [Thomas] Whimsical Walker, *From Sawdust to Windsor Castle* (London: Stanley Paul and Co., 1922), 61.

8. Letter from clerk of the London County Council to Mr. Hart, London Exhibition Buildings, Earl's Court, 7 October 1907, LCC/MIN/10, 842, London Metropolitan Archives.

9. Letter from Mr. Hart to Clerk of the London County Council, 12 October 1907, LCC/MIN/10, 842, London Metropolitan Archives.

10. Tom Norman, "Memoirs of Tom Norman," unpublished typescript, 1928, Q/Norm/575, 13, National Fairgrounds Archive, Sheffield.

11. *New York Times,* 15 August 1926, 20.

12. Robert W. Malcolmson, *Popular Recreations in English Society, 1700–1850* (Cambridge: Cambridge University Press, 1973), 118–57; Peter Bailey, *Leisure and Class in Victorian England* (London: Routledge, Kegan, and Paul, 1987).

13. *World's Fair,* 30 July 1910, 7.

14. Thomas Frost, *The Old Showmen and the Old London Fairs* (London: Tinsley Brothers, 1874), 376; Malcolmson, *Popular Recreations,* 89–117.

15. A. St. John Adcock, "Sideshow London," in *Living London,* ed. George Sims (London: Cassell, 1902), 285.

16. Ross McKibbin, *Classes and Cultures: England 1918–1951* (Oxford: Oxford University Press, 1998), 419.

17. Vanessa Toulmin, "Telling the Tale: The Story of the Fairground Bioscope Shows and the Showmen Who Operated Them," *Film History* 6 (1994): 219–37; Vanessa Toulmin, "Local Films for Local People: Travelling Showmen and the Commissioning of Local Films in Great Britain, 1900–1902," *Film History* 13 (2001): 118–37.

18. Mark E. Swartz, "An Overview of Cinema on the Fairgrounds," *Journal of Popular Film and Television* 15(3) (1987): 103.

19. "British Board of Film Censors Report for 1932," HO 45/24084, National Archives. Interestingly, the original epilogue to the movie, which was completely discarded save for the final shot, explicitly located the freak show in London. For more on the film, see David J. Skal and Elias Savada, *Dark Carnival* (New York: Anchor Books, 1995), 161–82.

20. I am grateful to Angela Smith for sharing her work on this subject with me. Her book manuscript is entitled "Hideous Progeny: Disability, Eugenics, and Classic Horror Cinema." See also Tom Johnson, *Censored Screams: The British Ban on Hollywood Horror in the Thirties* (Jefferson, N.C.: McFarland & Company, 1997).

21. *World's Fair*, 6 February 1915, 2; 13 February 1915, 11.

22. R. D. Sexton, "Travelling Showmen in Two World Wars," *Southern History* 10 (1988): 160–75.

23. For an interesting discussion of the possible existence of this category for a brief period in the seventeenth century, see Geoffrey L. Hudson, "Disabled Veterans and the State in Early Modern England," in *Disabled Veterans in History*, ed. David A. Gerber (Ann Arbor: University of Michigan Press, 2000), 117–44.

24. Deborah Cohen, *The War Come Home* (Berkeley: University of California Press, 2001), 19.

25. C. H. Unthan, *The Armless Fiddler* (London: George Allen and Unwin, 1935), 261–78.

26. Cohen, *War Come Home*, 15–60; Jeffrey Reznick, *Healing the Nation* (Manchester: Manchester University Press, 2004), 116–30.

27. This case has been made for the U.S. context by Thomas Fahy in his "Enfreaking War-Injured Bodies: Fallen Soldiers in Propaganda and American Literature of the 1920s," *Prospects* 25 (2000): 529.

28. See the classified advertisements in *World's Fair* from 1914 to 1918.

29. The details of both cases can be found in "Entertainments: Foreign Freaks," HO 45/20476, National Archives.

30. "A Collection of Handbills, Newspaper Cuttings, and Other Items, 1820–96," G.R.2.5.7, opposite 24, Guildhall Library.

31. Paula Black, *The Beauty Industry: Gender, Culture, Pleasure* (London: Routledge, 2004), 20.

32. Sander L. Gilman, *Making the Body Beautiful* (Princeton, NJ: Princeton University Press, 1999).

33. "Entertainments: Foreign Freaks," HO 45/20476, National Archives.

34. Grahame, *Fun O' The Fair*, 27.

35. Elizabeth Haiken, *Venus Envy* (Baltimore, MD: Johns Hopkins University Press, 1997), 123.

36. Duncan Dallas, *The Travelling People* (London: Macmillan, 1971), 156–57.

37. *World's Fair,* 30 July 1910, 7.

38. Dallas, *Travelling People,* 156–57.

39. Ruth Hubbard, "Abortion and Disability: Who Should and Should Not Inhabit the World?" in *The Disability Studies Reader,* 2nd ed., ed. Lennard J. Davis (New York: Routledge, 2006), 93–103.

40. Rosemarie Garland Thomson, "Integrating Disability, Transforming Feminist Theory," in Davis, *Disability Studies Reader,* 267.

BIBLIOGRAPHY

ARCHIVAL SOURCES

Ashmolean Museum, Oxford

"Curious Exhibition Bills of Giants, Dwarfs, Monstrosities, &c., &c." Hope Collection, Folder B29

British Library

A Collection of Advertisements . . . Relating to Bartholomew Fair
A Collection of Handbills, Programmes, and Admission Tickets Relating to Exhibitions in Leicester Square, 1800–1870
Evanion Collection of Ephemera
"Now Exhibiting at the Egyptian Hall, Piccadilly, The Bosjesmans, or Bush People," ca. 1847, 1856.g.15(16).
Playbills Collection

Brunel University Library

McKenzie, James. "Strange Truth. The Autobiography of a Circus Showman, Stage and Exhibition Man," unpublished manuscript, ca. 1944–50.

Circus World Museum, Baraboo, Wisconsin

Newspaper Advertisements, 1884–91

City of Westminster Archives Centre

Royal Aquarium Programs
St. Martin's Scrapbook, Leicester Square vol. 1(2)

Guildhall Library

A Collection of Handbills, Newspaper Cuttings, and Other Items, 1820–96
Circus Box, Barnum Folder
London Theatres, Playbills and Programmes
Noble Collection
Playbills Folder (Miscellaneous)

John Johnson Collection, Bodleian Library, Oxford University

Aquarium Programmes
Entertainments Folders 6 and 8
Human Freaks Boxes 1–4
London Play Places 10

London Hospital Museum and Archives

House Committee Minutes LH/A/5/43
Medical College Minute Book MC/A/2/3
Register of Bodies Used for Anatomical Examination MC/A/31/9
Register of Students MC/S/1/8

London Metropolitan Archives

London County Council Correspondence LCC/MIN/10

London Theatre Museum

Adelaide Gallery Folder
Piccadilly Hall Folder
Royal Aquarium Folders
Savile House Folder
Theatre Royal, Adelphi Folder

National Archives

COPY 1/439 Copyright Office: Entry Forms and Photographs
HO 45/20476 Entertainments: Foreign Freaks
HO 45/24084 British Board of Film Censors Report for 1932
HO 45/9710/A51137 Exhibitions at Westminster Aquarium
MEPO 3/1482 Fraud
Register of Marriages for the March Quarter of 1867 in the District of St. George's, Hanover Square.

National Fairgrounds Archive, Sheffield

Life of Miss Alice Bounds, The Bear Lady, ca. 1911
Norman, Tom. "Memoirs of Tom Norman," unpublished typescript, 1928
"What we know of Waino and Plutano, Wild Men of Borneo. And some of the latest Popular Songs," ca. 1878

Royal Anthropological Institute

Minutes of the Annual Meeting of the Ethnological Society Council
Minutes of the Ethnological Society Council

Royal College of Surgeons

Buckland, Francis T. *Commonplace Books,* vol. 1

Wellcome Library

Broadsides BF 24b
Ephemera Collections
Historical Images Collection
Iconographic Collection

NEWSPAPERS, MAGAZINES, AND JOURNALS

Anthropological Review
Athenaeum
Bell's Life in London
Billboard
Blackwood's Edinburgh Magazine
British Medical Journal

Broad Arrow
Daily Mail
Daily News
Daily Telegraph
Dublin Evening Mail
Dublin Evening Post
Dublin Medical Press
East London Advertiser
Encore
English Mechanic and World of Science
Era
Freeman's Journal
Guyoscope
Household Words
Illustrated Leicester Chronicle
Illustrated London News
Illustrated Magazine of Art
Indian Medical Gazette
Journal of the Anthropological Institute of Great Britain and Ireland
Journal of the Ethnological Society of London
Lancet
Land and Water
Leader
Liverpool Chronicle
Liverpool Mercury
London Figaro
Manchester Guardian
Medical Press and Circular
Morning Advertiser
Morning Post
Nature
New York Times
News of the World
Notes and Queries
Pearson's Weekly
Penny Illustrated Paper
Scotsman
Showman
Sporting and Dramatic News
Standard
Strand Magazine
Sunday Times

Times
Transactions of the Pathological Society of London
World's Fair

PUBLISHED PRIMARY SOURCES

Account of Miss Pastrana, the Nondescript; and the Double-Bodied Boy. London: E. Hancock, 1860.

Account of the Siamese Twin Brothers from Actual Observations. London: W. Turner, ca. 1830.

Adcock, A. St. John. "Sideshow London." In *Living London,* edited by George Sims. London: Cassell, 1902.

Adeler, Edwin, and Con West. *Remember Fred Karno? The Life of a Great Showman.* London: John Long, 1939.

Alden, W. L. *Among the Freaks.* London: Longmans, 1896.

Ballantyne, J. W. *The Diseases and Deformities of the Foetus.* Vol. 2. Edinburgh: Oliver and Boyd, 1892.

———. *Manual of Antenatal Pathology and Hygiene: The Foetus.* Edinburgh: William Green and Sons, 1902.

The Barnum and Bailey Songster. Railway Tour, Great Britain, 1899. London: Barnum and Bailey, 1899.

Barnum, P. T. *Struggles and Triumphs.* Buffalo, NY: The Courier Company, 1875.

Beddoe, John. *The Races of Britain.* London: Hutchinson, 1971 [1885].

Birnbaum, R. *A Clinical Manual of the Malformations and Congenital Diseases of the Foetus.* Trans. G. Blacker. London: J & A Churchill, 1912.

Bock, Carl. *The Head Hunters of Borneo.* London: Sampson Low, Marston, Searle & Rivington, 1881.

———. *Temples and Elephants: The Narrative of a Journey of Exploration through Upper Siam and Lao.* London: Sampson Low, Marston, Searle & Rivington, 1884.

Bolton, George Buckley. *On the United Siamese Twins.* London: Richard Taylor, 1830.

———. "Statement of the Principal Circumstances Respecting the United Siamese Twins Now Exhibiting in London." *Philosophical Transactions of the Royal Society of London* 120 (1830): 177–86.

Bradna, Fred. *The Big Top: My Forty Years with the Greatest Show on Earth.* London: Hamish Hamilton, 1953.

Buckland, Francis. *Curiosities of Natural History.* London: Macmillan, 1900.

———. *Curiosities of Natural History.* 4th series. London: Macmillan, 1905.

Burchett, George. *Memoirs of a Tattooist.* London: Oldbourne, 1958.

Catalogue of J. W. Reimer's Gallery of All Nations and Anatomical Museum. Leeds: Jackson and Asquith, 1853.

Chance, E. J. *On the Nature, Causes, Variety and Treatment of Bodily Deformities.* London: T. T. Lemare, 1862.

Conolly, John. *Address to the Ethnological Society of London Delivered at the Annual Meeting on the 25th of May 1855 and a Sketch of the Recent Progress of Ethnology by Richard Cull.* London: W. M. Watts, 1855.

————. *The Ethnological Exhibitions of London.* London: John Churchill, 1855.

Crawfurd, John. *Journal of an Embassy from the Governor-General of India to the Court of Ava in the Year 1827.* London: Henry Colburn, 1829.

Crocker, H. Radcliffe. *Diseases of the Skin.* London: H. K. Lewis, 1893.

Cull, Richard. "A Brief Notice of the Aztec Race." *Journal of the Ethnological Society of London* 4 (1856): 120–28.

————. "On the Recent Progress of Ethnology." *Journal of the Ethnological Society of London* 4 (1856): 297–316.

Dabney, William C. "Maternal Impressions." In *Cyclopaedia of the Diseases of Children,* edited by John M. Keating. Edinburgh: Young J. Petland, 1889.

Dallas, Duncan. *The Travelling People.* London: Macmillan, 1971.

Darwin, Charles. *The Variation of Animals and Plants Under Domestication.* Vol. 2. London: John Murray, 1868.

Dean, Clarence. *The Official Guide. Book of Marvels in the Barnum and Bailey Greatest Show on Earth with Full Descriptions of the Human Prodigies and Rare Animals.* London: Barnum and Bailey, 1899.

Down, John Langdon. *On Some of the Mental Affections of Childhood and Youth.* Oxford: Blackwell, 1990 [1887].

The Erdemanne; or, Earthmen from the Orange River in South Africa. London: John K. Chapman, 1853.

Frost, Thomas. *The Old Showmen and the Old London Fairs.* London: Tinsley Brothers, 1874.

Gorham, Maurice. *Showmen and Suckers.* London: Percival Marshall, 1951.

Gould, George M., and Walter L. Pyle. *Anomalies and Curiosities of Medicine.* London: Rebman Publishing, 1897.

Grahame, Kenneth. *Fun O' The Fair.* London: J. M. Dent and Sons, 1929.

Gray, D. M., ed. *Mandalay Massacres. Upper Burma During the Reign of King Theebaw.* Rangoon: Rangoon Gazette Press, 1884.

Grenfell, Sir Wilfred Thomason. *A Labrador Doctor.* London: Hodder and Staughton, 1929.

Halsted, D. G. *Doctor in the Nineties.* London: Christopher Johnson, 1959.

Handbook of Dr. Kahn's Museum. London: W. Snell, 1863.

Hirst, Barton Cooke, and George A. Piersol. *Human Monstrosities.* Philadelphia: Lea Brothers and Co., 1893.

History of Miss Annie Jones, Barnum and Bailey's Esau Lady. Glasgow: J. Lithgow, ca. 1891.

Houghton, W. "On a Hairy Family in Burmah." *Transactions of the Ethnological Society of London* 7 (1869): 53–59.

Illustrated Memoir of an Eventful Expedition into Central America Resulting in the Discovery of the Idolatrous City of Iximaya, in an Unexplored Region. London: R. S. Francis, 1853.

Illustrated Memoir of an Eventful Expedition into Central America Resulting in the Discovery of the Idolatrous City of Iximaya, in an Unexplored Region. London: n.p., 1853.

An Interesting Treatise on the Marvellous Indian Boy Laloo Brought to This Country by M. D. Fracis. Leicester: n.p., n.d.

Ireland, William W. "On the Diagnosis and Prognosis of Idiocy and Imbecility." *Edinburgh Medical Journal,* June 1882: 1072–85.

Jordan, R. J. *Catalogue of the London Anatomical Museum.* London: n.p., ca. 1861.

Knox, Robert. "Abstract of Observations on the Assyrian Marbles, and on Their Place in History and in Art." *Transactions of the Ethnological Society of London* 1 (1861): 146–54.

Law, John [Margaret Harkness]. *In Darkest London.* Cambridge: Black Apollo Press, 2003 [1889.]

Layard, Austen Henry. *Discoveries in the Ruins of Nineveh and Babylon.* London: John Murray, 1853.

———. *Nineveh and Its Remains.* London: John Murray, 1849.

Lever, Charles. *The Confessions of Harry Lorrequer.* New York: The Century Co., 1904 [1837].

The Life and Adventures of Joseph Carey Merrick. Leicester: H & A Cockshaw, ca. 1885.

Miller, David Prince. *The Life of a Showman: To Which Is Added Managerial Struggles.* London: Lacy, 1849.

Morley, Henry. *Memoirs of Bartholomew Fair.* London: Frederick Warne and Co., 1874 [1859].

Norman, Tom, and George Barnum Norman. *The Penny Showman: Memoirs of Tom Norman "Silver King."* London: Privately published, 1985.

Owen, Richard "A Description of the So-Called Aztec Children Exhibited on the Occasion, By Professor Owen, F.R.S." *Journal of the Ethnological Society of London* 4 (1856): 128–37.

Paré, Ambroise. *On Monsters and Marvels,* trans. Janis L. Pallister. Chicago: University of Chicago Press, 1982 [1573].

Pearson, Karl., E. Nettleship, and C. H. Usher. *A Monograph on Albinism in Man.* Part 1. London: Dulau and Co., 1911.

Pollocke, John, ed. *The Life of David Charles Donaldson, Better Known as "Showman Charlie."* London: Houlston and Son, 1875.

Reid, Robert. "Observations on the Dentition of the 'Lilliputian Aztecs.'" *Monthly Journal of Medical Science* 18 (1854): 119–23.

Sanger, Lord George. *Seventy Years a Showman.* London: C. Arthur Pearson, 1908.

Sherson, Erroll. *London's Lost Theatres of the Nineteenth Century.* London: John Lane, 1925.

The Siamese Twins: Chang and Eng. A Biographical Sketch. London: J. W. Last, ca. 1869.

Sims, George. *How the Poor Live.* London: Chatto and Windus, 1889.

Sutton, John Bland. *Tumours: Innocent and Malignant.* 7th ed. London: Cassell, 1922.

———. *The Story of a Surgeon.* London: Methuen, 1930.

Tibbles, J. A., and M. M. Cohen. "The Proteus Syndrome: The Elephant Man Diagnosed." *British Medical Journal* (Clinical Research Edition), 13 September 1986, 683–85.

Treves, Frederick. *The Elephant Man: Amplified from an Account Published in the 'British Medical Journal'. December, 1888.* London: John Bale and Sons, 1888.

———. *The Elephant Man and Other Reminiscences.* London: Cassell and Co., 1923.

———. *Physical Education.* London: J & A Churchill, 1892.

Tyler, J. S. *The Bosjesmans: A Lecture on the Mental, Moral, and Physical Attributes of the Bush Men.* Leeds: C. A. Wilson, 1847.

Tylor, E. B. *Anahuac.* London: Longman, Green, Longman and Roberts, 1861.

Unthan, C. H. *The Armless Fiddler.* London: George Allen and Unwin, 1935.

Vogt, Carl. *Lectures on Man: His Place in Creation and in the History of the Earth.* London: Longman, Green, Longman and Roberts, 1864.

Walker, [Thomas] Whimsical. *From Sawdust to Windsor Castle.* London: Stanley Paul and Co., 1922.

Warren, J. Mason. "An Account of Two Remarkable Indian Dwarfs Exhibited in Boston Under the Name of Aztec Children." *American Journal of the Medical Sciences,* April 1851, 288.

Webb, Sidney, and Beatrice Webb. *English Poor Law Policy.* London: Archon Books, 1963.

Weber, F. Parkes. "Cutaneous Pigmentation as an Incomplete Form of Recklinghausen's Disease, with Remarks on the Classification of Incomplete and Anomalous Forms of Recklinghausen's Disease." *British Journal of Dermatology* 21(2) (1909).

West, William Henry. "The Aztec Polka." London: J. Duncombe, ca. 1853.

Williams, Montagu. *Round London: Down East and Up West.* London: Macmillan and Co., 1894.

The Wonder Book of Freaks and Animals. London: Walter Hill and Co., 1898.

Wood, Edward J. *Giants and Dwarfs.* London: Richard Bentley, 1868.

Ackerknecht, Erwin. *Medicine at the Paris Hospital.* Baltimore, MD: Johns Hopkins University Press, 1967.

Adams, James Eli. *Dandies and Desert Saints.* Ithaca, NY: Cornell University Press, 1995.

Adams, Rachel. *Sideshow U.S.A.* Chicago: University of Chicago Press, 2001.

Aguirre, Robert D. "Exhibiting Degeneracy: The Aztec Children and the Ruins of Race." *Victorian Review* 29(2) (2003): 40–63.

———. *Informal Empire.* Minneapolis: University of Minnesota, 2005.

Alberti, Samuel J. M. M. "The Museum Affect: Visiting Collections of Anatomy and Natural History." In *Science in the Marketplace,* edited by Aileen Fyfe and Bernard Lightman. Chicago: University of Chicago Press, 2007.

Alexander, Sally. "St. Giles's Fair, 1830–1914." History Workshop Pamphlets No. Two. Oxford: History Workshop, 1970.

Altick, Richard D. *The Shows of London.* Cambridge: Belknap Press, 1978.

Ames, Eric. "From the Exotic to the Everyday: The Ethnographic Exhibition in Germany." In *The Nineteenth-Century Visual Culture Reader,* edited by Vanessa Schwarz and Jeannene Przyblyski. London: Routledge, 2004.

Anagol-McGinn, Padma. "The Age of Consent Act (1891) Reconsidered: Women's Perspectives and Participation in the Child Marriage Controversy in India." *South Asia Research* 12(2) (1992): 100–118.

Anderson, Nancy F. "The 'Marriage with a Deceased Wife's Sister Bill' Controversy: Incest, Anxiety, and the Defense of Family Purity in Victorian England." *Journal of British Studies* 21(2) (1982): 67–86.

Anemone, Anthony. "The Monsters of Peter the Great: The Culture of the St. Petersburg Kunstkamera in the Eighteenth Century." *Slavic and East European Journal* 44(4) (2000): 583–602.

Appleby, John H. "Human Curiosities and the Royal Society, 1699–1751." *Notes and Records of the Royal Society of London* 50(1) (1996): 13–27.

Arata, Stephen D. "The Occidental Tourist: *Dracula* and the Anxiety of Reverse Colonization." *Victorian Studies* 33(4) (1990): 621–45.

Arnstein, Walter L. "Victorian Prejudice Re-Examined." *Victorian Studies* 12(4) (1969): 452–57.

Assael, Brenda. *The Circus and Victorian Society.* Charlottesville: University of Virginia Press, 2005.

Auerbach, Jeffrey. *The Great Exhibition of 1851.* New Haven, CT: Yale University Press, 1999.

Augstein, H. F. "Aspects of Philology and Racial Theory in Nineteenth-Century Celticism—the Case of James Cowles Prichard." *Journal of European Studies* 28(4) (1998): 355–71.

Bailey, Peter. *Leisure and Class in Victorian England: Rational Recreation and the Contest for Control, 1830–1885.* London: Routledge and Kegan Paul, 1987.

Ballhatchet, Kenneth. *Race, Sex and Class Under the Raj: Imperial Attitudes and Policies and Their Critics, 1793–1905.* London: Weidenfeld and Nicolson, 1980.

Bancel, Nicolas, and Olivier Sirost. "Le corps de l'Autre: une nouvelle economie du regard." In *Zoos Humains,* edited by Nicholas Bancel et al. Paris: La Découverte, 2002.

Bancel, Nicolas, et al., eds. *Zoos Humains.* Paris: La Découverte, 2002.

Banton, Michael. *Racial Theories,* 2nd ed. Cambridge: Cambridge University Press, 1998.

Bates, A. W. *Emblematic Monsters: Unnatural Conceptions and Deformed Births in Early Modern Europe.* Amsterdam: Rodopi, 2005.

Bates, Alan W. "Good, Common, Regular, and Orderly: Early Modern Classifications of Monstrous Births." *Social History of Medicine* 18(2) (2005): 141–58.

Baynton, Douglas. "Disability: A Useful Category of Historical Analysis." *Disability Studies Quarterly* 17 (1997): 81–87.

———. "Disability History: No Longer Hidden." *Reviews in American History* 32(2) (2004): 282–92.

Behlmer, George. *Child Abuse and Moral Reform in England, 1870–1908.* Stanford, CA: Stanford University Press, 1982.

———. *Friends of the Family: The English Home and Its Guardians, 1850–1940.* Stanford, CA: Stanford University Press, 1998.

Belchem, John. "Comment: Whiteness and the Liverpool-Irish." *Journal of British Studies* 44(1) (2005): 146–52.

Benedict, Barbara. *Curiosity: A Cultural History of Early Modern Inquiry.* Chicago: University of Chicago Press, 2001.

Bickham, Troy. *Savages Within the Empire.* Oxford: Oxford University Press, 2005.

Black, Paula. *The Beauty Industry: Gender, Culture, Pleasure.* London: Routledge, 2004.

Bogdan, Robert. *Freak Show.* Chicago: University of Chicago Press, 1988.

Bohrer, Frederick N. *Orientalism and Visual Culture: Imagining Mesopotamia in Nineteenth-Century Culture.* Cambridge: Cambridge University Press, 2003.

Bolt, Christine. *Victorian Attitudes to Race.* London: Routledge and Kegan Paul, 1971.

Bondeson, Jan. *A Cabinet of Medical Curiosities.* London: I. B. Tauris, 1997.

Bonnett, Alastair. "How the British Working Class Became White: The Symbolic (Re)formation of Racialized Capitalism." *Journal of Historical Sociology* 11(3) (1998): 316–40.

Borsay, Anne. "Disciplining Disabled Bodies: The Development of Orthopaedic Medicine in Britain, c. 1800–1939." In *Social Histories of*

Disability and Deformity, edited by David M. Turner and Kevin Stagg. London: Routledge, 2006.

Boyer, Deborah Deacon. "Picturing the Other: Images of Burmans in Imperial Britain." *Victorian Periodicals Review* 35(3) (2002): 214–26.

Brammall, Kathryn M. "Monstrous Metamorphosis: Nature, Morality, and the Rhetoric of Monstrosity in Tudor England." *Sixteenth Century Journal* 27(1) (1996): 3–21.

Brantlinger, Patrick. *Dark Vanishings: Discourse on the Extinction of Primitive Races, 1800–1930*. Ithaca, NY: Cornell University Press, 2003.

———. *Rule of Darkness: British Literature and Imperialism, 1830–1914*. Ithaca, NY: Cornell University Press, 1988.

———. "Victorians and Africans: The Genealogy of the Myth of the Dark Continent." *Critical Inquiry* 12 (1985): 166–203.

Bratton, J. S. "British Heroism and the Structure of Melodrama." In *Acts of Supremacy*, edited by J. S. Bratton et al. Manchester: Manchester University Press, 1991.

———. "Introduction." In *Acts of Supremacy*, edited by J. S. Bratton et al. Manchester: Manchester University Press, 1991.

Brewer, Christopher. *The Hidden Consumer: Masculinities, Fashion, and City Life, 1860–1914*. Manchester: Manchester University Press, 1999.

Brewer, John, and Roy Porter. *Consumption and the World of Goods*. London: Routledge, 1994.

Broome, Richard. "Windows on Other Worlds: The Rise and Fall of Sideshow Alley." *Australian Historical Studies* 112 (1999): 1–22.

Browne, Janet. "Darwin in Caricature: A Study in the Popularisation and Dissemination of Evolution." *Proceedings of the American Philosophical Society* 145(4) (2001): 496–509.

Browne, Janet, and Sharon Messenger. "Victorian Spectacle: Julia Pastrana, the Bearded and Hairy Female." *Endeavour* 27(4) (2003): 155–59.

Buettner, Elizabeth. "Problematic Spaces, Problematic Races: Defining 'Europeans' in Late Colonial India." *Women's History Review* 9(2) (2000): 277–98.

Burgess, G. H. O. *The Curious World of Frank Buckland*. London: John Baker, 1967.

Burton, Antoinette. "From Child Bride to 'Hindoo Lady': Rukhmabai and the Debate on Sexual Respectability in Imperial Britain." *American Historical Review* 103(4) (1998): 1119–46.

Bynum, W. F. *Science and the Practice of Medicine in the Nineteenth Century*. Cambridge: Cambridge University Press, 1994.

Byrom, Brad. "Joseph F. Sullivan and the Discourse of 'Crippledom' in Progressive America." In *Disability Discourse*, edited by Mairian Corker and Sally French. Philadelphia: Open University Press, 1999.

Canguilhem, Georges. *The Normal and the Pathological*. New York: Zone, 1991.

Carroll, Victoria. "Natural History on Display: The Collection of Charles Waterton." In *Science in the Marketplace,* edited by Aileen Fyfe and Bernard Lightman. Chicago: University of Chicago Press, 2007.

Caudill, Edward. "Victorian Satire of Evolution." *Journalism History* 20(3/4) (1994): 107–15.

Cave, Richard Allen. "Staging the Irishman." In *Acts of Supremacy,* edited by J. S. Bratton et al. Manchester: Manchester University Press, 1991.

Chemers, Michael M. "Introduction: Staging Stigma: A Freak Studies Manifesto." *Disability Studies Quarterly* 25(3) (2005), available at www.dsq-sds-archives.org/_articles_html/2005/summer/intro_chemers.asp (accessed January 28, 2009).

Cheng, Vincent. *Joyce, Race, and Empire.* Cambridge: Cambridge University Press, 1995.

Clark, Anna. "Manhood, Womanhood and the Politics of Class in Britain, 1790–1845." In *Gender and Class in Modern Europe,* edited by Laura L. Frader and Sonya O. Rose. Ithaca, NY: Cornell University Press, 1996.

Clark, David L., and Catherine Myser. "Being Humaned: Medical Documentaries and the Hyperrealization of Conjoined Twins." In *Freakery: Cultural Spectacles of the Extraordinary Body,* edited by Rosemarie Garland Thomson. New York: New York University Press, 1996.

Cohen, Deborah. *The War Come Home.* Berkeley: University of California Press, 2001.

Cohen, Philip. "The Perversions of Inheritance." In *Multi-Racist Britain,* edited by P. Cohen and H. S. Bains. Houndmills: Macmillan, 1988.

Collini, Stefan. *Public Moralists: Political Thought and Intellectual Life in Britain, 1850–1930.* Oxford: Oxford University Press, 1991.

Cook, James W. *The Arts of Deception: Playing with Fraud in the Age of Barnum.* Cambridge, MA: Harvard University Press, 2001.

Cook, Jr., James W. "Of Men, Missing Links, and Nondescripts: The Strange Career of P. T. Barnum's 'What-is-It?' Exhibition." In *Freakery: Cultural Spectacles of the Extraordinary Body,* edited by Rosemarie Garland Thomson. New York: New York University Press, 1996.

Coombes, Annie. *Reinventing Africa.* New Haven, CT: Yale University Press, 1994.

Cooper, Wendy. *Hair: Sex, Society, Symbolism.* New York: Stein and Day, 1971.

Corbey, Raymond. "Ethnographic Showcases, 1870–1930." *Cultural Anthropology* 8(3) (1993): 338–69.

Corker, Mairian, and Tom Shakespeare. "Mapping the Terrain." In *Disability/Postmodernity: Embodying Disability Theory,* edited by Mairian Corker and Tom Shakespeare. London: Continuum, 2002.

Costello, Carrie Yang. "Teratology: 'Monsters' and the Professionalization of Obstetrics." *Journal of Historical Sociology* 19(1) (2006): 1–33.

Cowling, Mary. *The Artist as Anthropologist.* Cambridge: Cambridge University Press, 1989.

Crawford, Julie. *Marvelous Protestantism: Monstrous Births in Post-Reformation England.* Baltimore, MD: Johns Hopkins University Press, 2005.

Crowhurst, Andrew. "Empire Theatres and the Empire: The Popular Geographical Imagination in the Age of Empire." *Environment and Planning D: Society and Space* 15(2) (1997): 155–73.

Cunningham, Hugh. *Leisure in the Industrial Revolution c. 1780–1880.* London: Croom Helm, 1980.

Curran, Andrew, and Patrick Graille. "The Faces of Eighteenth-Century Monstrosity." *Eighteenth-Century Life* 21(2) (1997): 1–15.

Curtin, Philip. *The Image of Africa.* Madison: University of Wisconsin Press, 1964.

Curtis, L. Perry. *Anglo-Saxons and Celts.* New York: New York University Press, 1968.

———. *Apes and Angels.* Washington, D.C.: Smithsonian Press, 1996.

———. "Comment: The Return of Revisionism." *Journal of British Studies* 44(1) (2005): 134–45.

Daston, Lorraine, and Katharine Park. *Wonders and the Order of Nature, 1150–1750.* New York: Zone Books, 1998.

Davies, Alun C. "Ireland's Crystal Palace, 1853." In *Irish Population, Economy and Society,* edited by J. M. Goldstrom and L. A. Clarkson. Oxford: Oxford University Press, 1981.

Davis, Lennard J. "Constructing Normalcy: The Bell Curve, the Novel and the Invention of the Disabled Body in the Nineteenth Century." In *The Disability Studies Reader,* edited by Lennard J. Davis. New York: Routledge, 1997.

———. "Crips Strike Back: The Rise of Disability Studies." *American Literary History* 11(3) (1999): 500–512.

Davis, Tracy C. "The Actress in Victorian Pornography." *Theatre Journal* 41(3) (1989): 294–315.

———. "Sex in Public Places: The Zaeo Aquarium Scandal and the Victorian Moral Majority." *Theatre History Studies* 10 (1990): 1–13.

De Camp, L. Sprague. *Lost Continents: The Atlantis Theme in History, Science, and Literature.* New York: Dover, 1970.

De Nie, Michael. *The Eternal Paddy: Irish Identity and the British Press, 1798–1882.* Madison: University of Wisconsin Press, 2004.

———. "The Famine, Irish Identity, and the British Press." *Irish Studies Review* 6(1) (1998): 27–35.

Dennett, Andrea Stulman. "The Dime Museum Freak Show Reconfigured as Talk Show." In *Freakery: Cultural Spectacles of the Extraordinary Body,* edited by Rosemarie Garland Thomson. New York: New York University Press, 1996.

———. *Weird and Wonderful: The Dime Museum in America.* New York: New York University Press, 1997.

Devlieger, Patrick. "'Handicap' and Education in the United States of the 1930s: Discursive Formations in the *New York Times*." *Paedagogica Historica* 37(2) (2001): 279–89.

Dikotter, Frank. "Hairy Barbarians, Furry Primates, and Wild Men: Medical Science and Cultural Representations of Hair in China." In *Hair: Its Power and Meaning in Asian Cultures,* edited by Alf Hiltebeitel and Barbara D. Miller. Albany: State University of New York Press, 1998.

Douglas, R. M. "Anglo-Saxons and Attacotti: The Racialization of Irishness in Britain Between the World Wars." *Ethnic and Racial Studies* 25(1) (2002): 40–63.

Douthwaite, Julia V. *The Wild Girl, Natural Man, and the Monster: Dangerous Experiments in the Age of Enlightenment.* Chicago: University of Chicago Press, 2002.

Dreger, Alice. *Hermaphrodites and the Medical Invention of Sex.* Cambridge, MA: Harvard University Press, 1998.

———. *One of Us: Conjoined Twins and the Future of the Normal.* Cambridge, MA: Harvard University Press, 2004.

Duggan, G. C. *The Stage Irishman.* New York: B. Blom, 1969.

Durbach, Nadja. "The Missing Link and the Hairy Belle: Krao and the Victorian Discourses of Evolution, Imperialism and Primitive Sexuality." In *Victorian Freaks: The Social Context of Freakery in Britain,* edited by Marlene Tromp. Columbus: Ohio State University Press, 2008.

———. "Monstrosity, Masculinity and Medicine: Re-Examining 'the Elephant Man.'" *Cultural and Social History* 4(2) (2007): 193–213.

Dyer, Richard. *White.* London: Routledge, 1997.

Engels, Dagmar. "The Age of Consent Act of 1891: Colonial Ideology in Bengal." *South Asia Research* 3(2) (1983): 107–34.

Fabian, Johannes. *Time and the Other: How Anthropology Makes Its Object.* New York: Columbia University Press, 1983.

Fahy, Thomas. "Enfreaking War-Injured Bodies: Fallen Soldiers in Propaganda and American Literature of the 1920s." *Prospects* 25 (2000): 529–63.

———. "Exotic Fantasies, Shameful Realities: Race in the Modern American Freak Show." In *A Modern Mosaic,* edited by Townsend Ludington. Chapel Hill: University of North Carolina Press, 2000.

Fausto-Sterling, Anne. "Gender, Race, and Nation: The Comparative Anatomy of 'Hottentot' Women in Europe, 1815–17." In *The Gender and Science Reader,* edited by Muriel Lederman and Ingrid Bartsch. London: Routledge, 2001.

———. *Sexing the Body: Gender Politics and the Construction of Sexuality.* New York: Basic Books, 2000.

Fauvelle-Aymar, Francois-Xavier. "Les Khoisan: entre science et spectacle." In *Zoos Humains,* edited by Nicholas Bancel et al. Paris: La Découverte, 2002.

Featherstone, Ann. "Shopping and Looking: Trade Advertisements in the *Era* and Performance History Research." *Nineteenth Century Theatre* 28(1) (2000): 26–61.

———. "Showing the Freak: Photographic Images of the Extraordinary Body." In *Visual Delights,* edited by Simon Popple and Vanessa Toulmin. Trowbridge: Flicks Books, 2000.

Ferguson, Christine C. "Elephant Talk: Language and Enfranchisement in the Merrick Case." In *Victorian Freaks: The Social Context of Freakery in Britain,* edited by Marlene Tromp. Columbus: Ohio State University Press, 2008.

Ferreira, Patricia. "All But 'A Black Skin and Wooly Hair': Frederick Douglass's Witness of the Irish Famine." *American Studies International* 37(2) (1999): 69–83.

Fiedler, Leslie. *Freaks: Myths and Images of the Secret Self.* New York: Simon and Schuster, 1978.

———. *Tyranny of the Normal.* Boston: David R. Godine, 1996.

Findling John E., ed. *Historical Dictionary of World's Fairs and Expositions, 1851–1988.* New York: Greenwood Press, 1988.

Fissell, Mary E. "Hairy Women and Naked Truths: Gender and the Politics of Knowledge in Aristotle's Masterpiece." *William and Mary Quarterly* 60(1) (2003): 43–74.

Flores, Jorge. "Distant Wonders: The Strange and the Marvelous Between Mughal India and Habsburg Iberia in the Early Seventeenth Century." *Comparative Studies in Society and History* 49(3) (2007): 553–81.

Foster, R. F. *Paddy and Mr. Punch.* Harmondsworth: Penguin, 1993.

Francis, Martin. "The Domestication of the Male? Recent Research on Nineteenth- and Twentieth-Century British Masculinity." *The Historical Journal* 45(3) (2002): 637–52.

Frost, Linda. *Never One Nation: Freaks, Savages, and Whiteness in U.S. Popular Culture, 1850–1877.* Minneapolis: University of Minnesota Press, 2005.

Fryer, Peter. *Staying Power.* Atlantic Highlands, NJ: Humanities Press, 1984.

Fyfe, Aileen, and Bernard Lightman. "Science in the Marketplace: An Introduction." In *Science in the Marketplace,* edited by Aileen Fyfe and Bernard Lightman. Chicago: University of Chicago Press, 2007.

Gerber, David. "The 'Careers' of People Exhibited in Freak Shows." In *Freakery: Cultural Spectacles of the Extraordinary Body,* edited by Rosemarie Garland Thomson. New York: New York University Press, 1996.

———. "Pornography or Entertainment? The Rise and Fall of the Freak Show." *Reviews in American History* 18(1) (1990): 15–21.

Gerzina, Gretchen Holbrook, ed. *Black Victorians/Black Victoriana.* New Brunswick, NJ: Rutgers University Press, 2003.

Gibbons, Luke. "Race Against Time: Racial Discourse and Irish History." *Oxford Literary Review* 13(1–2) (1991): 95–117.

Gilbert, Pamela. "'Scarcely to Be Described': Urban Extremes as Real Spaces and Mythic Places in the London Cholera Epidemic of 1854." *Nineteenth Century Studies* 14 (2000): 149–72.

Gilbert, Ruth. "Seeing and Knowing: Science, Pornography, and Early Modern Hermaphrodites." In *At the Borders of the Human,* edited by Erica Fudge, Ruth Gilbert, and Susan Wiseman. Houndmills: Macmillan, 1999.

Gilley, Sheridan. "English Attitudes to the Irish in England, 1780–1900." In *Immigrants and Minorities in British Society,* edited by Colin Holmes. London: Allen and Unwin, 1978.

Gilman, Sander L. "Black Bodies, White Bodies: Toward an Iconography of Female Sexuality in Late Nineteenth-Century Art, Medicine and Literature." In *"Race," Writing and Difference,* edited by Henry Louis Gates Jr. Chicago: University of Chicago Press.

———. *The Jew's Body.* New York: Routledge, 1991.

———. *Making the Body Beautiful.* Princeton, NJ: Princeton University Press, 1999.

Gitter, Elisabeth G. "The Power of Women's Hair in the Victorian Imagination." *PMLA* 99(5) (1984): 936–54.

Goodall, Jane R. *Performance and Evolution in the Age of Darwin.* London: Routledge, 2002.

Goodwin, Gordon. "King, Edward, Viscount Kingsborough (1795–1837)," rev. Alan Bell. In *Oxford Dictionary of National Biography.* Oxford: Oxford University Press, 2004.

Graham, Peter W., and Fritz H. Oehlschlaeger. *Articulating the Elephant Man: Joseph Merrick and His Interpreters.* Baltimore, MD: Johns Hopkins University Press, 1992.

Gray, Robert. *The Factory Question and Industrial England, 1830–1860.* Cambridge: Cambridge University Press, 1996.

Greenhalgh, Paul. *Ephemeral Vistas.* Manchester: Manchester University Press, 1991.

Grosz, Elizabeth. "Intolerable Ambiguity: Freaks as/at the Limit." In *Freakery: Cultural Spectacles of the Extraordinary Body,* edited by Rosemarie Garland Thomson. New York: New York University Press, 1996.

Gruner, Elisabeth Rose. "Born and Made: Sisters, Brothers, and the Deceased Wife's Sister Bill." *Signs* 24(2) (1999): 423–47.

Hagner, Michael. "Enlightened Monsters." In *The Sciences in Enlightened Europe,* edited by William Clark, Jan Golinski, and Simon Schaffer. Chicago: University of Chicago Press, 1999.

Haiken, Elizabeth. *Venus Envy.* Baltimore, MD: Johns Hopkins University Press, 1997.

Halberstam, Judith. *Skin Shows: Gothic Horror and the Technology of Monsters.* Durham, NC: Duke University Press, 1995.

Haley, Bruce. *The Healthy Body and Victorian Culture.* Cambridge, MA: Harvard University Press, 1978.

Hall, Catherine. "The Nation Within and Without." In *Defining the Victorian Nation,* edited by Catherine Hall, Keith McClelland, and Jane Rendall. Cambridge: Cambridge University Press, 2000.

Harvey, Karen. "The History of Masculinity, circa 1650–1800." *Journal of British Studies* 44(2) (2005): 296–311.

———. *Reading Sex in the Eighteenth Century.* Cambridge: Cambridge University Press, 2004.

Harvey, Karen, and Alexandra Shepard. "What Have Historians Done with Masculinity? Reflections on Five Centuries of British History, circa 1500–1950." *Journal of British Studies* 44(2) (2005): 274–80.

Hays, J. N. "The London Lecturing Empire, 1800–1850." In *Metropolis and Province: Science and British Culture, 1780–1850,* edited by Ian Inkster and Jack Morrell. London: Hutchinson, 1983.

Hechter, Michael. *Internal Colonialism.* Berkeley: University of California Press, 1975.

Henkin, Leo. *Darwinism in the English Novel, 1860–1910.* New York: Corporate Press, 1940.

Herman, Arthur. *The Idea of Decline in Western History.* New York: The Free Press, 1997.

Hickman, Mary J. "The Irish in Britain: Racism, Incorporation and Identity." *Irish Studies Review* 10 (1995): 16–19.

———. "Reconstructing Deconstructing 'Race': British Political Discourses About the Irish in Britain." *Ethnic and Racial Studies* 21(2) (1998): 288–307.

———. *Religion, Class and Identity: The State, the Catholic Church and the Education of the Irish in Britain.* Aldershot: Averbury, 1995.

Himmelfarb, Gertrude. *The Idea of Poverty.* New York: Vintage, 1983.

Hinley, Curtis M. "The World as Marketplace: Commodification of the Exotic at the World's Columbian Exposition, Chicago, 1893." In *Exhibiting Cultures: The Poetics and Politics of Museum Display,* edited by Ivan Karp and Steven D. Lavine. Washington, D.C.: Smithsonian Institution Press, 1991.

Hitchcock, Tim. *English Sexualities, 1700–1800.* New York: St. Martin's Press, 1997.

Hoffenberg, Peter H. *An Empire on Display.* Berkeley: University of California Press, 2001.

Hoffmann, Kathryn A. "Of Monkey Girls and a Hog-Faced Gentlewoman: Marvel in Fairytales, Fairgrounds, and Cabinets of Curiosities." *Marvels & Tales* 19(1) (2005): 67–85.

———. "Sutured Bodies: Counterfeit Marvels in Early-Modern Europe." *Seventeenth-Century French Studies* 24 (2002): 57–70.

Holladay, William E., and Stephen Watt. "Viewing the Elephant Man." *PMLA* 104(5) (1989): 868–81.

Hollis, Patricia. "Anti-Slavery and British Working-Class Radicalism in the Years of Reform." In *Anti-Slavery, Religion, and Reform,* edited by Christine Bolt and Seymour Drescher. Folkestone: W. Dawson, 1980.

Holloway, Steven W. "Biblical Assyria and Other Anxieties in the British Empire." *Journal of Religion and Society* 3 (2001): 1–19.

Hopfl, H. M. "From Savage to Scotsman: Conjectural History in the Scottish Enlightenment." *Journal of British Studies* 17(2) (1978): 19–40.

Houlbrook, Matt. "'The Man with the Powder Puff' in Interwar London." *The Historical Journal* 50(1) (2007): 145–71.

Howell, Michael, and Peter Ford. *The True History of the Elephant Man.* London: Allison and Busby, 1983.

Hubbard, Ruth. "Abortion and Disability: Who Should and Should Not Inhabit the World?" In *The Disability Studies Reader.* 2nd ed., edited by Lennard J. Davis. New York: Routledge, 2006.

Hudson, Geoffrey L. "Disabled Veterans and the State in Early Modern England." In *Disabled Veterans in History,* edited by David A. Gerber. Ann Arbor: University of Michigan Press, 2000.

Hudson, Nicholas. "'Hottentots' and the Evolution of European Racism." *Journal of European Studies* 34(4) (2004): 308–32.

Huet, Marie-Hélène. *Monstrous Imagination.* Cambridge, MA: Harvard University Press, 1993.

Huff, Joyce L. "Freaklore: The Dissemination, Fragmentation, and Reinvention of the Legend of Daniel Lambert, King of Fat Men." In *Victorian Freaks: The Social Context of Freakery in Britain,* edited by Marlene Tromp. Columbus: Ohio State University Press, 2008.

Hurley, Kelly. "The Victorian Mummy Fetish: H. Rider Haggard, Frank Aubrey, and the White Mummy." In *Victorian Freaks: The Social Context of Freakery in Britain,* edited by Marlene Tromp. Columbus: Ohio State University Press, 2008.

Hyslop, Jonathan. "The Imperial Working Class Makes Itself 'White': White Labourism in Britain, Australia, and South Africa Before the First World War." *Journal of Historical Sociology* 12(4) (1999): 398–421.

Ignatiev, Noel. *How the Irish Became White.* New York: Routledge, 1995.

Isherwood, Robert M. "Entertainment in the Parisian Fairs in the Eighteenth Century." *Journal of Modern History* 53(1) (1981): 24–48.

Jackson, Louise A. *Child Sexual Abuse in Victorian England.* London: Routledge, 2000.

Jay, Ricky. *Jay's Journal of Anomalies.* New York: Farrar, Straus and Giroux, 2001.

Jewson, N. D. "The Disappearance of the Sick Man from Medical Cosmology, 1770–1870." *Sociology* 10 (1976): 225–44.

———. "Medical Knowledge and the Patronage System in Eighteenth-Century England." *Sociology* 12 (1974): 369–85.

Johnson, Tom. *Censored Screams: The British Ban on Hollywood Horror in the Thirties.* Jefferson, N.C.: McFarland & Company, 1997.

Jones, Gareth Stedman. *Outcast London.* Oxford: Clarendon Press, 1971.

Jones, Greta. *Social Darwinism and English Thought.* Atlantic Highlands, NJ: Humanities Press, 1980.

Keating, Peter. *Into Unknown England.* Manchester: Manchester University Press, 1976.

Keen, Benjamin. *The Aztec Image in Western Thought.* New Brunswick, NJ: Rutgers University Press, 1990.

Kessler, Suzanne. *Lessons from the Intersexed.* New Brunswick, NJ: Rutgers University Press, 1998.

Kiernan, V. G. "Britain, Siam, and Malaya: 1875–1885." *Journal of Modern History* 28(1) (1956): 1–20.

Kincaid, James R. *Child-Loving: The Erotic Child and Victorian Culture.* New York: Routledge, 1992.

Kirsch, Stuart. "Lost Tribes: Indigenous People and the Social Imaginary." *Anthropological Quarterly* 70(2) (1997): 58–67.

Kirshenblatt-Gimblett, Barbara. *Destination Culture.* Berkeley: University of California Press, 1998.

Knoppers, Laura Lunger, and Joan B. Landes, eds. *Monstrous Bodies/Political Monstrosities in Early Modern Europe.* Ithaca, NY: Cornell University Press, 2004.

Kochanek, Lisa. "Reframing the Freak: From Sideshow to Science." *Victorian Periodicals Review* 30(3) (1997): 227–43.

Kondo, Dorinne. *About Face: Performing Race in Fashion and Theater.* New York: Routledge, 1997.

Koven, Seth. "Remembering and Dismemberment: Crippled Children, Wounded Soldiers and the Great War in Great Britain." *American Historical Review* 99 (1994): 1167–1202.

———. *Slumming: Sexual and Social Politics in Victorian London.* Princeton, NJ: Princeton University Press, 2004.

Kriegel, Lara "Narrating the Subcontinent: India at the Crystal Palace in 1851." In *The Great Exhibition of 1851,* edited by Louise Purbrick. Manchester: Manchester University Press, 2001.

Kuchta, David. *The Three-Piece Suit and Modern Masculinity: England, 1550–1850.* Berkeley: University of California Press, 2002.

Kudlick, Catherine J. "Disability History: Why We Need Another 'Other.'" *American Historical Review* 108(3) (2003): 763–93.

Kuklick, Henrika. *The Savage Within: The Social History of British Anthropology, 1885–1945.* Cambridge: Cambridge University Press, 1991.

Kuper, Adam. "Incest, Cousin Marriage, and the Origin of the Human Sciences in Nineteenth-Century England." *Past and Present* 174(1) (2002): 158–83.

Laqueur, Thomas. *Making Sex.* Cambridge, MA: Harvard University Press, 1994.

———. *Solitary Sex.* New York: Zone, 2004.

Lebow, Ned. *White Britain and Black Ireland.* Philadelphia: Institute for the Study of Human Issues, 1976.

Leerssen, Joep. "Wildness, Wilderness, and Ireland: Medieval and Early-Modern Patterns in the Demarcation of Civility." *Journal of the History of Ideas* 56(1) (1995): 25–39.

Lightman, Bernard. "Lecturing in the Spatial Economy of Science." In *Science in the Marketplace,* edited by Aileen Fyfe and Bernard Lightman. Chicago: University of Chicago Press, 2007.

Lindfors, Bernth. "Charles Dickens and the Zulus." In *Africans on Stage: Studies in Ethnological Show Business,* edited by Bernth Lindfors. Bloomington: Indiana University Press, 1999.

———. "Circus Africans." *Journal of American Culture* 6(2) (1983): 9–14.

———. "Clicks and Clucks: Victorian Reactions to San Speech." *Africana Journal* 14(1) (1983): 10–17.

———. "Ethnological Show Business." In *Freakery: Cultural Spectacles of the Extraordinary Body,* edited by Rosemarie Garland Thomson. New York: New York University Press, 1996.

———. "Hottentot, Bushman, Kaffir: Taxonomic Tendencies in Nineteenth-Century Racial Iconography." *Nordic Journal of African Studies* 5(2) (1996): 1–28.

———. "A Zulu View of Victorian London." *Munger Africana Library Notes* 48 (1979): 3–19.

———, ed. *Africans on Stage: Studies in Ethnological Show Business.* Bloomington: Indiana University Press, 1999.

Linton, Simi. *Claiming Disability: Knowledge and Identity.* New York: New York University Press, 1998.

Litvack, Leon. "Exhibiting Ireland, 1851–3: Colonial Mimicry in London, Cork, and Dublin." In *Ireland in the Nineteenth Century: Regional Identity,* edited by Leon Litvack and Glenn Hooper. Dublin: Four Courts Press, 2000.

Lohrli, Anne. *Household Words: A Weekly Journal 1850–1859 Conducted by Charles Dickens.* Toronto: University of Toronto Press, 1973.

Long, Kathleen Perry. "Sexual Dissonance: Early Modern Scientific Accounts of Hermaphrodites." In *Wonders, Marvels, and Monsters in Early Modern Culture,* edited by Peter G. Platt. Newark: University of Delaware, 1999.

Longmore, Paul K., and David Goldberger. "The League of the Physically Handicapped and the Great Depression: A Case Study in the New Disability History." *Journal of American History* 87(3) (2000): 888–922.

Lorimer, Douglas. *Colour, Class, and the Victorians.* Leicester: Leicester University Press, 1978.

———. "Science and the Secularization of Victorian Images of Race." In *Victorian Science in Context,* edited by Bernard Lightman. Chicago: University of Chicago Press, 1997.

Loughlin, Kelly. "Spectacle and Secrecy: Press Coverage of Conjoined Twins in 1950s Britain." *Medical History* 49 (2005): 197–212.

Low, Gail Ching-Liang. *White Skins/Black Masks: Representation and Colonialism.* New York: Routledge, 1996.

Lund, Roger. "Laughing at Cripples: Ridicule, Deformity and the Argument from Design." *Eighteenth-Century Studies* 39(1) (2005): 91–114.

MacLaughlin, Jim. " 'Pestilence on Their Backs, Famine in Their Stomachs': The Racial Construction of Irishness and the Irish in Victorian Britain." In *Ireland and Cultural Theory,* edited by Colin Graham and Richard Kirkland. Houndmills: Macmillan, 1999.

MacKenzie, John. *Propaganda and Empire.* Manchester: Manchester University Press, 1984.

Magubane, Zine. "Which Bodies Matter? Feminism, Poststructuralism, Race, and the Curious Theoretical Odyssey of the 'Hottentot Venus.' " *Gender and Society* 15(6) (2001): 816–34.

Malcolmson, Robert W. *Popular Recreations in English Society, 1700–1850.* Cambridge: Cambridge University Press, 1973.

Malik, Kenan. *The Meaning of Race.* New York: New York University Press, 1996.

Malley, Shawn. "Austen Henry Layard and the Periodical Press: Middle Eastern Archaeology and the Excavation of Cultural Identity in Mid-Nineteenth Century Britain." *Victorian Review* 22(2) (1996): 152–70.

Mangan, J.A., ed. *Making European Masculinities: Sport, Europe, Gender.* London: Frank Cass, 2000.

Mangan, J.A., and James Walvin, eds. *Manliness and Morality: Middle-Class Masculinity in Britain and America 1800–1940.* Manchester: Manchester University Press, 1991.

Martin, Charles. *The White African American Body: A Cultural and Literary Exploration.* New Brunswick, NJ: Rutgers University Press, 2002.

Mathur, Saloni. "Living Ethnological Exhibits: The Case of 1886." *Cultural Anthropology* 15(4) (2000): 492–524.

McClelland, Keith. "England's Greatness, the Working Man." In *Defining the Victorian Nation,* edited by Catherine Hall, Keith McClelland, and Jane Rendall. Cambridge: Cambridge University Press, 2000.

McClintock, Anne. *Imperial Leather.* New York: Routledge, 1995.

McDevitt, Patrick. *May the Best Man Win: Sport, Masculinity, and Nationalism in Great Britain and the Empire, 1880–1935.* Houndmills: Palgrave, 2004.

McHold, Heather. "Even as You and I: Freak Shows and Lay Discourse on Spectacular Deformity." In *Victorian Freaks: The Social Context of Freakery in*

Britain, edited by Marlene Tromp. Columbus: Ohio State University Press, 2008.

McKendrick, Neil, John Brewer, and J. H. Plumb, eds. *The Birth of a Consumer Society.* Bloomington: Indiana University Press, 1982.

McKibbin, Ross. *Classes and Cultures: England 1918–1951.* Oxford: Oxford University Press, 1998.

Merians, Linda E. "What They Are, Who We Are: Representations of the 'Hottentot' in Eighteenth-Century Britain." *Eighteenth-Century Life* 17 (1993): 14–39.

Merish, Lori. "Cuteness and Commodity Aesthetics: Tom Thumb and Shirley Temple." In *Freakery: Cultural Spectacles of the Extraordinary Body,* edited by Rosemarie Garland Thomson. New York: New York University Press, 1996.

Metz, Nancy Aycock. "*Little Dorrit's* London: Babylon Revisited." *Victorian Studies* 33(3) (1990): 465–86.

Mitchell, David T., and Sharon L. Snyder. "Introduction: Disability Studies and the Double Bind of Representation." In *The Body and Physical Difference,* edited by David T. Mitchell and Sharon L. Snyder. Ann Arbor: University of Michigan Press, 1997.

———. "Exploitations of Embodiment: *Born Freak* and the Academic Bally Plank." *Disability Studies Quarterly* 25(3) (2005), available at www.dsq-sds.-archives.org/_articles_html/2005/summer/mitchell_snyder.asp (accessed January 28, 2009).

Mitchell, Michael. *Monsters: Human Freaks in America's Gilded Age.* Toronto: ECW Press, 2002.

Mitchell, Sarah. "Exhibiting Monstrosity: Chang and Eng, the 'Original' Siamese Twins." *Endeavour* 27(4) (2003): 150–54.

———. "From 'Monstrous' to 'Abnormal': The Case of Conjoined Twins in the Nineteenth Century." In *Histories of the Normal and the Abnormal,* edited by Waltraud Ernst. London: Routledge, 2006.

Montagu, Ashley. *The Elephant Man: A Study in Human Dignity.* New York: Outerbridge and Dienstfrey, 1971.

Mort, Frank. *Dangerous Sexualities: Medico-Moral Politics in England Since 1830.* London: Routledge and Kegan Paul, 1987.

Morus, Iwan Rhys. "'More the Aspect of Magic Than Anything Natural': The Philosophy of Demonstration." In *Science in the Marketplace,* edited by Aileen Fyfe and Bernard Lightman. Chicago: University of Chicago Press, 2007.

Moscoso, Javier. "Monsters as Evidence: The Uses of the Abnormal Body During the Early Eighteenth Century." *Journal of the History of Biology* 31 (1998): 355–82.

Muldoon, James. *Identity on the Medieval Irish Frontier.* Gainesville: University Press of Florida, 2003.

————. "The Indian as Irishman." *Essex Institute Historical Collections* III (1975): 267–89.

Neil, Timothy. "White Wings and Six-Legged Muttons: The Freakish Animal." In *Victorian Freaks: The Social Context of Freakery in Britain,* edited by Marlene Tromp. Columbus: Ohio State University Press, 2008.

Nelson, James Malcolm. "From Rory and Paddy to Boucicault's Myles, Shaun and Conn: The Irishman on the London Stage, 1830–1860." *Eire-Ireland* 13(3) (1978): 70–105.

Nord, Deborah. "The Social Explorer as Anthropologist: Victorian Travellers Among the Urban Poor." In *Visions of the Modern City,* edited by William Sharpe and Leonard Wallock. Baltimore, MD: Johns Hopkins University Press, 1987.

O'Connor, Erin. *Raw Material: Producing Pathology in Victorian Culture.* Durham, NC: Duke University Press, 2000.

O'Day, Alan. "Home Rule and the Historians." In *The Making of Modern Irish History: Revisionism and the Revisionist Controversy,* edited by David George Boyce and Alan O'Day. London: Routledge, 1996.

Park, Katharine, and Lorraine J. Daston. "Unnatural Conceptions: The Study of Monsters in Sixteenth-Century France and England." *Past and Present* 92 (1981): 20–54.

Parsons, Neil. "No Longer Rare Birds in London: Zulu, Ndebele, Gaza, and Swazi Envoys to England, 1882–1894." In *Black Victorians, Black Victoriana,* edited by Gretchen Holbrook Gerzina. New Brunswick, NJ: Rutgers University Press, 2003.

Peacock, Shane. "Africa Meets the Great Farini." In *Africans on Stage: Studies in Ethnological Show Business,* edited by Bernth Lindfors. Bloomington: Indiana University Press, 1999.

————. *The Great Farini: The High-Wire Life of William Hunt.* Toronto: Viking, 1995.

Peatling, G. K. "A Response to the Commentators." *Journal of British Studies* 44(1) (2005): 161–66.

————. "The Whiteness of Ireland." *Journal of British Studies* 44(1) (2005): 115–33.

Pender, Stephen. "In the Bodyshop: Human Exhibition in Early Modern England." In *"Defects": Engendering the Modern Body,* edited by Helen Deutsch and Felicity Nussbaum. Ann Arbor: University of Michigan Press, 2000.

Pick, Daniel. *Faces of Degeneration.* Cambridge: Cambridge University Press, 1993.

————. *Svengali's Web.* New Haven, CT: Yale University Press, 2000.

Pickering, Michael. "John Bull in Blackface." *Popular Music* 16(2) (1997): 181–201.

———. "Mock Blacks and Racial Mockery: The 'Nigger' Minstrel and British Imperialism." In *Acts of Supremacy,* edited by J. S. Bratton, et al. Manchester: Manchester University Press, 1991.

———. *Stereotyping: The Politics of Representation.* Houndmills: Palgrave, 2001.

———. "White Skin, Black Masks: 'Nigger' Minstrelsy in Victorian England." In *Music Hall: Performance and Style,* edited by J. S. Bratton. Milton Keynes: Open University Press, 1986.

Pingree, Allison. "America's 'United Siamese Brothers.'" In *Monster Theory,* edited by Jeffrey Jerome Cohen. Minneapolis: University of Minnesota Press, 1996.

———. "The 'Exceptions That Prove the Rule': Daisy and Violet Hilton, the 'New Woman,' and the Bonds of Marriage." In *Freakery: Cultural Spectacles of the Extraordinary Body,* edited by Rosemarie Garland Thomson. New York: New York University Press, 1996.

Poignant, Roslyn. *Professional Savages.* New Haven, CT: Yale University Press, 2004.

Pollock, Griselda. *Vision and Difference.* London: Routledge, 1988.

Qureshi, Sadiah. "Displaying Sara Baartman, the 'Hottentot Venus.'" *History of Science* 42(2) (2004): 233–57.

Ragussis, Michael. "Jews and Other 'Outlandish Englishmen': Ethnic Performance and the Invention of British Identity under the Georges." *Critical Inquiry* 26 (2000): 773–97.

Ramaswamy, Sumathi. *The Lost Land of Lemuria.* Berkeley: University of California Press, 2004.

Rappaport, Erika. *Shopping for Pleasure.* Princeton, NJ: Princeton University Press, 2000.

Reece, R. H. W. Introduction to *The Head Hunters of Borneo,* by Carl Bock. Oxford: Oxford University Press, 1985.

Reid, Douglas A. "Interpreting the Festival Calendar: Wakes and Fairs as Carnivals." In *Popular Culture and Custom in Nineteenth-Century England,* edited by Robert D. Storch. London: Croom Helm, 1982.

Reznick, Jeffrey S. *Healing the Nation.* Manchester: Manchester University Press, 2004.

Riach, Douglas C. "Blacks and Blackface on the Irish Stage, 1830–60." *Journal of American Studies* 7(3) (1973): 231–42.

Rich, Paul B. "Social Darwinism, Anthropology and English Perspectives of the Irish, 1867–1900." *History of European Ideas* 19(4–6) (1994): 777–85.

Richards, Evelleen. "A Political Anatomy of Monsters, Hopeful and Otherwise: Teratogeny, Transcendentalism, and Evolutionary Theorizing." *Isis* 85(3) (1994): 377–411.

Richards, Thomas. *The Commodity Culture of Victorian England.* Stanford, CA: Stanford University Press, 1990.

Ritvo, Harriet. *The Platypus and the Mermaid.* Cambridge, MA: Harvard University Press, 1997.

Roper, Michael. "Between Manliness and Masculinity: The 'War Generation' and the Psychology of Fear in Britain, 1914–1950." *Journal of British Studies* 44(2) (2005): 343–62.

Rose, Sarah F. "'Crippled' Hands: Disability in Labor and Working-Class History." *Labor* 2(1) (2005): 27–54.

Ross, Ellen. *Love and Toil: Motherhood in Outcast London, 1870–1918.* Oxford: Oxford University Press, 1993.

Roston, Bill. "Are the Irish Black?" *Race and Class* 41(1/2) (1999): 94–102.

Rothfels, Nigel "Aztecs, Aborigines, and Ape-People: Science and Freaks in Germany, 1850–1900." In *Freakery: Cultural Spectacles of the Extraordinary Body,* edited by Rosemarie Garland Thomson. New York: New York University Press, 1996.

Samuel, Raphael. "The Elephant Man as a Fable of Class." *New Society,* 19 November 1981.

Saris, A. Jamie. "Imagining Ireland in the Great Exhibition of 1853." In *Ireland in the Nineteenth Century: Regional Identity,* edited by Leon Litvack and Glenn Hooper. Dublin: Four Courts Press, 2000.

Schiebinger, Londa. *Nature's Body.* Boston: Beacon Press, 1993.

———. "Skeletons in the Closet: The First Illustrations of the Female Skeleton in Eighteenth-Century Anatomy." *Representations* 14 (1986): 42–82.

Schneer, Jonathan. *London 1900: The Imperial Metropolis.* New Haven, CT: Yale University Press, 1999.

Schneider, William. "Race and Empire: The Rise of Popular Ethnography in the Late Nineteenth Century." *Journal of Popular Culture* 11(1) (1977): 98–109.

Scully, Pamela, and Clifton Crais. "Race and Erasure: Sara Baartman and Hendrik Cesars in Cape Town and London." *Journal of British Studies* 47(2) (2008): 301–23.

Semonin, Paul. "Monsters in the Marketplace: The Exhibition of Human Anomalies in Early Modern England." In *Freakery,* edited by Rosemarie Garland Thomson. New York: New York University Press, 1996.

Senelick, Laurence. "Enlightened By Morphodites: Narratives of the Fairground Half-and-Half." *Amerikastudien* 44(3) (1999): 357–78.

Sexton, R. D. "Travelling Showmen in Two World Wars." *Southern History* 10 (1988): 160–75.

Shannon, Brent. "ReFashioning Men: Fashion, Masculinity, and the Cultivation of the Male Consumer in Britain, 1860–1914." *Victorian Studies* 46(4) (2004): 597–630.

Shepard, Alexandra. "From Anxious Patriarchs to Refined Gentlemen? Manhood in Britain, circa 1500–1700." *Journal of British Studies* 44(2) (2005): 281–95.

Shephard, Ben. "Showbiz Imperialism: The Case of Peter Lobengula." In *Imperialism and Popular Culture,* edited by John MacKenzie. Manchester: Manchester University Press, 1986.

Sinha, Mrinalini. "Nationalism and Respectable Sexuality in India." *Genders* 21 (1995): 30–57.

Skal, David J., and Elias Savada. *Dark Carnival.* New York: Anchor Books, 1995.

Smit, Christopher R. "A Collaborative Aesthetic: Levinas's Idea of Responsibility and the Photographs of Charles Eisenmann and the Late Nineteenth-Century Freak-Performer." In *Victorian Freaks: The Social Context of Freakery in Britain,* edited by Marlene Tromp. Columbus: Ohio State University Press, 2008.

Smith, Andrew. *Victorian Demons: Medicine, Masculinity, and the Gothic at the Fin-de-Siècle.* Manchester: Manchester University Press, 2004.

Snigurowicz, Diana. "The Phenomène's Dilemma: Teratology and the Policing of Human Anomalies in Nineteenth- and Early Twentieth-Century Paris." In *Foucault and the Government of Disability,* edited by Shelley Tremain. Ann Arbor: University of Michigan Press, 2005.

———. "Sex, Simians, and Spectacle in Nineteenth-Century France; or, How to Tell a 'Man' From a Monkey." *Canadian Journal of History* 34(1) (1999): 51–81.

Stagg, Kevin. "Representing Physical Difference: The Materiality of the Monstrous." In *Social Histories of Disability and Deformity,* edited by David M. Turner and Kevin Stagg. London: Routledge, 2006.

Stallybrass, Peter, and Allon White. *The Politics and Poetics of Transgression.* Ithaca, NY: Cornell University Press, 1986.

Stauffer, Andrew M. "Dante Gabriel Rossetti and the Burdens of Nineveh." *Victorian Literature and Culture* 33(2) (2005): 369–94.

Stepan, Nancy. *The Idea of Race in Science: Great Britain, 1800–1960.* London: Macmillan, 1982.

Stephens, Elizabeth. "Cultural Fixions of the Freak Body: Coney Island and the Postmodern Sideshow." *Continuum: Journal of Media & Cultural Studies* 20(4) (2006): 485–98.

———. "Twenty-First Century Freak Show: Recent Transformations in the Exhibition of Non-Normative Bodies." *Disability Studies Quarterly* 25(3) 2005, available at www.dsq-sds.-archives.org/_articles_html/2005/summer/ stephens.asp (accessed January 28, 2009).

Stern, Rebecca. "Our Bear Women, Ourselves: Affiliating With Julia Pastrana." In *Victorian Freaks: The Social Context of Freakery in Britain,* edited by Marlene Tromp. Columbus: Ohio State University Press, 2008.

Stiker, Henri-Jacques. *A History of Disability.* Ann Arbor: University of Michigan Press, 2000.

Stocking Jr., George W. *Victorian Anthropology.* New York: Free Press, 1987.

Stoler, Ann. *Race and the Education of Desire.* Durham, NC: Duke University Press, 1996.

Stone, Deborah A. *The Disabled State.* Philadelphia: Temple University Press, 1985.

Street, Brian. "British Popular Anthropology: Exhibiting and Photographing the Other." In *Anthropology and Photography,* edited by Elizabeth Edwards. New Haven, CT: Yale University Press, 1992.

Strother, Z. S. "Display of the Body Hottentot." In *Africans on Stage: Studies in Ethnological Show Business,* edited by Bernth Lindfors. Bloomington: Indiana University Press, 1999.

Swartz, Mark E. "An Overview of Cinema on the Fairgrounds." *Journal of Popular Film and Television* 15(3) (1987): 102–8.

Sweet, Matthew. *Inventing the Victorians.* New York: St. Martin's Press, 2001.

Tagliacozzo, Eric. "Ambiguous Commodities, Unstable Frontiers: The Case of Burma, Siam, and Imperial Britain, 1800–1900." *Comparative Studies in Society and History* 46(2) (2004): 354–77.

Thomas, Deborah. "Uncovering Nineveh." *Archaeology Odyssey* 7 (2004): 24–31, 54.

Thompson, E. P. *The Making of the English Working Class.* London: Victor Gollancz, 1963.

Thomson, Rosemarie Garland. *Extraordinary Bodies: Figuring Physical Disability in American Culture and Literature.* New York: Columbia University Press, 1997.

———. "Freakery Unfurled." In *Victorian Freaks: The Social Context of Freakery in Britain,* edited by Marlene Tromp. Columbus: Ohio State University Press, 2008.

———. "Integrating Disability, Transforming Feminist Theory." In *The Disability Studies Reader.* 2nd ed., edited by Lennard J. Davis. New York: Routledge, 2006.

———. "Narratives of Deviance and Delight: Staring at Julia Pastrana, the 'Extraordinary Lady.'" In *Beyond the Binary: Reconstructing Cultural Identity in a Multicultural Context,* edited by Timothy B. Powell. New Brunswick, NJ: Rutgers University Press, 1999.

———. "Preface" and "Introduction." In *Freakery: Cultural Spectacles of the Extraordinary Body,* edited by Rosemarie Garland Thomson. New York: New York University Press, 1996.

———. "Redrawing the Boundaries of Feminist Disability Studies." *Feminist Studies* 20(3) (1994): 583–95.

———. "Staring at the Other." *Disability Studies Quarterly* 25(4) (2005), available at www.dsq-sds-archives.org/_articles_html/2005/fall/garland-thomson.asp (accessed January 28, 2009).

Thorne, Susan. "'The Conversion of Englishmen and the Conversion of the World Inseparable': Missionary Imperialism and the Language of Class in

Early Industrial Britain." In *Tensions of Empire,* edited by Frederick Cooper and Ann Laura Stoler. Berkeley: University of California Press, 1997.

Todd, Dennis. *Imagining Monsters: Miscreations of the Self in Eighteenth-Century England.* Chicago: University of Chicago Press, 1995.

Topham, Jonathan R. "Publishing 'Popular Science' In Early Nineteenth-Century Britain." In *Science in the Marketplace,* edited by Aileen Fyfe and Bernard Lightman. Chicago: University of Chicago Press, 2007.

Tosh, John. "Gentlemanly Politeness and Manly Simplicity in Victorian England." *Transactions of the Royal Historical Society* 12 (2002): 455–72.

———. "Masculinities in Industrializing Society: Britain 1800–1914." *Journal of British Studies* 44(2) (2005): 330–42.

———. "What Should Historians Do with Masculinity: Reflections on Nineteenth-Century Britain." *History Workshop Journal* 38 (1994): 179–202.

Toulmin, Vanessa. "'Curios Things in Curios Places': Temporary Exhibition Venues in the Victorian and Edwardian Entertainment Environment." *Early Popular Visual Culture* 4(2) 2006: 113–37.

———. "'It was not the show it was the tale that you told': The Life and Legend of Tom Norman, Silver King," available at www.shef.ac.uk/nfa/history/shows/norman.php (accessed January 28, 2009).

———. "Local Films for Local People: Travelling Showmen and the Commissioning of Local Films in Great Britain, 1900–1902." *Film History* 13 (2001): 118–37.

———. "Telling the Tale: The Story of the Fairground Bioscope Shows and the Showmen Who Operated Them." *Film History* 6 (1994): 219–37.

Tremain, Shelley. "On the Subject of Impairment." In *Disability/Postmodernity: Embodying Disability Theory,* edited by Mairian Corker and Tom Shakespeare. London: Continuum, 2002.

Trombley, Stephen. *Sir Frederick Treves: The Extra-Ordinary Edwardian.* London: Routledge, 1989.

Tromp, Marlene. "Empire and the Indian Freak: The 'Miniature Man' from Cawnpore and the 'Marvellous Indian Boy' on Tour in England." In *Victorian Freaks: The Social Context of Freakery in Britain,* edited by Marlene Tromp. Columbus: Ohio State University Press, 2008.

Tromp, Marlene, and Karyn Valerius. "Introduction." In *Victorian Freaks: The Social Context of Freakery in Britain,* edited by Marlene Tromp. Columbus: Ohio State University Press, 2008.

Tucker, Jennifer. *Nature Exposed: Photography as Eyewitness in Victorian Science.* Baltimore, MD: Johns Hopkins University Press, 2005.

Twitchell, James B. *Dreadful Pleasures: An Anatomy of Modern Horror.* Oxford: Oxford University Press, 1985.

———. *Forbidden Partners: The Incest Taboo in Modern Culture.* New York: Columbia University Press, 1987.

Walkowitz, Judith. *City of Dreadful Delight.* Chicago: University of Chicago Press, 1992.

———. *Prostitution and Victorian Society.* Cambridge: Cambridge University Press, 1980.

———. "The 'Vision of Salome': Cosmopolitanism and Erotic Dancing in Central London, 1908–1918." *American Historical Review* 108(2) (2003): 336–76.

Wallace, Irving, and Amy Wallace. *The Two.* New York: Simon and Schuster, 1978.

Walter, Bronwen. *Outsiders Inside: Whiteness, Place and Irish Women.* London: Routledge, 2001.

Walvin, James. *Black and White: The Negro and English Society, 1555–1945.* London: Allen Lane, 1973.

———. *Leisure and Society, 1830–1950.* London: Longman, 1978.

Waters, Hazel. "The Great Irish Famine and the Rise of Anti-Irish Racism." *Race and Class* 37(1) (1995): 95–108.

Wauchope, Robert. *Lost Tribes and Sunken Continents: Myth and Method in the Study of American Indians.* Chicago: University of Chicago Press, 1962.

Wilson, David A. "Comment: Whiteness and Irish Experience in North America." *Journal of British Studies* 44(1) (2005): 153–61.

Wilson, Dudley. *Signs and Portents.* London: Routledge, 1993.

Wohl, Anthony S. *Endangered Lives: Public Health in Victorian Britain.* Cambridge, MA: Harvard University Press, 1983.

———. "Sex and the Single Room: Incest Among the Victorian Working Classes." In *The Victorian Family: Structure and Stresses,* edited by Anthony S. Wohl. New York: St. Martin's Press, 1978.

Woodward, Christopher. *In Ruins.* New York: Vintage, 2003.

Zanger, Jules. "A Sympathetic Vibration: Dracula and the Jews." *English Literature in Transition* 34(1) (1991): 33–44.

UNPUBLISHED SECONDARY SOURCES

Chemers, Michael Mark. "Monsters, Myths, and Mechanics: Performance of Stigmatized Identity in the American Freak Show." PhD dissertation, University of Washington, 2001.

McHold, Heather. "Diagnosing Difference: The Scientific, Medical, and Popular Engagement with Monstrosity in Victorian Britain." PhD dissertation, Northwestern University, 2002.

Moss, Jami. "'A Body of Organized Truth': Freaks in Britain, 1830–1900." PhD dissertation, University of Wisconsin–Madison, 1999.

Snigurowicz, Diana. "Spectacles of Monstrosity and the Embodiment of Identity in France, 1829–1914." PhD dissertation, University of Chicago, 2000.

WEBSITES

http://dictionary.oed.com
http://library.syr.edu/information/spcollections/digital/eisenmann
http://www.thai2english.com
http://www.victorian-cinema.net/doyen.htm

INDEX

response, 1, 13, 32; freaks engaging in, 9–11; sexual, 83

Text:	11.25/13.5 Adobe Garamond
Display:	Adobe Garamond
Compositor:	International Typesetting and Composition
Printer & Binder:	Thomson-Shore, Inc.